Communications in Computer and Information Science 1818

Rationale

The CCIS series is devoted to the publication of proceedings of computer science conferences. Its aim is to efficiently disseminate original research results in informatics in printed and electronic form. While the focus is on publication of peer-reviewed full papers presenting mature work, inclusion of reviewed short papers reporting on work in progress is welcome, too. Besides globally relevant meetings with internationally representative program committees guaranteeing a strict peer-reviewing and paper selection process, conferences run by societies or of high regional or national relevance are also considered for publication.

Topics

The topical scope of CCIS spans the entire spectrum of informatics ranging from foundational topics in the theory of computing to information and communications science and technology and a broad variety of interdisciplinary application fields.

Information for Volume Editors and Authors

Publication in CCIS is free of charge. No royalties are paid, however, we offer registered conference participants temporary free access to the online version of the conference proceedings on SpringerLink (http://link.springer.com) by means of an http referrer from the conference website and/or a number of complimentary printed copies, as specified in the official acceptance email of the event.

CCIS proceedings can be published in time for distribution at conferences or as post-proceedings, and delivered in the form of printed books and/or electronically as USBs and/or e-content licenses for accessing proceedings at SpringerLink. Furthermore, CCIS proceedings are included in the CCIS electronic book series hosted in the SpringerLink digital library at http://link.springer.com/bookseries/7899. Conferences publishing in CCIS are allowed to use Online Conference Service (OCS) for managing the whole proceedings lifecycle (from submission and reviewing to preparing for publication) free of charge.

Publication process

The language of publication is exclusively English. Authors publishing in CCIS have to sign the Springer CCIS copyright transfer form, however, they are free to use their material published in CCIS for substantially changed, more elaborate subsequent publications elsewhere. For the preparation of the camera-ready papers/files, authors have to strictly adhere to the Springer CCIS Authors' Instructions and are strongly encouraged to use the CCIS LaTeX style files or templates.

Abstracting/Indexing

CCIS is abstracted/indexed in DBLP, Google Scholar, EI-Compendex, Mathematical Reviews, SCImago, Scopus. CCIS volumes are also submitted for the inclusion in ISI Proceedings.

How to start

To start the evaluation of your proposal for inclusion in the CCIS series, please send an e-mail to ccis@springer.com.

M. A. Jabbar · Fernando Ortiz-Rodríguez ·
Sanju Tiwari · Patrick Siarry
Editors

Applied Machine Learning and Data Analytics

5th International Conference, AMLDA 2022
Reynosa, Tamaulipas, Mexico, December 22–23, 2022
Revised Selected Papers

Editors
M. A. Jabbar ⓘ
Vardhaman College of Engineering
Hyderabad, India

Fernando Ortiz-Rodríguez ⓘ
Autonomous University of Tamaulipas
Ciudad Victoria, Mexico

Sanju Tiwari ⓘ
Autonomous University of Tamaulipas
Ciudad Victoria, Mexico

Patrick Siarry ⓘ
University of Paris-Est Creteil
Vitry sur Seine, France

ISSN 1865-0929   ISSN 1865-0937 (electronic)
Communications in Computer and Information Science
ISBN 978-3-031-34221-9   ISBN 978-3-031-34222-6 (eBook)
https://doi.org/10.1007/978-3-031-34222-6

This Springer imprint is published by the registered company Springer Nature Switzerland AG
The registered company address is: Gewerbestrasse 11, 6330 Cham, Switzerland

Preface

This volume contains the main proceedings of the 2022 edition of Applied Machine Learning and Data Analytics (AMLDA 2022). AMLDA is established as a yearly venue for discussing the latest scientific results and technology innovations related to Machine Learning.

The International Conference on Applied Machine Learning and Data Analytics (AMLDA) is the premier conference in this branch of artificial intelligence. AMLDA renowned for presenting cutting-edge research on all aspects of machine learning as well as important application areas such as healthcare and medical imaging informatics, biometrics, forensics, precision agriculture, risk management, robotics, and satellite imaging. Participants at AMLDA 2022 included academic and industrial researchers and engineers, graduate students, and postdocs.

AMLDA is convened annually to provide a platform for knowledge exchange on the most recent scientific and technological advances in the field of applied machine learning and data analytics.

The main scientific program of the conference comprised 20 papers: 16 full research papers and four short research papers selected out of 89 reviewed submissions, which corresponds to an acceptance rate of 22.4% for the research papers submitted. The program also included two exciting, invited keynotes (Stefan Kramer and Edlira Kalemi), with novel topics.

The General and Program Committee chairs would like to thank the many people involved in making AMLDA 2022 a success. First, our thanks go to the four co-chairs of the main event and more than 50 reviewers for ensuring a rigorous review process that led to an excellent scientific program and an average of three reviews per article.

Further, we thank the kind support of all people from Tamaulipas Autonomous University, particularly the Faculty at the venue, the Reynosa Rodhe campus. We are thankful for the kind support of the staff of Springer. We finally thank our sponsors and our community for their vital support of this edition of AMLDA.

The editors would like to close the preface with warm thanks to our supporting keynotes, the program committee for rigorous commitment in carrying out reviews, and finally, our enthusiastic authors who made this event truly International.

December 2022

M. A. Jabbar
Fernando Ortiz-Rodriguez
Sanju Tiwari
Patrick Siarry

Organization

General Chairs

M. A. Jabbar   Vardhaman College of Engineering, India
Fernando Ortiz Rodriguez   Universidad Autónoma de Tamaulipas, Mexico
Sanju Tiwari   Universidad Autónoma de Tamaulipas, Mexico
Patrick Siarry   University of Paris-Est Créteil, France

Program Chairs

Millie Pant   IIT Roorkee, India
Shishir Kumar Shandilya   VIT Bhopal University, India
José Melchor Medina-Quintero   Universidad Autónoma de Tamaulipas, Mexico
Andries Engelbrecht   University of Stellenbosch, South Africa

Publicity Chairs

P. Sivakumara   University of Malaya, Malaysia
Vania V. Estrela   Universidade Federal Fluminense, Brazil
Patience Usoro Usip   University of Uyo, Nigeria

Workshop Chairs

Yusniel Hidalgo Delgado   Universidad de las Ciencias Informáticas, Cuba
Shikha Mehta   JIIT Noida, India
C. A. Dhawale   P R Pote Patil College of Engineering and Management, India

Special Session Chairs

Tanima Datta   IIT BHU, India
David Hicks   Texas A & M University Kingsville, USA
Antonio De Nicola   ENEA, Italy
Patrice Boursier   International Medical University, Malaysia

Tutorial Chairs

Hari Prabhat Gupta   IIT BHU, India
Ayush Goyal   Texas A & M University Kingsville, USA
Smita Shandilya   Sagar Institute of Research and Technology, India

Program Committee

Fatima Zahra Amara   Abbès Laghrour University of Khenchela, Algeria
Dridi Amna   Birmingham City University, UK
Ivan Armuelles Voinov   University of Panama, Panama
Debajyoty Banik   Kalinga Institute of Industrial Technology, India
Bilal Ben Mahria   Sidi Mohamed Ben Abdellah University, Morocco
Semih Bitim   İzmir Bakırçay Üniversitesi, Turkey
Orchid Chetia Phukan   University of Tartu, Estonia
Gerard Deepak   Manipal Institute of Technology Bengaluru, India
Burcu Devrim İçtenbaş   Ankara Bilim University, Turkey
Onur Dogan   İzmir Bakırçay University, Turkey
Houda El Bouhissi   University of Bejaja, Algeria
Orhan Er   İzmir Bakırçay University, Turkey
Christian Estay-Niculcar   FUNIBER, Spain
Abid Ali   Halmstad University, Sweden
Devottam Gaurav   Indian Institute of Technology Delhi, India
Orlando Toledano   Universidad de las Ciencias Informáticas, Cuba
Sven Groppe   Universität zu Lübeck, Germany
Shankru Guggari   BMS College of Engineering, India
Mounir Hemam   Khenchela University, India
Yuseniel Hidalgo   Universidad de las Ciencias Informáticas, Cuba
Hanieh Khorashadizadeh   Universität zu Lübeck, Germany
Ajit Kumar   Soongsil University, South Korea
Kusum Lata   NIT Hamirpur, India
Yoan Antonio Lopez   Universidad de las Ciencias Informáticas, Cuba
Víctor López   Universidad Tecnológica de Panama, Panama
Thangavel M.   VIT Bhopal University, India
Melchor Medina   Universidad Autónoma de Tamaulipas, Mexico
José Eladio Medina Pagola   Universidad de las Ciencias Informáticas, Cuba
M. A. Jabbar   Vardhaman College of Engineering, India
Shikha Mehta   JIIT Noida, India
Vladimir Milián Núñez   Universidad de las Ciencias Informáticas, Cuba
Mohamed Madani Hafidi   Abbès Laghrour University of Khenchela, Algeria
Mounir Hemam   Abbès Laghrour University of Khenchela, Algeria

Ron Ojino	Cooperative University of Kenya, Kenya
Fernando Ortiz-Rodriguez	Universidad Autónoma de Tamaulipas, Mexico
Piyush Pareek	Nitte Meenakshi Institute of Technology, India
Krishna Ponnekanti	Anil Neerukonda Institute of Technology & Sciences, India
Hector Raúl	Universidad de las Ciencias Informáticas, Cuba
Shishir Shandilya	VIT Bhopal University, India
Serge Sonfack	INP-Toulouse, France
Tagaram Soni Madhulatha	Telangana Social Welfare Residential Degree College for Women, India
Sanju Tiwari	Universidad Autónoma de Tamaulipas, Mexico
Patience Usoro Usip	University of Uyo, Nigeria
Edlira Vakaj	Birmingham City University, UK
David Valle-Cruz	Universidad Autónoma del Estado de México, Mexico
Miguel Vargas-Lombardo	Universidad Tecnológica de Panama, Panama
Sonali Vyas	University of Petroleum and Energy Studies, Dehradun, India
Bezza Youcef	Abbès Laghrour University of Khenchela, Algeria

Contents

Deep Learning Methods to Automate Embryo Classification and Evaluation

Rani B R Shobha[1]([✉])[ID], S. Bharathi[1][ID], and Piyush Kumar Pareek[2][ID]

[1] Dr. Ambedkar Institute of Technology, Bengaluru, Karnataka, India
shobhakrishna8@gmail.com
[2] Nitte Meenakshi Institue of Technology, Bengaluru, Karnataka, India

Abstract. Every one in seven people face fertility issues in India due to surge in stress levels and changes in lifestyle, IVF (In Vitro Fertilization) comes as boon [1]. Artificial Intelligence methods increase the performance of assisted reproductive technology (ART) over past decade. Manual approaches in grading embryos are prone to human errors and show slight variations in grading embryos by different embryologists. Science and technology can improve the grading of embryos to some extent by using time lapse imaging systems use of high-resolution microscopes. Artificial intelligence, machine learning and deep learning in particular automates and standardizes the embryo grading process, their by minimising the variations and increasing the chances of successful pregnancy. This paper evaluates different approaches involving machine learning and deep learning techniques to identify embryo and extract the features of embryos such as ICM and TE which help in grading embryos.

Keywords: IVF · ICM · TE · Convolutional Neural Network · R-CNN · DCNN architectures · Embryo Classification

1 Introduction

1.1 About IVF

Despite tremendous advancements in the field of assisted reproduction, the clinical pregnancy rates are still modest at about 30% per embryo transfer. Indian Society of Assisted Reproduction estimates that 10–14% of the Indian urban population face infertility problems that amounts to roughly one in every six couples. In India, the success rate in IVF ranges from 30% to 35% depending on factors such as woman's age, infertility type, cause of infertility, quality of the sperm, egg and embryo. assisted reproductive treatment (ART) procedures [1] such as IVF (in-vitro fertilization) and ICSI (intra cytoplasmic sperm injection) used in which eggs are injected with men's sperm in a specialized laboratory. The fertilized egg (embryo) is then allowed to grow in an incubator before being transferred in to womb thus, increasing the chances of pregnancy.

M. A. Jabbar et al. (Eds.): AMLDA 2022, CCIS 1818, pp. 1–12, 2023.
https://doi.org/10.1007/978-3-031-34222-6_1

1.2   IVF Procedure

Based on morphological criteria, best one to two good quality embryos are selected to implant in to patient's uterus. Evaluation of embryo is performed by skilled embryologist by observing, assessing and manually grading the blasto-cysts. A Good quality embryo selection is a major process in In Vitro Fertilization (IVF) era. Conventional morphological evaluation is used for embryo selection since years, where grading of the embryos is done manually by monitoring the embryos under stereo zoom or inverted microscopy [2]. Whereas, in Time-Lapse Imaging technology, embryo images are extracted in frequent intervals helping embryologist to choose a good quality oocyte or embryo. Thus, recurrent preg-nancy loss and recurrent implantation failures can be reduced when evaluation is done based on morphological assessment either by traditional way or by using latest technology called Time lapse method.

1.3   Embryo Development

Embryo grading and evaluation is crucial step for the success of IVF. The selec-tion procedure includes morphological assessment of embryos under microscope by an embryologist at every 20 to 24 hrs. to identify good quality embryo as shown in Fig. 1 from day-1 to day-6. The other method called Time-Lapse Imag-ing system is used to extract the development of embryos from video frames and grade them. Time-lapse embryo monitoring is the latest technology [1] used during an IVF or ICSI treatment that enables the embryologists to assess the embryos in detail. This is a special type of incubator that has camera built in it which takes pictures of the developing embryos at regular intervals. This cam-era unit connects to a microscope system. The captured pictures are processed using a software that combines these pictures to form a time-lapse video [13]. This helps the embryologist to assess every vital stage of a developing embryo.

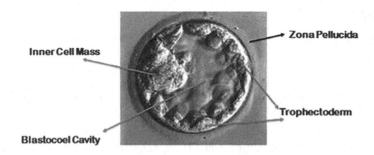

Fig. 1. Embryo features-Inner Cell Mass, Trophectoderm, Zona Pellucida, Blastocoel Cavity

1.4   Importance of Embryo Grading

Two letter grades for the two different parts of each blastocyst (the inner cell mass, or ICM, which becomes the fetus and the outer layer is called the trophectoderm, or TE, which becomes the placenta). The number, from 1 to 6, indicates the expansion of blastocyst and the letters indicate the quality of the ICM and the TE. The grade A indicates excellent quality, B as good quality, C as fair quality, and D as poor quality. In general, poor quality embryos have few cells and a more of fragmentation. Good quality blastocysts get expanded between day-3 to day-5 and further begin to hatch during day-6. The below Fig. 2 depicts the poor quality embryos in first column of day-1 and day-5 respectively and good quality embryos in second column of day-1 and day-5 respectively. The reproductive endocrinologist and the embryologists will identify the embryos and assess the quality in increasing the chances of successful IVF treatment.

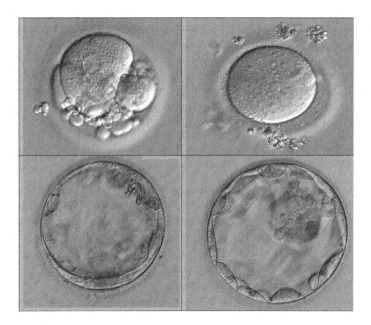

Fig. 2. Poor quality embryos in column 1 and Good quality embryo images in column 2 of day-1 & day-5

2   Material and Methods

2.1   Image Datasets

Image datasets play an important role in solving classification, feature extraction and object segmentation using deep learning techniques. These datasets train, validate and test based on object detection and object segmentation. There are only few image data sets such as Imagenet, COCO, GoogleAI open datasets with annotations of the features that enhance deep neural network methodologies and rise in computational capabilities. ImageNet is a large-scale dataset that has contributed in the development of Deep learning and Artificial Intelligence in detecting objects. It has 14 million hand annotated bounding boxes for at least million images with 200 classes. COCO dataset is another important large image dataset that helps in image detection, image segmentation and detecting key points in the image. It has 164 K images with training and test datasets separately. Google AI open image dataset has around 12 million images having 500 object classes with image labelled annotations, object bounding boxes, object segmentations, visual relationships, localized narratives, and more.

There are no standard embryo datasets available in any repositories, all embryo images used for analysis are taken from IVF centers, captured either from Time Lapse Imaging system or through traditional camera mounted microscopic system. The performance of detection system also depends on the which day embryos, either day-3 or day-5 images used for analysis.

2.2   Embryo Development Stages

Artificial Intelligence methods have shown a drastic change in detecting embryo or oocyte [20] which classifies and selects embryos in IVF method. High quality embryo selection can be done when machine learning is combined with prediction model by forming an Artificial Intelligence approach [22]. This process takes less time by embryologist in selecting the matured and good quality embryos as shown in Fig3, thus showing great potential in taking decisions within short duration with greater depth and precision.

There are different machine learning techniques [18, 20] which classifies and identifies stages of embryos and select quality ones using following i) Supervised Learning Algorithms ii) Convolutional Neural Network iii) Region based CNN iv) Deep Neural Network with different Models.

2.3   Supervised Learning Algorithms

Supervised learning is the most widely used approach where segmentation, feature extraction and classification can be performed based on class labels. Thus, Image Processing with Machine Learning algorithms helps in giving high performance with complex images. In prediction of embryo quality and oocytes was done using Machine Learning methods. Preprocessing procedure [9] was applied as first step to extract the boundaries or edges of the image, next images

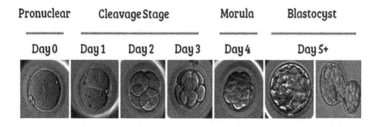

Fig. 3. Stages of embryo from day-0 & day-5

with noise, blur or varying illumination conditions are removed. Further feature extraction was used on the images which extracts useful patterns using LBP (Local Binary Pattern) with good texture descriptors. The paper suggests that a single classifier does not have better performance when compared ensemble of classifiers. Hence the system combines all the features extracted and applied to ensemble of classifiers and final score (sum rule) is obtained.

Bayesian Classifier.
Given the uncertainty of the treatment, this paper [14] proposes an expert decision support system that uses a Bayesian classifier which helps in selecting good quality embryos [5] that will form the batch to be implanted to the woman's uterus. With supervised classification success rate can be higher for each IVF treatment as each time a batch of embryos are transferred to get positive pregnancy results. Thus supervised classification techniques are identified as a classification model to solve the problem of human embryo selection.

In this paper, model is created using Bayesian Classifier that determines the probability of hypothesis using prior probability. Consider a vector of a feature X= (x1, x2,..... xn) with a class variable C, then Posterior probability(C—X) is obtained as a product of likelihood P(X—C) and P(C) given the prior probability P(X). Applying conditional probability to the feature vector, Bayes Classification problem is formulated as in the equation below.

$$y(x) = argmax P(C) \prod P(X|C) \qquad (1)$$

The classification problem is resulted as 0,1 that assigns the labels to the observations which detects whether an embryo is a good or bad quality when the prior probability of class P(C) computed up on applied on training data set of embryos images.

The Bayesian classifier implementation helps to analyse the probabilistic classification process and to derives the set of features that help embryologist to interpret the results. This methodology is applied as a decision support system by embryologist experts in to decide viable embryos that help in increasing the successful implantation and to improve the process in selecting quality embryos for transfer [3]. Predictor variables [1] like thickness of zona pellucida, degree of fragmentation, multinucleate and blastomere size improves the performance of Classification technique.

Variables used as predictor features such as woman's age, sperm quality, cell number, zygote score, blastomeres size, inner cell mass (ICM), thickness zona pellucida (ZP), number of transferred embryos etc. help in detecting good embryos for successful implantation. In this paper an account of different cases of batches where set of three embryos are used to transfer in each treatment.

3   Methodology

3.1   Convolutional Neural Network

In recent years, Deep learning algorithms were used in different image processing problems especially in medical domain. Convolutional neural network is one of the most popular architecture used in recent years implemented for image recognition and image classification problems. It trains the machine for any computer vision problems, detects the objects, identify the features and classify them. CNN architecture has input layer, convolv layer, pooling layer, fully connected layer, softmax layer and output layer with suitable activation functions to process pixel level data as shown in Fig4. One of medical problem answered is on IVF treatment, where, the neural network that mimics human brain helps in predicting embryos and grade them automatically. But Convolutional Neural Network [4,6] implemented in most of medical problems are with supervised learning where both inputs and their labels are with training data producing labelled outputs. Embryo classification is done with morphological features by convoluting image pixels in hidden layers. Whereas using time-lapse incubation systems in IVF clinics, results in high quality video files that records the stages of pre implantation embryo development.

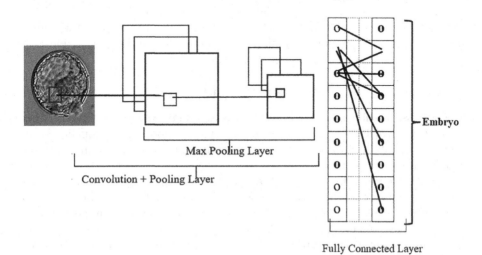

Fig. 4. An overview of Convolutional Neural Network Architecture

In this paper [4], an automatic grading system is developed based on morphological structure of blastocyst obtained from time lapse imaging system. A convolution neural network [6] is applied to detect the embryo features such as inner cell mass (ICM) and trophectoderm (TE) and grades them from a single image frame. After identifying the ICM and TE, recurrent neural network is applied over the selected features to incorporate temporal information of the growing blastocysts from multiple frames. Convolutional Neural Network is applied on Time Lapse Imaging (TLI) images to asses right from day-one human embryo images. Day-one human embryo images are detected using region based CNN and segment them in to three distinct features [8] termed as zona pellucida (ZP), cytoplasm and pronucleus (PN). The performance of CNN algorithm is compared with images labelled by embryologist manually beginning from day one embryo images.

The images that are collected from Time Lapse Imaging System [7] are extracted and converted them into grey images. The grey scaled images ranging from 0 to 255 are compressed to 512 *512 pixels. Pre-processing is done on the images to reduce the noise and smooth the input images by applying filters. Then, enhanced image dataset after denoising segments the images using Convolutional Neural network for entire training data set.

Convolution is a function of image pixels matrix and computed with filter that results on to a feature map or activation function. Thus, this convolutional layer helps to detect and select the features of embryo images. These activation maps [4] generated from the convolutional layer are processed repeatedly multiple times and finally the extracted information is processed by the fully connected layer. Cross validation is a process which is applied on training and test image datasets to reduce the risk of high performance of the proposed system. Thus, the network has enhanced images as input and predicts the features of embryo such as background of the cell, Zona Pellucida Cytoplasm based on pixel probabilities.

3.2 Region Based Convolutional Neural Network

Region based Convolutional Neural Network (R-CNN) is an effective learning technique which minimizes learnable parameters by using the same basis function across different image locations [8,9]. It is a region-based search selection which segments the image based on color, shape and size and combines the similar regions. In R-CNN pipeline, the regions are segmented using selective search and later CNN is applied on the features extracted and finally Support Vector Machine (SVM) classifier is applied to predict the required features of the image. Hence, this methodology is more effective approach compared to only CNN for automatic learning-based cell detection framework executed on both 2D and 3D images.

In [9], cell regions are identified and irrelevant background regions are discarded. CNN helps in detecting background regions and thus cell regions are detected in more efficient way using SVM classifier [10]. Then the cell regions are identified using SVM-RGB Histogram detector, later cell and patches are extracted. Probability is increased in detecting correct cells and even background and overlapping pixels. The architecture used in the paper suggests 1 input layer, 13 hidden layers (convolutional, Relu, Max Pooling, Fully Connected, Softmax) and output layer that classifies the required output in out layer. Thus, predicted position and size of embryos were compared with expert embryologist with labeled embryo size and their position results with smaller error and good prediction rate.

3.3 Mask R-CNN

Masked RCNN [21] is a new state of art method to segment the objects or images. It first segments region of interest with region-based CNN on the input images and next mask the similar pixel entities in a bounding box and predicts the class of the object. This method gives better performance on the images of embryos to identify the Inner Cell Mass (ICM) and Trophectoderm (TE) with the help of masked RCNN and need to helps in grading them further. In recent years, Masked RCNN has helped to solve instance segmentation problem in machine learning or computer vision. It has been the new state of art in terms of instance segmentation. There are two stages of Mask RCNN.

- The first stage generates proposals about the regions where there might be an object based on the input image.
- Second,it predicts the class of the object, refines the bounding box and generates a mask in pixel level of the object based on the first stage proposal.

3.4 Deep Convolutional Neural Network Architectures

Deep Neural Network is an advanced neural network effective on image classification. It has different architectures used to build models like AlexNet, VGG16, Inception V1, Inception V3, ResNet50, U-Net and GoogleNet enhancing the performance of image segmentation, classification and image processing.

In the paper [12,16], convolutional networks with different architectures are used to detect the embryos and predict the quality of human embryos. First, images of embryos from Time Lapse Imaging system are extracted and labelled as good and poor quality images further grade them. An efficient transfer learning algorithm called Inception-V1 architecture is used initially to fine-tuning of the parameters for all of the layers. After pre-processing good quality images are selected randomly and bad quality images are removed using STORK framework. Finally, a decision tree method referred as a chi-squared automatic interaction detection (CHAID) algorithm was used to integrate patients age and embryo quality which has effect on the pregnancy rate.

The paper [16] proposes a multi-task deep learning with dynamic programming (MTDL-DP) which pre-classify each frame extracted from a time-lapse video to identify different stages of embryo development. They used a combination of CONV Pooling and LATE Fusion approaches which are mainly applied for videos classification to extract image features. MTDL frameworks like one-to-many, many-to-one are verified and found that one-to-many gives performance and computational cost. Further dynamic programming was used to adjust the classifications based on the constraint and DP-based decoder performs on fusion of CovNet and Late Fusion pooling approaches for predicting embryo features in time-lapse videos.

In [11], methodology is based on a deep convolutional neural network models applied on images extracted from time lapse imaging. Features obtained from a recurrent neural network (RCNN) helps to predict ICM grades (A, B, or C) and TE grades (A, B, or C) [14] . It is an automatic grading system to detect features of all embryos. Paper proposes that an ordinal variation of categorical cross-entropy loss function is used to detect the correct grading of ICM and TE helping in predicting and showing high performance.

The paper [17] propose an automated system to improve the speed, repeatability, and accuracy of embryo detection and grading. Individual oocytes are identified which have potential to become embryos based on their principal components using CNN (U-Net) segmentation. Paper suggests on localization of the cell, extracts background and foreground regions and performs the oocyte segmentation using U-Net with the powerful ResNet50 architecture [3]. This model predicts the features with descriptors based on geometry and texture were ran with feature significance and evaluated for higher classification accuracy.

4   Comparative Analysis

With latest advancements in Machine and Deep neural networks, embryo detection and classification of features has significant state in automatic grading of embryos. Data collection stage plays an important role in implementation of any methodology, since there are no standard repositories or open datasets for embryo images. Images from time-lapse imaging systems and traditional camera mounted microscopes also have an effect in performance of the algorithms. Comparative analysis is done based on methodology used, size of dataset used, accuracy obtained, strengths and weakness of the algorithms implemented are discussed. Different metrics such as as accuracy,precision, F1 score, recall, specificity and commonly used performance measures for assessing the performance of the algorithms. Analysis of image classification techniques are performed with day-1, day-3 and day-5 embryo images and neural networks such as CNN, RCNN and D-CNN are compared in the Table1 given below.

Table 1. Comparison of different Deep Learning methods to detect and classify embryos.

Reference	Algorithms Applied	Accuracy	strengths	Weakness
Morales Dinora et al. [14]	Bayesian Network	68.5%	zona pellucida thickness, degree of fragmentation, multinucleate and blastomere size considered for good classification results	Other parameters also to be considered for evaluation of embryo False positive and false negatives have to be verified
Pegah Khosravi et al. [15]	DNN with STORK frame work & In-ception V1	98%	CNN and SVM for embryo grading	Pregnancy outcome prediction is not verified
Z. Liu et al. [16]	Multi task Deep Learning with Dynamic Programming	89%	Identifies zona pellucida (ZP), cytoplasm and pronucleus (PN) with early-stage classification	Classification accuracy is lower due to fewer samples
Denis Baruci et al. [17]	CNN(U-Net) Segmentation with SVM Classifier	70%	Automatic detection of oocytes with textural and geometrical features	Classification Accuracy has to be improved
Zhao, M et al. [6]	CNN algorithm	97%	Segment cytoplasm, PN and ZP in high speed with high accuracy	–
Hakim et al. [9]	YOLOv3	100%	Scheme using training datawith 70%, validation at 15% and testing at 15%	Model fails at higher grades
Santos Filho E et al. [19]	SVM Classifier	92%	Semi-automatic Blastocyst grading on day 1,5,6	Fully automated method to grade embryos
Brian D. Leahy et al. [21]	D-CNN	87.9%	Masked CNN with improved embryo features	Performance to be enhanced with multi-task learning

5 Conclusion

IVF treatment serves as an important approach to solve the infertility issues. This paper evaluates machine learning and deep learning algorithms in identifying and classifying the features of embryos. Comparative analysis of different architectures are assessed in this paper on CNN architectures and traditional image processing techniques on embryo images. The comparison of methodologies used concludes that CNN with YOLOv3 [9] model with an accuracy of 100% is used to identify the embryos with higher accuracy and ResNet works better in extracting the features of embryos like Inner Cell Mass and Trophectoderm better in comparison to other architectures. The future work involves use of stacked Mask R-CNN models to identify and grade day-3 and day-5 images. This process will automate and improve embryo grading and their by increasing the changes of positive pregnancy helping doctors and embryologists.

References

1. Kushnir, V.A., Smith, G.D., Adashi, E.Y. The Future of IVF: The New Normal in Human Reproduction. Reprod. Sci. **29**, 849–856 (2022). https://doi.org/10.1007/s43032-021-00829-3
2. Choucair, F., Younis, N., Hourani, A.: The value of the modern embryologist to a successful IVF system: revisiting an age-old question. Middle East Fertility Society J. **26**(1), 1–6 (2021). https://doi.org/10.1186/s43043-021-00061-8
3. Bormann CL, et al.: Performance of a deep learning based neural network in the selection of human blastocysts for implantation. Elife. 2020 Sep 15;9:e55301. PMID: 32930094; PMCID: PMC7527234. https://doi.org/10.7554/eLife.55301
4. Amitai, T., Kan-Tor, Y., Srebnik, N., Buxboim, A.: Embryo classification beyond pregnancy: early prediction of first trimester miscarriage using machine learning medRxiv **11**(24), 20237610 (2020). https://doi.org/10.1101/2020.11.24.20237610
5. Wu, Y.G., et al.: Different effectiveness of closed embryo culture system with time-lapse imaging (EmbryoScope(TM)) in comparison to standard manual embryology in good and poor prognosis patients: a prospectively randomized pilot study. Reprod Biol Endocrinol. 2016 Aug 24; **14**(1):49. PMID: 27553622; PMCID: PMC4995783. https://doi.org/10.1186/s12958-016-0181-x
6. Zhao, M., Xu, M., Li, H., et al.: Application of convolutional neural network on early human embryo segmentation during in vitro fertilization. J Cell Mol Med. **25**, 2633–2644 (2021). https://doi.org/10.1111/jcmm.16288
7. Seshadri, S., Saab, W., Serhal, P.: Time lapse imaging of embryos is useful in in vitro fertilisation (IVF) or intracytoplasmic sperm injection (ICSI) treatment: FOR: Time-lapse monitoring of embryos. BJOG: Int. J. Obstet. Gy. 126 287–287 (2019). https://doi.org/10.1111/1471-0528.15159
8. Girshick, R., Donahue, J., Darrell, T., Malik, J.: Region-Based Convolutional Networks for Accurate Object Detection and Segmentation. In: IEEE Transactions on Pattern Analysis and Machine Intelligence, vol. 38, no. 1, pp. 142–158, 1 (2016) https://doi.org/10.1109/TPAMI.2015.2437384
9. Hakim, D., Jamal, A., Nugroho, A., Septiandri, A., Wiweko, B.: Embryo Grading after In Vitro Fertilization using YOLO. Lontar Komputer?: Jurnal Ilmiah Teknologi Informasi **13**(3), 137–149 (2022). https://doi.org/10.24843/LKJITI.2022.v13.i03.p01
10. Wang, R., et al.: Artificial intelligence in reproductive medicine. Reproduction (Cambridge, England) **158**(4), R139–R154 (2019). https://doi.org/10.1530/REP-18-0523
11. Kragh, M.F., Rimestad, J., Berntsen, J., Karstoft, H.: Automatic grading of human blastocysts from time-lapse imaging. Comput. Biol. Med. 2019 Dec; 115:103494. Epub 2019 Oct 15. PMID: 31630027. https://doi.org/10.1016/j.compbiomed.2019.103494

12. Chen, T.-J., Zheng, W.-L., Liu, C.-H., Huang, I., Lai, H.-H., Liu, M.: Using deep learning with large dataset of microscope images to develop an automated embryo grading system. Fertility Reproduction. **01**, 1–6 (2019). https://doi.org/10.1142/S2661318219500051

13. Conaghan, J., et al.: Improving embryo selection using a computer-automated time-lapse image analysis test plus day 3 morphology: results from a prospective multicenter trial. Fertil Steril. 2013 Aug; 100(2):412–9.e5. Epub 2013 May 28. PMID: 23721712. https://doi.org/10.1016/j.fertnstert.2013.04.021

14. Morales, D.A., et al.: Bayesian classification for the selection of in-vitro human embryos using morphological and clinical data. Computer methods and programs in **90** 104-16. https://doi.org/10.1016/j.cmpb.2007.11.018

15. Khosravi, P., Kazemi, E., Zhan, Q., Toschi, M., Malmsten, J., Hickman, C., Meseguer, M., Rosenwaks, Z., Elemento, O., Zaninovic, N., Hajirasouliha, I.: Robust automated assessment of human blastocyst quality using deep learning. Preprints (2018). https://doi.org/10.1101/394882

16. Khosravi, P., et al.: Robust automated assessment of human blastocyst quality using deep learning. Preprints (2018). https://doi.org/10.1101/394882

17. Liu, Z., et al.: Multi-task deep learning with dynamic programming for embryo early development stage classification from time-lapse videos. Ieee Access, 7, 122153-122163 (2019)

18. Gaurav, D., Rodriguez, F. O., Tiwari, S., Jabbar, M. A. (2021). Review of machine learning approach for drug development process. In: Deep Learning in Biomedical and Health Informatics (pp. 53–77). CRC Press (2021)

19. Carrasco, B., et al.: Selecting embryos with the highest implantation potential using data mining and decision tree based on classical embryo morphology and morphokinetics. J. Assisted Reproduct. Genetics **34**(8), 983–990 (2017). https://doi.org/10.1007/s10815-017-0955-x

20. Tiwari, S., Dogan, O., Jabbar, M. A., Shandilya, S. K., Ortiz-Rodriguez, F., Bajpai, S., & Banerjee, S. (2022). Applications of machine learning approaches to combat COVID-19: a survey. Lessons from COVID-19, pp. 263–287

21. Fernandez, E.I., et al.: Artificial intelligence in the IVF laboratory: overview through the application of different types of algorithms for the classification of reproductive data. J. Assisted Reprod. Genetics **37**(10), 2359–2376 (2020). https://doi.org/10.1007/s10815-020-01881-9

22. Leahy, B., et al.: Automated Measurements of Key Morphological Features of Human Embryos for IVF (2020)

23. Raef, B., Ferdousi, R.: A Review of Machine Learning Approaches in Assisted Reproductive Technologies. Acta. Inform. Med. 2019 Sep; **27**(3), 205–211. PMID: 31762579; PMCID: PMC6853715. https://doi.org/10.5455/aim.2019.27.205-211

24. Barucic, D., Kybic, J., Teplá, O., Topurko, Z., & Kratochvílová, I. (2021). Automatic evaluation of human oocyte developmental potential from microscopy images. arXiv preprint arXiv:2103.00302

25. Filho, E.S., Noble, J.A., Poli, M., Griffiths, T., Emerson, G., Wells, D.: A method for semi-automatic grading of human blastocyst microscope images. Human Reproduction **27**(9), 2641–2648 (2012)

Univariate Feature Fitness Measures for Classification Problems: An Empirical Assessment

Emon Asad[(✉)], Atikul Islam, Asfaque Alam, and Ayatullah Faruk Mollah

Department of Computer Science and Engineering, Aliah University, IIA/27 New Town,
Kolkata 700160, India
mailtoemonasad@gmail.com

Abstract. This paper offers a brief assessment of leading filter-based feature selectors i.e. chi-square, symmetrical uncertainty, ANOVA f-statistic, mutual information, fisher score, gini index and ReliefF. Each of these measures are evaluated by correlating univariate feature fitness scores with corresponding accuracies obtained using support vector machine with stratified 10-fold cross-validation over a diversified collection of datasets like mobile pricing, digits, wine, breast cancer, microarray gene expression, etc. Multiple correlation methods such as pearson, spearman and kendall rank have been adopted in this empirical study. It is found that none of these feature selectors have appeared as the best for all types of datasets. However, ANOVA f-statistic and mutual information have topped most often, which are followed by fisher score, SU, Chi-square and ReliefF. Such study is imperative in choosing appropriate feature selectors for a given classification problem, and therefore may be useful for research fraternity.

Keywords: Feature selection · Filter-based methods · Univariate feature selectors · Chi-square · ANOVA · Symmetrical uncertainty · Mutual information · Fisher score · Gini index · ReliefF · Correlation measure · Classification

1 Introduction

In recent years, data from various fields such as text mining, genome projects, proteomics analysis, computational chemistry, multivariate imaging etc. have increased enormously. These datasets usually come up with very high dimensions (about hundreds or thousands of variables) and numerous samples. But, only a handful of features from these high dimensional datasets are truly responsible for class determination and helpful for revealing important patterns from the datasets. Feature selection paves the way to select the most informative subset of features and remove the least significant or redundant ones from a given dataset. The selected subset of features may enhance the classification accuracy and reduce computation cost.

Feature selection techniques are largely divided into four categories - filter, wrapper, hybrid, and embedded methods [1]. Most filter-based feature selection methods rank the features according to some calculated scores, or determine the statistical significance

M. A. Jabbar et al. (Eds.): AMLDA 2022, CCIS 1818, pp. 13–26, 2023.
https://doi.org/10.1007/978-3-031-34222-6_2

like p-value, confidence intervals etc. to identify the most informative features. On the other hand, the wrapper-based feature selection methods, hybrid methods and embedded methods apply at least one predominant learning algorithm based on global greedy search approach which evaluates possible combination of features to identify the optimal feature subset. As wrapper-based feature selection methods often evaluate all possible combination of features, these methods are computationally expensive in comparison to filter-based feature selection methods since for n number of features there are 2^n possible solutions [2]. Therefore, selection of features from high dimensional data exerts difficult challenges for data mining. Such methods may not always find the optimal subset of features from the high dimensional data. Moreover, the optimal subset of features selected by a method may not produce equally good results when applied to other classifiers.

As the dimensionality of dataset increases, applying wrapper-based method becomes very expensive in terms of computation time and selection of optimal subset of features. On the contrary, univariate feature selection methods are quite fast and reasonably effective. However, there are a number of such univariate feature fitness measures, and one may wonder which of these to use for a given feature selection cum classification problem. Therefore, a comparative study of these fitness measures is a necessity to figure out relatively effective filter-based feature fitness measures which may cope with the above challenges.

In this paper, an empirical study of feature fitness measures has been carried out wherein we have evaluated seven univariate feature fitness measures on six different types of datasets with a number of features ranging from 13 to 7129 and a number of samples ranging from 62 to 2000. The seven filter-based methods have been used for finding the feature scores of the datasets and Support Vector Machine has been used for measuring the classification accuracy. Also, Pearson correlation score, Spearman correlation score and Kendall tau correlation score have been used to determine the strength for feature selection of the filter-based method. A higher correlation score suggests that the corresponding feature selection method is more efficient in detecting the most informative features. In this study, multiple correlation methods have been applied to correlate features fitness measures and corresponding accuracies.

2 Related Works

Filter-based feature selection methods are widely used as a preprocessing step before applying wrapper techniques by hybrid methods. Filter-based feature selection method ranks the features according to certain calculated scores, and these methods are preferred due to their computational and statistical scalability [3]. Recently, there are many works on filter-based feature selection methods and obtained good classification accuracy. Dashtban et al. [1] employed Laplacian and Fischer score based Genetic Algorithm techniques for gene selection from microarray data. This method obtained very high accuracy by selecting only a few genes from five microarray datasets. In [2], Ghosh et al. used 10 different filter-based feature selection techniques on 10 different microarray datasets to access the potential for feature selection of those methods. Their results reflect that Mutual Information produced the best classification accuracy whereas Chi-square and ReliefF also produced good results. In [4], Jain et al. applied a correlation-based filter method followed by improved binary particle swarm optimization on eleven microarray datasets. They achieved 100 percent classification accuracy for seven out of eleven datasets with only a few selected genes. In [5], a symmetrical uncertainty-based filter method followed by random forest classifier shows very high performance on colon cancer and leukemia dataset.

Dabba et al. [6] implemented Mutual Information Maximization based on a modi-fied Moth Flame Algorithm for gene selection from sixteen benchmark gene expression datasets and obtained very impressive results. In [7], Baliarsingh et al. applied a novel ANOVA based enhanced Jaya and forest optimization algorithm on seven microarray datasets for cancer classification. It shows very high classification accuracy and very low computation time for small round blue cell tumors and Leukemia dataset with few selected features. Bolón-Canedo et al. [8] applied seven feature selection techniques such as Correlation-based Feature Selection (CFS), Fast Correlation-based Filter Selec-tion, INTERACT, Information Gain, ReliefF, Minimum Redundancy Maximum Rele-vance (MRMR) and SVM Recursive Feature Elimination, and applied on nine datasets to determine best feature selection methods. Other popular feature selection methods include MRMR filter-based method with Genetic Bee Colony and Genetic Algorithm [9], Symmetrical Uncertainty [10], Markov Blanket [11], Chi-square [12].

In short, the studies carried out so far on evaluation of univariate feature selectors neither focus on diversity of datasets nor the essence of generality. For instance, Ghosh et al. [2] have applied some feature selectors on microarray gene expression datasets only. Moreover, statistical correlation in evaluating such measures is quite uncommon. In this paper, we apply multiple correlation methods to correlate individual feature fitness scores with their classification ability measured in terms of classification accuracy over a wide range of datasets.

3   Feature Fitness Measures

The univariate filter methods prove to be very effective for large datasets or limited resources due to its low computational cost as it doesn't involve any learning algorithm like wrapper or hybrid methods. Therefore, in this work, seven filter-based univariate feature selection techniques - Chi-square [12], Symmetrical Uncertainty [10], ANOVA [13], Mutual Information [14], Fisher score [2], Gini index [2] and ReliefF [2] have been considered. Using these methods, fitness scores of all features of a dataset under consideration are determined along with their classification ability in terms of accuracy. Followed by this, statistical relationship between feature fitness scores and their cor-responding accuracies are studied using Pearson correlation, Spearman correlation and Kendall tau correlation method. Correlation scores are normalized so as to vary from -1 to + 1, where -1 suggests extreme negative correlation, + 1 indicates extreme positive correlation and 0 indicates no correlation. Below, we present a brief outline of the feature fitness measures taken into consideration in this experiment.

3.1 Chi-Square

Chi-square statistic is widely used for feature selection. Chi-square test checks for independence between two categorical variables simultaneously, which will determine if the feature is related to the class or not. The formula for X^2 score for a feature f is given in Eq. 1 [2, 12].

$$X^2(f) = \sum_{j=1}^{r} \sum_{s=1}^{c} \frac{\left(n_{js} - \mu_{js}\right)^2}{\mu_{js}} \tag{1}$$

where r represents the number of distinct values in the feature and c is the number of distinct values in a class, n_{js} stands for frequency of jth element of sth class. Here , $\mu_{js} = \frac{n_{*s}n_{j*}}{n}$, n_{*s} denotes the number of data elements in class r and n_{j*} indicates the number of data instances in j^{th} feature. A larger value of chi-square implies that the feature is relatively more informative in nature. Theoretically, χ^2 value ranges from 0 to ∞. Though, chi-square test is robust with respect to the distribution of data, it cannot produce satisfactory results for less number of observations (less than 20) and for frequency less than 5.

3.2 Analysis of Variance (ANOVA)

Analysis of Variance F (ANOVA-F) is a statistical test to determine the difference between multiple groups (classes) in a given sample [13]. The ANOVA F-test measures the ratio between variance values of two different samples. The F ratio can be calculated as follows.

$$F = MSB / MSW \tag{2}$$

Here, MSB signifies Mean Squares Between the groups and MSW signifies Mean Squares Within the groups. MSB can also be explained as the variance between the groups and MSW is the variance within the groups. MSB and MSW are defined as in Eqs. 3 and 4.

$$MSB = \left(SSB / df_b\right) \tag{3}$$

$$MSW = \left(SSW / df_w\right) \tag{4}$$

where SSB denotes the Sum of Squares Between the groups and SSW signifies the Sum of Squares Within the groups, df_b is the degrees of freedom between groups and we can calculate $df_b =$ Number of groups -1. Also, df_w is the degrees of freedom within groups and we can calculate $df_w =$ Total observations- Number of groups. The SSB and SSW are defined as in Eqs. 5 and 6 [15].

$$SSB = \sum_{g} n_g \left(\bar{x}_g - \bar{\bar{x}}\right)^2 \tag{5}$$

$$SSW = \sum_{i,g} (x_i - \overline{x}_g)^2 \tag{6}$$

Here, n_g is the number of samples from group g, $\overline{x}_g$ is the mean of group g, $\overline{\overline{x}}$ is the grand mean of the samples, and x_i represents each observation from a group g. Theoretically, F value ranges from 0 to infinite. Though, ANOVA-F is robust when the observations are normally distributed, it may not produce exact p-values when the distribution of the observations are heavier in the tails compared to the normal distribution. Also, ANOVA-F may produce suboptimal results for a specific hypothesis rather than any alternate to the null hypothesis.

3.3 Mutual Information

Mutual Information (MI) is an information theoretic feature fitness measure. MI uses Shannon's entropy formula [14] and the concept of conditional entropy [14] to calculate feature score. MI between two random variables X and Y is defined as shown in Eq. 7.

$$MI(X, Y) = H(X) - H(X|Y)$$
$$or \tag{7}$$
$$MI(X, Y) = H(Y) - H(Y|X)$$

Shannon's entropy H(X) of a random variable X having probability density function p, can be calculated as per Eq. 8.

$$H(X) = -\sum_i p(x_i) * \log_2 p(x_i) \tag{8}$$

The conditional entropy H(X|Y) of two random variables X and Y having probability density function p can be calculated as shown in Eq. 9.

$$H(X|Y) = -\sum_j p(y_j) \sum_i p(x_i|y_j) * \log_2 [p(x_i|y_j)] \tag{9}$$

Here, $p(x_i|y_j)$ is the conditional probability of x_i having occurred y_j. The conditional entropy can also be written as follows.

$$H(X|Y) = -\sum_{x \varepsilon X} p(x, y) \sum_{y \varepsilon Y} p(x, y) * \log_2 \frac{p(x, y)}{g(x)} \tag{10}$$

Here, $p(x, y)$ is the joint probability distribution at (x, y) between the observation x and y, and $g(x)$ is the marginal probability of x. Theoretically, MI value ranges from 0 to ∞. A value 0 means that X and Y are independent. The higher is value of MI(X,Y), the more the information is shared between X and Y. The main limitation for measuring MI is that any distribution-free high-confidence lower bound on MI estimated from N samples cannot be larger than $O(\ln N)$.

3.4 Symmetrical Uncertainty

Symmetrical Uncertainty (SU) is another information theoretic feature fitness measure. Mutual Information is bent in favor of features with more values. So, the values should be normalized to confirm that they can be compared and have the same effect. SU determines the correlation between the features and class values, and can be calculated as shown in Eq. 11 [10].

$$SU(X, Y) = 2 * \frac{MI(X, Y)}{H(X) + H(Y)} \tag{11}$$

Here, MI(X,Y) is mutual information between two random variables X and Y, H(X) is the entropy of X and H(Y) is the entropy of random variable Y. SU value lies between 1 and 0, value 1 indicates the feature X and Y are completely correlated and value 0 indicates X and Y are uncorrelated. The major drawback of SU is that this method exhibits a linear bias in favour of non-informative attributes with more values.

3.5 Fisher Score

Fisher score-based feature selection method is widely used because of its good performance. Say, X is the feature and Y is the label having c classes. Also, n_i is the number of elements with label i, μ_i and σ_i respectively denotes the mean and standard deviation of the elements of X having label i. Additionally, μ and σ respectively denotes mean and standard deviation of all the elements of X. Now, the Fisher score is computed as shown in Eq. 12 [2]. Theoretically, the Fisher score value ranges from 0 to ∞.

$$F_i = \frac{\sum_{i=1}^{c} n_i * (\mu_i - \mu)^2}{\sum_{i=1}^{c} n_i * \sigma_i^2} \tag{12}$$

Fisher-score based feature selector has many advantages. However, it may sometimes select suboptimal subset of features as it considers each feature individually.

3.6 Gini Index

Gini index is used for feature selection in decision tree algorithm like CART (Classification and Regression Tree), SLIQ (Supervised Learning In Quest), SPRINT (Scalable Parallelizable Induction of Decision Trees) and others algorithms [2]. Let, S is the set of s samples and these samples have m different groups. As samples belong to m different groups we can divide S into m different subsets, $(S_i, i = 1, ..., m)$. Say, S_i is the sample set which falls under class C_i, where s_i is the sample number of the set S_i. Then, we can calculate Gini index of set S using Eq. 13 [16].

$$Gini(S) = 1 - \sum_{i=1}^{m} p_i^2 \tag{13}$$

Here, p_i is the probability of any sample in S that belongs to class C_i. We calculate the probability as s_i/s, the sum is computed over m classes. Gini coefficient lies between

0 (complete equality) and 1 (complete inequality). If the set is divided into n different subsets, the *Gini* after splitting is shown in Eq. 14. The minimum $Gini_{split}$ is desirable for splitting an attribute. As Gini index computes according to the ordinal metric, this may sometimes result in poor performance.

$$Gini_{split}(S) = \sum_{j=1}^{n} \frac{s_j}{s} * Gini(s_j) \tag{14}$$

3.7   ReliefF

Relief was first introduced by Kira and Rendell for binary class classification by applying Euclidian distance measure. Later, Relief was modified with Manhattan distance measurements for multi class problem solving and was named ReliefF [2]. For a randomly selected instance R_i, ReliefF searches for k of its nearest neighbors from the same class called nearest hits H_j, and also k nearest neighbors from each of the different classes, called nearest misses $M_j(C)$. The ReliefF algorithm then updates the quality estimation $W[A]$ for all attributes A depending on their values for R_i, hits H_j and misses $M_j(C)$. Also, $P(C)$ signifies the probability of class C, and $1-P(class\ (R_i))$ represents probability of misses' classes. The process is repeated m times. The estimation of quality of a feature A is given in Eq. 15 [17].

$$W[A] = W[A] - \sum_{j=1}^{k} \frac{diff(A, R_i, H_j)}{m.k} + \sum_{c \neq classR_i} [\frac{P(C)}{1 - P(class(R_i))} \sum_{j=1}^{k} diff(A, R_i, M_j(C))]/m.k \tag{15}$$

The *diff(X,Y,Z)* function measures the difference between the values of attribute X for two instances Y and Z. The *diff(X,Y,Z)* function is defined for numerical attributes as follows:

$$diff(X, Y, Z) = \frac{|(value(X, Y) - value(X, Z))|}{max(X) - min(X)} \tag{16}$$

For nominal attributes, *diff(X,Y,Z)* gives value 0 if $value(X,Y) = value(X,Z)$, otherwise *diff(X,Y,Z)* produces 1. The function *diff(X,Y,Z)* is used also for computing the distance between instances to find out the nearest neighbors. The sum of distances over all attributes applying Manhattan distance method offers the total distance. ReliefF values range within -1 (worst) to 1 (best). Though, Relief based feature selectors have low time complexity, the redundant features cannot be removed by excluding features with low weights.

3.8   Correlation Estimation

The above discussed seven univariate filter-based methods were used to compute feature scores for all features from Mobile, Colon cancer, Digits, Breast cancer, Wine and Leukemia datasets. The datasets are diversified in many aspects i.e. in their dimensions and samples (number of features ranging from 13 to 7129 and number of samples ranging from 62 to 2000) as well as data type, such as survey data, microarray data, pathological data, physico-chemical data etc. To test the robustness of the univariate fitness measures such diversified datasets have been considered in this study. Accuracies of each individual feature were determined using the SVM classifier with stratified 10-fold cross validation [18]. Parameters for the SVM classifier were adjusted according to the dataset in the experiment. Next, statistical relationship between the features (score) and its corresponding classification accuracy was established by calculating Pearson correlation score [19], Spearman correlation score [20] and Kendall tau correlation score [21]. This process offers a relationship score for the corresponding Filter based method. The Pearson, Spearman and Kendall tau correlation values range from -1 to $+1$, where -1 indicates strong negative correlation, $+1$ indicates strong positive correlation and 0 indicates no correlation. A higher score of Pearson correlation, Spearman correlation, Kendall tau correlation suggest that the Filter-based method is more efficient to identify the most informative features from those datasets.

4   Experimental Results

The experiments for univariate feature fitness measures have been carried out on six diversified datasets i.e. Mobile [22], Colon cancer [23], Digits [24], Breast cancer [25], Wine [26] and Leukemia [27]. Among them, Colon cancer and Leukemia are microarray gene expression datasets. Configuration of the system on which these experiments have been conducted includes Intel Core i3 processor, 4 GB RAM, Windows 10 operating system and Python 3.8 environment. As discussed in Sect. 3, for a good feature fitness measure, features with higher fitness scores should yield higher accuracy and vice-versa, which leads to stronger correlation. In Fig. 1, feature fitness scores (x-axis of each individual graph) and their corresponding accuracies (y-axis of each individual graph) are shown for all feature fitness measures over all the six datasets.

Quantitative performance of the seven measures on six datasets are summarized in Table 1. From Table 1, it may be observed that for Mobile dataset Chi-square method obtained the highest score when Pearson correlation is used, but ANOVA method scored the highest when Spearman correlation and Kendall tau correlation are used. For the same dataset, ReliefF method scored the second highest and Mutual Information scored the third highest using Pearson correlation method. When Spearman correlation is used, Chi-square method scored the second highest and Fisher score method scored the third highest. For Kendall tau correlation, Chi-square method scored the second highest and Fisher score method scored the third highest. Gini index method scored the lowest for all three correlation methods. According to sum of correlation scores, ANOVA method is found to be the best one (shown in bold font in the table) and Chi-square and Fisher score are consecutively the second and the third best method for this dataset.

From Digits dataset, Mutual Information scored the best considering Pearson correlation, Spearman correlation and Kendall tau correlation method. SU and ANOVA based method consecutively scored the second and the third best using Pearson correlation. When Spearman correlation is considered, ANOVA method scored the second best and SU method scored the third best. For Kendall tau correlation, ANOVA method scored the second best and SU method scored the third best. Gini index-based method scored the lowest for all three correlation methods from the same Digits dataset. Considering sum of correlation scores, Mutual Information method is found to be the best one, and ANOVA and SU consecutively are the second and the third best method.

For the Breast cancer dataset, MI is the best method, and ANOVA and Fisher score consecutively are the second and the third best method according to sum of correlation score. Gini index method overall performed the worst for this dataset. Considering Pearson correlation, MI method performed the best, ANOVA method is the second best and Chi-square is the third best method. When Spearman correlation is considered, ANOVA method performed the best, Fisher score the second best and MI the third best. According to Kendall tau correlation, ANOVA method is found to be the best one, MI and Fisher score consecutively are the second and the third best methods.

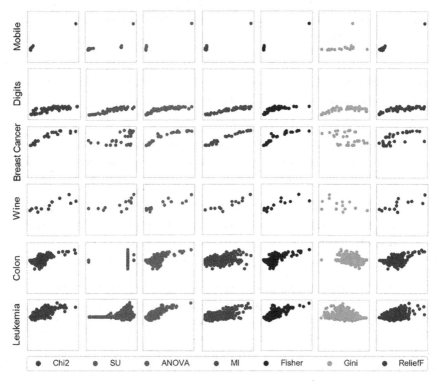

Fig. 1. Feature fitness scores vs. accuracy graph for all six datasets. The vertical axis of each graph represents accuracy and the horizontal axis of each graph represents normalized values of feature fitness scores of a particular dataset.

For Wine dataset, Fisher score method overall performed the best for feature selection, MI is the second best and ANOVA method is the third best method according to sum of correlation score. Again, Gini index based method overall performed the worst in this data set. When Pearson correlation is considered, ANOVA method is found to be the best one, MI is the second best and Fisher score is the third best method. Considering both Spearman and Kendall tau correlation score, Fisher score is the best one, MI is the second best and ANOVA is the third best method for feature selection.

For Colon cancer microarray dataset, Fisher score method scored the best using Pearson correlation, but SU based method scored the best when Spearman correlation and Kendall tau correlation are considered. The second and the third best score according to Pearson correlation from the same dataset consecutively are Chi-square and ANOVA method. According to Spearman correlation, the second and the third best scores are obtained by Gini index and Mutual Information respectively. Also, according to Kendall tau correlation method the second and the third best scores are obtained consecutively by Gini index and Mutual Information method from colon cancer dataset. According to the sum of correlation scores, SU method is the best one and Mutual Information and ReliefF consecutively are the second and the third best method.

For Leukemia microarray dataset, ANOVA is found to be the best feature selection method, whereas Chi-square is the second best and Fisher score is the third best method as per the sum of correlation score. Again, Gini index overall performed the worst in this dataset. According to Pearson correlation score, ANOVA is the best method, Fisher score is the second best one and Chi-square is the third best method. Considering both Spearman and Kendall tau correlation score, MI is the best feature selection method, Chi-square is the second best and ANOVA is the third best method.

Thus, it may be realized from the above results that univariate feature fitness measures taken into consideration in this study responded differently for different datasets. None of these measures performed consistently well in all types of datasets. This is due to the properties of the datasets and the nature of the feature selection algorithm. However, a closer look reveals that ANOVA f-statistic and MI method often topped in the experiments carried out. For instance, ANOVA f-statistic topped in Mobile and Leukemia datasets while it performed well in Digits, Breast cancer and Wine datasets. MI method topped in Digits and Breast cancer datasets and it also performed well in Colon cancer and Wine datasets. Fisher score method is found to be another efficient feature selection technique besides ANOVA and MI. Followed by ANOVA f-statistic and MI, few other measures such as SU, Chi-square and ReliefF also performed reasonably well.

The datasets used for this experiment varied in instances, in features, and in classes. The number of samples varied from 62 to 2000, number of features varied from 13 to 7129, and class size ranges from 2 to 10. Among these six datasets, colon cancer and Leukemia are microarray datasets. The datasets having 2 classes are mobile, breast cancer, colon cancer, and leukemia. Wine data have 3 classes and digits data have 10 classes. The experimental results reveal that ANOVA is the most promising feature selection method for binary class datasets. For 3 or higher number of classes, MI appears to be the most promising feature selection criterion.

Table 1. Pearson, Spearman and Kendall correlation scores for the seven filter-based feature selection methods applying to Mobile, Colon cancer, Digits dataset, Breast cancer, Wine and Leukemia dataset.

Dataset	Methods	Pearson Corr.	Spearman Corr.	Kendall tau	Sum
Mobile dataset [22]	Chi-square	0.9921	0.8372	0.6491	2.4784
	SU	0.7334	0.6265	0.4908	1.8507
	ANOVA	0.9851	0.9484	0.8391	**2.7726**
	MI	0.9887	0.5729	0.4554	2.0170
	Fisher score	0.9812	0.6912	0.5435	2.2159
	Gini index	0.2813	0.6551	0.5013	1.4377
	ReliefF	0.9891	0.4137	0.3113	1.7141
Digits dataset [24]	Chi-square	0.7742	0.7830	0.5974	2.1546
	SU	0.9092	0.8654	0.7124	2.4870
	ANOVA	0.8509	0.8964	0.7463	2.4936
	MI	0.9438	0.9031	0.7663	**2.6132**
	Fisher score	0.7589	0.8518	0.6949	2.3056
	Gini index	0.6972	0.5413	0.3898	1.6283
	ReliefF	0.8383	0.8220	0.6517	2.3120
Breast cancer [25]	Chi-square	0.9312	0.9553	0.8243	2.7108
	SU	0.5283	0.5354	0.3819	1.4456
	ANOVA	0.9320	0.9760	0.8802	2.7882
	MI	0.9837	0.9722	0.8755	**2.8314**
	Fisher score	0.9060	0.9731	0.8708	2.7499
	Gini index	-0.3433	−0.2301	−0.1583	-0.7317
	ReliefF	0.6730	0.7528	0.5775	2.0033
Wine [26]	Chi-square	0.8072	0.8406	0.6923	2.3401
	SU	0.6977	0.8132	0.6410	2.1519
	ANOVA	0.8751	0.8791	0.6923	2.4465
	MI	0.8750	0.8792	0.7436	2.4978
	Fisher score	0.8259	0.9121	0.7692	**2.5072**
	Gini index	-0.4541	−0.4340	−0.3077	-1.1958
	ReliefF	0.7361	0.6868	0.4872	1.9101
Colon cancer [23]	Chi-square	0.3082	−0.2033	−0.1732	-0.0683
	SU	0.0174	0.0402	0.0386	**0.0962**

(continued)

Table 1. (*continued*)

Dataset	Methods	Pearson Corr.	Spearman Corr.	Kendall tau	Sum
	ANOVA	0.2636	−0.2051	−0.1743	−0.1158
	MI	0.1583	−0.0448	−0.0394	0.0741
	Fisher score	0.3104	−0.2089	−0.1791	−0.0776
	Gini index	-0.1528	−0.0114	−0.0081	−0.1723
	ReliefF	0.1978	−0.0995	−0.0827	0.0156
Leukemia [27]	Chi-square	0.7206	0.1599	0.1259	1.0064
	SU	0.0997	0.0514	0.0415	0.1926
	ANOVA	0.7309	0.1588	0.1253	**1.0150**
	MI	0.4906	0.1837	0.1541	0.8284
	Fisher score	0.7233	0.1558	0.1223	1.0014
	Gini index	-0.2557	−0.1451	−0.1159	−0.5167
	ReliefF	0.2460	0.0512	0.0405	0.3377

5 Conclusion

This work is a modest attempt to reveal effective filter-based feature selection measures by establishing correlation between feature fitness scores and corresponding accuracies. Seven leading univariate feature fitness measures i.e. Chi-square, Symmetrical Uncertainty, ANOVA f-statistic, Mutual Information, Fisher score, Gini index and ReliefF are taken into consideration for this empirical study. Experiments on diversified datasets like Mobile, Colon cancer, Digits, Breast cancer, Wine and Leukemia with multiple correlation methods revealed that performance of univariate feature selectors vary on different datasets. While none of these measures performed equally well for all types of datasets, Mutual Information and ANOVA f-statistic produced the best results in most cases, followed by Fisher score, SU, Chi-square and ReliefF. This study may equip researchers in choosing appropriate selector(s) for a given feature selection cum classification problem. As a possible extension to this work, separate studies on similar type of datasets as well as different type of datasets may be conducted to investigate if there is any measure good for specific dataset-type. Additionally, other univariate feature selectors may be included in such studies.

References

1. Dashtban, M., Balafar, M.: Gene selection for microarray cancer classification using a new evolutionary method employing artificial intelligence concepts. Genomics **109**(2), 91–107 (2017)
2. Ghosh, K.K., et al.: Theoretical and empirical analysis of filter ranking methods: experimental study on benchmark DNA microarray data. Expert Sys. with Appl. **169**(114485), (2021)

3. Saeys, Y., Inza, I., Larranaga, P.: Review of feature selection techniques in bioinformatics. Bioinformatics **23**(19), 2507–2517 (2007)
4. Jain, I., Jain, V.K., Jain, R.: Correlation feature selection based improved-binary particle swarm optimization for gene selection and cancer classification. Appl. Soft Comput. **62**, 203–215 (2018)
5. Asad, E., Mollah, A.F.: Biomarker identification from gene expression based on symmetrical uncertainty. Int. J. Intel. Info. Techno. **17**(4), 19–37 (2021)
6. Dabba, A., Tari, A., Meftali, S., Mokhtari, R.: Gene selection and classification of microarray data method based on mutual information and moth flame algorithm. Expert Sys. with Appl. **166**(114012) (2021)
7. Baliarsingh, S.K., Vipsita, S., Dash, B.: A new optimal gene selection approach for cancer classification using enhanced Jaya-based forest optimization algorithm. Neural Comput. Appl. **32**(12), 8599–8616 (2019). https://doi.org/10.1007/s00521-019-04355-x
8. Bolón-Canedo, V., Sánchez-Maroño, N., Alonso-Betanzos, A., Benítez, J.M., Herrera, F.: A review of microarray datasets and applied feature selection methods. Information Sci. **282**, 111–135 (2014)
9. Alshamlan, H.M., Badr, G.H., Alohali, Y.A.: Genetic bee colony (GBC) algorithm: A new gene selection method for microarray cancer classification. Comput. Biol. Chem. **56**(C), 49-60 (2015)
10. Shreem, S.S., Abdullah, S., Nazri, M.Z.A.: Hybrid feature selection algorithm using symmetrical uncertainty and a harmony search algorithm. Int. J. Syst. Sci. **47**(6), 1312–1329 (2016)
11. Yu, K., Wu, X., Ding, W., Mu, Y., Wang, H.: Markov blanket feature selection using representative sets. IEEE Trans. on Neural Net. and learn. Sys. **28**(11), 2775–2788 (2017)
12. Li, J., et al.: Feature selection: a data perspective. ACM Comput. Surv. **50**(6), 1–45 (2017)
13. Kumar, M., Rath, N.K., Swain, A., Rath, S.K.: Feature selection and classification of microarray data using mapreduce based anova and k-nearest neighbor. Procedia Comp. Sci. **54**, 301–310 (2015)
14. Beraha, M., Metelli, A. M., Papini, M., Tirinzoni, A., Restelli, M.: Feature selection via mutual information: new theoretical insights. In: International Joint Conference on Neural Network. IEEE, Budapest, Hungary (2019)
15. Ding, H., Feng, P.M., Chen, W., Lin, H.: Identification of bacteriophage virion proteins by the ANOVA feature selection and analysis. Mol. Bio. Sys **10**(8), 2229–2235 (2014)
16. Shang, W., Huang, H., Zhu, H., Lin, Y., Qu, Y., Wang, Z.: A novel feature selection algorithm for text categorization. Expert Sys. With Appl. **33**(1), 1–5 (2007)
17. Robnik-Šikonja, M., Kononenko, I.: Theoretical and empirical analysis of ReliefF and RReliefF. Machine Learn. **53**, 23–69 (2003)
18. Ojala, M., Garriga, G. C.: Permutation tests for studying classifier performance. In: 2009 Ninth IEEE International Conference on Data Mining, pp. 908–913. IEEE, USA (2009)
19. Chandrashekar, G., Sahin, F.: A survey on feature selection methods. Comput. Electr. Engg. **40**(1), 16–28 (2014)
20. Mukaka, M.M.: Statistics corner: A guide to appropriate use of correlation coefficient in medical research. Malawi Medical J. The J. Medical Assoc. Malawi **24**(3), 69–71 (2012)
21. Lapata, M.: Automatic evaluation of information ordering: Kendall's Tau. Comput. Linguist. **32**(4), 471–484 (2006)
22. Mobile Pricing Dataset. https://raw.githubusercontent.com/krishnaik06/Feature-Engineering-Live-sessions/master/mobile_dataset.csv. (Accessed 2 July 2021)
23. Alon, U., et al.: Broad patterns and normal colon tissues probed by oligonucleotide arrays. In: Proceedings of the National Academy of Sciences of the United States of America, vol. 96(12), pp. 6745–6750 (1999)

24. Optical Recognition of Handwritten Digits. https://archive.ics.uci.edu/ml/datasets/Optical+
    Recognition+of+Handwritten+Digits, (Accessed 2 July 2021)

25. Wolberg, W.H., Street, W.N., Mangasarian, O.L.: Machine learning techniques to diagnose
    breast cancer from fine-needle aspirates. Cancer Lett. **77**(2–3), 163–171 (1994)

26. Forina, M., Leardi, R., Armanino, C., Lanteri, S.: PARVUS: An extendable package of
    programs for data exploration, classification and correlation. J. Chemom. **4**(2), 191–193
    (1990)

27. Golub, T.R., et al.: Molecular classification of cancer: class discovery and class prediction by
    gene expression monitoring. Science **286**(5439), 531–537 (1999)

Securing Advanced Metering Infrastructure Using Blockchain for Effective Energy Trading

Yuvraj Singh[1(✉)], Agni Datta[1], Smita Shandilya[2], and Shishir Kumar Shandilya[1]

[1] VIT Bhopal University, Bhopal, India
yuvrajsingh3440@gmail.com
[2] Sagar Institute of Research and Technology, Bhopal, India

Abstract. To effectively regulate the energy supply, Advanced Metering Infrastructure (AMI) deployment is gaining momentum in various parts of the world. Energy distributors, service providers, and consumers must work together to address several issues. All the transactions need to be documented properly and securely. Third parties can be trusted in those transactions by using blockchain. With the deployment of Advanced Metering Infrastructure (AMI) and distributed ledgers, blockchain may aid in safeguarding and facilitating the movement of data. This paper discusses the viability of utilizing blockchain for advanced metering infrastructure, along with the security risks and threat landscape. For the exchange of energy, we have proposed an Ethereum-based blockchain model, and results are discussed for the scenario when an independent house's smart meter and distribution system operator trades energy.

Keywords: Blockchain · Advanced Metering Infrastructure · Smart Meters · Smart Grids · Distribution System Operator

1 Introduction

"If it's smart, it's vulnerable," they say. This study discusses the viability of utilizing blockchain for advanced metering infrastructure and electronic devices that transmit information such as power use, pricing, and advanced metering that serve as the point of contact between homeowners and Distribution System Operators (DSOs). Since it may affect the transaction and billing information, secure communication between the two parties is crucial [1].

Smart grids play a vital role in creating and implementing the digital paradise, just as we are on the verge of creating smart cities. The smart grids may be thought of as the basis for the same since smart homes, buildings, streets, and other places include intelligent gadgets that require real-time monitoring and scheduling of power use [2].

The main purpose of smart meters is to report real-time use, sending the recorded data to the smart grid at frequent intervals. The extra capabilities also include a smart interface to manage electricity consumption in home appliances during peak hours and the ability to analyze usage trends and disconnect customers from electricity usage directly from the smart grid when a problem arises. Many security challenges like Distributed Denial of

Service (DDoS) attacks, Man in the Middle (MITM) attacks, adjusting/altering invoices, stealing payment information, etc., may affect smart meters. Blockchain technology can be used to address these problems and to have secure and trusted financial transactions.

Blockchain helps to make transactions comprehensive and safe. It is not just restricted to cryptocurrency and is being employed in the majority of other sectors as well. Among Distributed Energy Resources (DER) transactions, the demand for blockchain implementation is very high as it facilitates peer-to-peer energy exchanges at microgrids. The distribution system operators enable the sale of excess energy produced by electric cars without the intervention of the distributed system operators by monitoring energy consumption, load balancing, and demand-supply at negotiated prices. With many different applications of blockchain, one such application paves the way for a sustainable environment and a digitally driven society by including an automated smart metering system. It considers how much energy home appliances use to secure blockchain for power production and transparent bill generation. American company Bankymoons was the first to integrate blockchain technology into a smart grid's smart metering system. The full implementation of peer-to-peer technology is still fraught with difficulties, but it allows for a secure flow of transactions between smart meters and DSOs through the distributed trust that is built up among peers using cryptographic techniques, which ultimately takes care of security attacks like eavesdropping, data tampering, and unauthorized access to data. In this study, we suggest a blockchain based on Ethereum to improve the security of transactions between SMEs and DSOs.

2 Related Works

Blockchain saves transactions in blocks and through a timestamp and interconnected hash links, each block in Blockchain is linked to the one before it. Hash values ensure that no data or value is ever updated by an unauthorized person. Blockchain is a distributed ledger with no single point of failure since all parties adhere to the no-trust policy. Data is completely decentralized, with no involvement from outside parties. A chain of the ledger made up of several blocks is known as a blockchain. Because no individual block can be changed without also changing the entire chain of blocks, systems are protected from attacks and may carry out transactions in a secure manner without the intervention of a third party Fig. 1. The blockchain serves as a public ledger for all transactions that take place when entities participate in digital activities. The act of mining is known as the creation of new blocks, and a method known as consensus helps the user ensure the reliability and integrity of blocks. A network of linked nodes may be used to create blockchain-enabled systems, and several computer languages are already being utilized to create blockchains [3].

In 2015, the blockchain-based system, Ethereum launched the first smart contracts. Additionally, it offers an interactive environment for creating and deploying smart contracts written in a Turing-complete programming language for the user-defined deployment of robust, effective, and smart contracts. The ability to evaluate the account's current balance, save the address in 20 bytes, and execute it are only a few of its numerous benefits. Ethereum has its cryptocurrency, called ether. Smart contracts and other autonomous agents are utilized for inter-account transactions. To provide a run environment, smart contract prototypes created for smart grids are executed on the EVM

(Environment Virtual Machine). New nodes are verified by using the entire nodes that EVM has produced. In Ethereum, blocks are generated every 15 s. Gas is used as a transaction charge to stop attacks. The product of gas usage and gas price is the definition of a transaction in Ethereum. Gas consumption can be improved as every transaction uses 5 USD for buyers and sellers and there is a need for the development of a more reliant smart contract that might serve the demands and specifications of bidders and auctioneers more generally [4].

Hyperledger is a private, permissioned blockchain that was created and is now maintained by the Linux Foundation. It was first implemented as a private network for users to monitor their transactions and communicate with their digital assets. One of the main characteristics of the programming languages known as chain codes that are used on the Hyperledger network is support for distributed applications [5]. It doesn't have many highly qualified programmers. Additionally, it has failed to provide any use cases. Its architecture is intricate. It has the bare minimum of SDKs and APIs also It is not a fault-tolerant network [6].

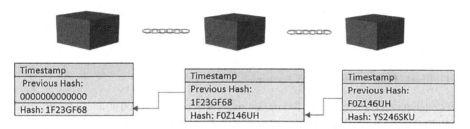

Fig. 1. Chain of blocks in the blockchain

The design makes use of elements including ordering, peer, and endorsing nodes as well as client applications. Peers are a type of component that is not restricted to any one node; they can act as a committer for certain tasks and an endorser for others for some time. They carry out tasks that are not all that dissimilar from those carried out by miners in other blockchain architectures. Hash functions might be held accountable for ensuring the robustness and security of blockchain in that instance, however even these hash functions could be compromised by some superfast machines, such as supercomputers or quantum computers. [5] To overcome these challenges consensus algorithms [7] were introduced in the blockchain. Some of the primary consensus algorithms are:

Proof of Work (PoW): Cryptocurrency system secured by a proof of work mechanism. E.g., in Bitcoin, each block consists of two components: block headers with important characteristics, such as the time the block was created and a reference to the preceding block and the block of transactions' Merkle tree root [8] and List of transactions in a block. The SHA-256 algorithm [9] is used to hash a block twice, and the resultant integer value is used to reference a specific block.

Proof of Stake (PoS): Proof of stake algorithms change inequality [10] such that it now depends on the user's possession of the specific coin used with the PoS protocol rather than block attributes.

Delegated Proof of Stake (DPoS): "Delegated proof of stake (DPoS) is a generic term describing an evolution of the basic PoS consensus protocols." DPoS is utilized in BitShares, as are other proposed algorithms such as Slasher and Tendermint. As compared to PoS and PoW, this algorithm promises to be more effective and efficient.

Practical Byzantine Fault Tolerance (PBFT): Depending on the technique, 2/3 of the network's nodes must vote in favor of the transaction being included in the next block to be considered legitimate. This approach is often employed in semi-trusted or trusted settings. Hyperledger makes use of the PBFT algorithm [11].

It might be challenging to predict how much resources would cost and how long a smart contract will take to execute. It is necessary to create a more robust smart contract formalism that is similar to Ethereum so that smart contracts on LC can do practically all distributed computing jobs [12].

2.1 Blockchain in the Energy Sector

To develop smart energy, a self-maintaining, self-rectifying, robust, and decentralized system is needed. With improvements in several technologies, the blockchain timeline is illustrated in Fig. 2.

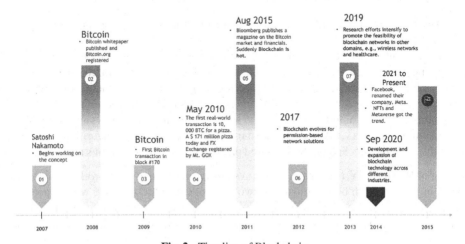

Fig. 2. Timeline of Blockchain

A variety of technologies have been combined to create blockchain technology. Blockchain was built on the principles of distributed computing, which were initially discussed in 1982. With the publication of his white paper "Blockchain: A Peer-to-Peer Electronic Cash System" in 2008, Satoshi Nakamoto introduced the first project. Since then, a variety of blockchain technologies have been created, but the real-world use of blockchain only began with the introduction of smart contracts in 2013. Even at that time, a dependable and adaptable platform was still required, so the Linux Foundation introduced Hyperledger in 2015 to address this issue. Since then, the energy sector has been utilizing blockchain to transform the existing grid infrastructure into intelligent grids [13].

The primary use of energy blockchain is decentralized energy trade. Every transaction in traditional energy trading often involves a power company acting as an intermediary. Prosumers (i.e., customers who own power-producing equipment like solar panels or wind turbines) and consumers can conduct peer-to-peer power trading without the requirement for a centralized provider where there are direct physical power connections (see Fig. 3). In greater detail, using a P2P blockchain-based platform operated by the neighborhood, prosumers and consumers converse about transactional information. When a transaction is authorized, electricity will be physically transferred from the prosumer to the consumer in the equivalent quantity.

2.2 Blockchain-Based Smart Grid

In comparison to the traditional system of the centralized ledger, the digital immutable ledger has been demonstrated as a financial game changer with the arrival of blockchain technology. Similarly, modern smart grids use blockchain technology to eliminate the central entity and, simultaneously, increase stakeholder trust by dispersing power among them.

If blockchain algorithms like Ethereum are used, performance may be improved overall as a way to overcome power limitations in difficult circumstances by making it more robust and quicker. A block is a specific sort of chain, a timestamped tuple of transactions where each transaction is recorded and results in the creation of a blockchain [14].

Consumers based on dynamic, real-time power use. Smart meters act as regulatory bodies to manage data and keep an eye on user behavior. The aforementioned model aims to clarify the elements of the smart grid as well as how to create a market based on energy for the bidirectional flow and trading of energy. Smart meters act as regulatory bodies to manage data and provide consumers with access to track their power usage. The following functions are accomplished by smart contracts, which were created taking into account the characteristics of the energy market:

1. Element energy transactions are offered using currencies.
2. Trustworthiness of Smart Grids is ensured by blockchain and smart contracts by posing as an autonomous third party.
3. Features like enquire balance, payments, and adding new clients are presented by smart contracts.
4. Smart contracts also offer features like tracking carbon emissions.

Blockchain offers a framework for an open market between suppliers and customers. Smart contracts provide integrity for deposits and energy trading since blockchain is

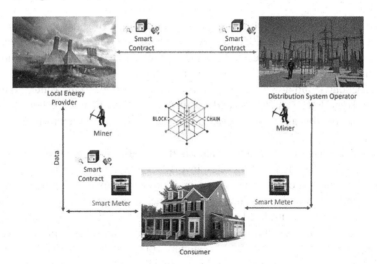

Fig. 3. Smart Grid based on Blockchain

now the main entity and they serve as a leader between energy suppliers and consumers. The inherited payment system used by energy companies is called "ether" Due to the blockchain, participants in smart grids may actively swap energy rather than rely on a single central authority. Customers and service providers now have a platform for a free market. Since blockchain is now the dominant entity, serving as a leader between energy providers and customers, smart contracts enable integrity for energy deposits.

Energy Trading Process: The Trade of energy with the help of blockchain in a virtual smart grid is illustrated above in Fig. 3 Distribution System Operators (DSOs) control the vast bulk of the energy market, while local distributors only control a small portion of it. Given that energy exchange in smart grids is bidirectional, local distributors can transfer more energy to the grid than distributed system operators.

Depending on the energy purchases, consumers might also be purchasers and prosumers. Smart contracts that are driven by smart meters make it possible to reach agreements between buyers and sellers. Implementation on Ethereum.

The configuration of the system is shown in Fig. 4 with the DSO, three regional energy suppliers, three miners, and three Ethereum full nodes acting as customers. The many local energy sources, such as sun, wind, and biogas, are depicted in Fig. 4. Local energy suppliers are prosumers with a two-way flow of energy. The miners in the discussed system are local energy suppliers and DSO, who produce a block of transactions every 15 s throughout the mining process, employing a Proof of Work consensus method. All prosumers receive their allotted mining pay-outs through transfers to their Ethereum wallets. Consumers' energy use has grown similarly. For consumers and prosumers, each transaction is recorded in a block, and the market payment mechanism is run using Ethereum tokens.

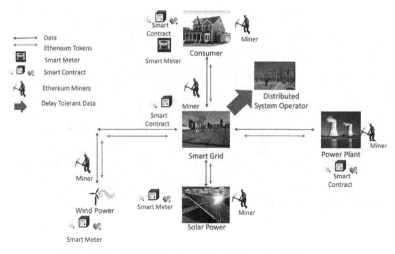

Fig. 4. Smart Grid Based on Blockchain using Ethereum

2.3 Ethereum Transaction and Fee System

In Ethereum, a transaction is a data packet that has been acknowledged by an externally owned account. The quantity of ether, the receiver of the message STARTGAS, GASPRICE, and an optional data field are all included in an Ethereum transaction. The STARTGAS and GASPRICE fields are a crucial first line of defense to stop denial of attack and are required to stop accidental or hostile loops. The quantity of computing steps required to execute code is a transaction cost. Its basic unit called "gas" is used to determine how much bandwidth and storage space a transaction may have gas may be used by Ethereum transactions in a variety of ways. The basic charge for every Ethereum transaction is 21,000 gas. Depending on the smart contract's complexity, each transition for the deployment of a smart contract has a gas cost.

2.4 Virtual Smart Grid Deployed on EVM

Ethereum Virtual Machine (EVM) is a virtual platform, the state of the Ethereum network as soon as a new block is added to the chain. There are many advantages of using Ethereum Virtual Machine and among them is that it does not require any hardware specifications and anticipates an indistinguishable environment to set up the accomplished blockchain network.

The authors implemented a Smart grid virtually on Ethereum Virtual Machine (EVM) and an Ethereum-based smart contract was deployed for the execution of the features and functionality of the smart grid. Figure 5 is the illustration of the Ethereum Virtual Machine environment. Smart contracts are programmed in Turing complete programming language called "Solidity" along with compiler version "solc:0.8.17 + commit.9c3226ce.Emscripten.clang" was used for the deployment of Ethereum-based Smart Grid (Fig. 6).

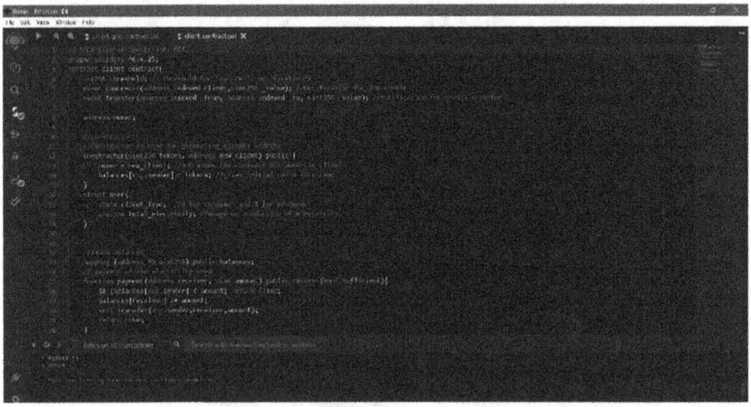

Fig. 5. Virtual smart grid using EVM

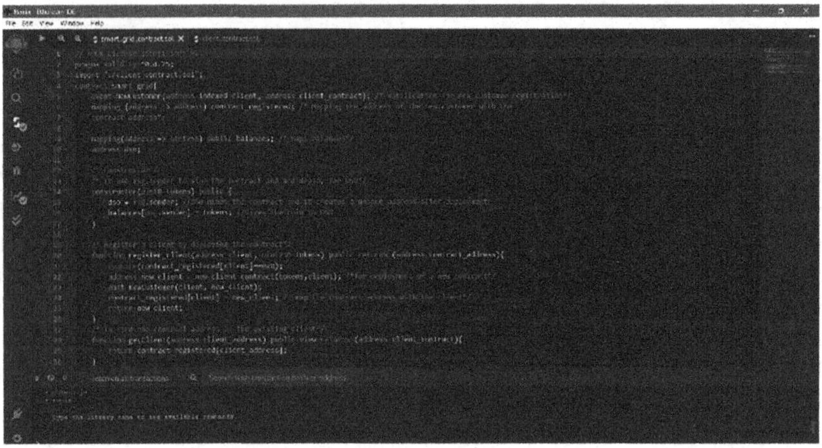

Fig. 6. Virtual smart grid using EVM

3 SM-DSO Interaction Implementation with Blockchain

With the use of smart meters, customers and DSOs may exchange information about generating, consumption, and energy costs in both directions. The adoption of smart metering infrastructure will be a turning point in the digital revolution of the energy industry. It mainly offers customers access to utilities so they may consciously take part in real-time energy trading platforms that enable transparency in usage and pricing. The infrastructure for smart meters has various security flaws because of these benefits. If an attacker is successful in obtaining illegal access, it may result in complete access to and control of household equipment. Smart Meter sends the data of consumption in an interval of every 15 min [15, 16] and in, between that interval, an eavesdropper may access the channel and use the consumption data for malicious purposes [17]. The attacker can even perform slide attacks [18]. The attack's axis may stretch into other domains, like how an attacker may launch gray outs, blackouts, or even modify price details [19].

Blockchain technology can be used to address the aforementioned security issues when trading energy between distributed system operators and smart meters (DSO). The blockchain's concatenation-like characteristic makes it possible to connect block meters, each of which contains two hash meters for the current block and the other for the preceding block—helping to build a peer-to-peer trust model and guarantee data validity.

As per Fig. 7, smart meters authorize the sale and trade of energy contracts with the auxiliary market. For instance, when smart meters submit a tacit request, the system operator replies with a signed copy of the contract. The advantages of using smart contracts for the exchange of energy between smart meters and DSOs are shown in 7.

This data is added to the blockchain as soon as a smart contract between the two DSOs and the Smart meter is formed. A genuine and authorized node must be chosen to create and include a new block in the blockchain. In the presented work, the node for block validation is decided using the proof of stake (PoS) consensus technique.

It is assumed that ancillary Market SC1, shown in Fig. 7, and SM1 enter into a contract. Solc compiler version: "-solc:0.8.17 + commit.9c3226ce.Emscripten.clang" was used to compile the contract. The produced bytes of code was installed on SM1, a blockchain node running on Ethereum. Now, SM1 is selected as the validator node after taking into account the consensus PoS process. In the case shown in Fig. 7, SM1 is identified as the authorized 3 nodes for node validation, meaning that it will determine whether to add additional blocks through PoS and then announce its decision to network peers. A copy of the newly created block is distributed to network peers and added to the system (Fig. 8).

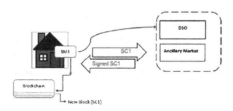

Fig. 7. Energy Trading contracts with ancillary market

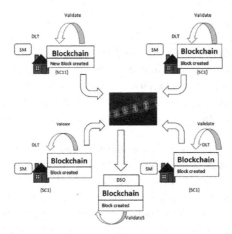

Fig. 8. Addition of New block to blockchain and validation by its network peers

4   Proposed Method

The choice of blockchain protocol is mostly influenced by the implementation function-ality and consensus algorithm. Depending on the kind of case study, this could change. The problems with sustainability and scalability have been addressed. However, there are still a lot of issues that need to be resolved:

1. Cost analysis is crucial for every technology to have a substantial impact. The present power rates are too high for Ethereum and Hyperledger implementations to compete with. Due to the high transaction costs associated with blockchain, the system's total cost has skyrocketed.
2. The smart grid's meter capacity is without a doubt the biggest obstacle. The choice of blockchain protocol depends solely on how much real-time data must be linked.
3. In the same way that any network system does, blockchain has security issues. Even though data is kept on a secure network in possibly unmodified chunks, blockchain. A P2P electrical transaction between the buyer and the seller still involves some risk. The outcome will not always be settled definitively. If a third party learns about a user's daily activities and transactional logs, their privacy may have been violated.
4. According to a market case study, incentives for local energy suppliers who simul-taneously work as miners need to be regulated. These incentives may encourage additional investment in the market for renewable energy.
5. There must be regulatory norms for new technologies, and there are none for blockchain at the moment. It is challenging to be broadly adopted without stan-dardization and compatibility, especially by major businesses.
6. The algorithms used by blockchain protocols today have significant energy require-ments and a large carbon footprint. The architecture of the smart grid is significantly influenced by the physical hardware implementation. To address this difficulty, more study is needed.

5 Cost Analysis

In the Ethereum network, any operation, such as the execution of a smart contract or a function that modifies the contract's state, requires a certain quantity of gas. As a result, Solidity requires a certain gas amount to run each line of code. Therefore, defining the precise quantity of gas required is crucial for the timely and effective execution of smart contracts. Executing and submitting Ethereum transactions to the blockchain largely come at two fees. The first is called the "execution cost", which covers all expenses relating to internal storage and contract modifications. The second is called the "transaction cost", which covers both the execution cost and expenses incurred when sending data to the blockchain, such as the deployment and input costs for transactions.

6 Conclusion

Blockchain technology is getting attention due to its versatility in distributed control and system utilities' stronger defense against attacks and data manipulation. Researchers are also becoming more concerned about cybersecurity and, are experimenting with various cryptographic methods to give reliability and security to utility communications. Alternatives to third-party trust-based cryptographic primitives include blockchain technology. This paper suggests and, creates a blockchain implementation for the energy industry transactions taking place in a smart meter's setting. It exemplifies how the blockchain may be used by smart meters and DSOs. The Solidity platform is used to model smart meter transactions. Blockchain implementation is demonstrated with DSO over the Ethereum network. The experiments indicate that the proposed method can be implemented in DSOs and smart meters as it consumes less gas and provides more security, which opens new doors for future work on less gas consumption and more security. The effective implementation of blockchain for fully distributed peer-to-peer energy transactions can also be extended.

References s

1. Hussain, S.M.S., Tak, A., Ustun, T.S., Ali, I.: Communication modeling of solar home system and smart meter in smart grids. IEEE Access **6**, 16985–16996 (2018). https://doi.org/10.1109/ACCESS.2018.2800279
2. Malik, H., Manzoor, A., Ylianttila, M., Liyanage, M.: Performance analysis of blockchain based smart grids with Ethereum and Hyperledger implementations. In: 2019 IEEE International Conference on Advanced Networks and Telecommunications Systems (ANTS), pp. 1–5 (2019). https://doi.org/10.1109/ANTS47819.2019.9118072
3. Tama, A., Bayu, Kweka, B., Park, Y., Rhee, K.H.: A critical review of blockchain and its current applications, pp. 109–113 (2017). https://doi.org/10.1109/ICECOS.2017.8167115
4. Omar, I.A., Hasan, H.R., Jayaraman, R., Salah, K., Omar, M.: Implementing decentralized auctions using blockchain smart contracts. Technol. Forecast. Soc. Chang. **168**, 120786 (2021). https://doi.org/10.1016/j.techfore.2021.120786
5. Androulaki, E., et al.: Hyperledger fabric: A distributed operating system for permissioned blockchains. In: Proceedings of the Thirteenth EuroSys Conference (EuroSys 2018), pp. 1–15 (2018). https://doi.org/10.1145/3190508.3190538

6. Cachin, C.: Architecture of the hyperledger blockchain fabric. In: Workshop on Distributed Cryptocurrencies and Consensus Ledgers (2016)
7. Moubarak, J., Filiol, E., Chamoun, M.: On blockchain security and relevant attacks. In: 2018 IEEE Middle East and North Africa Communications Conference (MENACOMM) (2018). https://doi.org/10.1109/MENACOMM.2018.8465575
8. Wikipedia Merkle tree (2023). https://en.wikipedia.org/wiki/Merkle_tree
9. Wikipedia. SHA-2 (2023). https://en.wikipedia.org/wiki/SHA-2
10. Lund, A.: Wikipedia, work and capitalism. Springer (2017). https://doi.org/10.1007/978-3-319-55092-9
11. Mingxiao, D., Xiaofeng, M., Zhe, Z., Xiangwei, W., Qijun, C.: A review on consensus algorithm of blockchain. In: 2017 IEEE International Conference on Systems, Man, and Cybernetics (SMC), pp. 2567–2572 (2017). https://doi.org/10.1109/SMC.2017.8123011
12. Sun, X., Sopek, M., Wang, Q., Kulicki, P.: Towards quantum-secured permissioned blockchain: signature, consensus, and logic. Entropy 21(9), 887 (2019). https://doi.org/10.3390/e21090887
13. Nakamoto, S.: Bitcoin: A peer-to-peer electronic cash system. Bitcoin.org (2009). https://bitcoin.org/en/bitcoin-paper
14. Scherrer, A., Larrieu, N., Owezarski, P., Borgnat, P., Abry, P.: Non-gaussian and long memory statistical characterizations for internet traffic with anomalies. IEEE Trans. Dependable Secure Comput. 4(1), 56–70 (2007). https://doi.org/10.1109/TDSC.2007.12
15. Cusumano, M.A., Selby, R.W.: Microsoft Secrets: How the World's Most Powerful Software Company Creates Technology. Free Press, Shapes Markets and Manages People (1995)
16. Beaird, J., George, J.: The Principles of Beautiful Web Design (2007)
17. Wang, W., Lu, Z.: Cybersecurity in the smart grid: survey and challenges. Comput. Netw. 57(5), 1344–1371 (2013)
18. Mbitiru, R., Ustun, T.S.: Using input-output correlations and a modified slide attack to compromise IEC 62055–41. In: 2017 IEEE International Autumn Meeting on Power, Electronics and Computing (ROPEC), pp. 1–6 (2017)
19. Case, D.U.: Analysis of the cyber attack on the Ukrainian power grid. In: Electricity Information Sharing and Analysis Center (E-ISAC), 1–29 (2016)

Keratoconus Classification Using Feature Selection and Machine Learning Approach

E. Smily Yeya Jothi[1], J. Anitha[2], and Jude Hemanth[2(✉)]

[1] Department of Biomedical Instrumentation Engineering, Avinashilingam Institute for Home Science and Higher Education for Women, Coimbatore, India
[2] Department of Electronics and Communication, Karunya Institute of Technology and Sciences, Coimbatore, India
judehemanth@karunya.edu

Abstract. The development and design of new tools that can help identify the disease at an early stage may aid in preventing or delaying the progression of the disease. The preservation of young populations' vision is crucial because Keratoconus (KC) typically affects people at puberty, with children being the most affected. The goal of this research is to identify the most pertinent variables in relation to the various keratoconus classifiers employed in the Harvard Dataverse keratoconus dataset. Out of 3162 observations, a total of 446 parameters are examined by 3 feature selection techniques, Sequential Forward, and Backward Selection (SFS and SBS), Genetic Algorithm (GA) and Particle Swarm Optimisation (PSO). The prediction is done through machine learning algorithms. The experimental results implied that Sequential forward selection and PSO provided the highest classification accuracy by the application of Negative Correlation based Deep Ensemble Network (NC-DEN), with an accuracy of 96.14%.

Keywords: Keratoconus · SFS · GA · PSO · SVM · Ensemble · Neural network

1 Introduction

Noninflammatory corneal disease known as keratoconus frequently affects both eyes. Usually, the cornea is shaped like a ball and is round. However, occasionally the cornea's structure is insufficiently robust to maintain this spherical shape. The eye's normally round surface might develop a cone-like outgrowth over time. Keratoconus is the medical term for this condition. In keratoconus, the cornea is bent into a conical shape and the stroma is subsequently thinned as portrayed in Fig. 1. The development of an uneven astigmatism, which is frequently difficult to regulate and typically results in vision deterioration. Progressive keratoconus may result in a slow loss of eyesight that eventually affects the patient's quality of life [1]. Figure 2 shows the Corneal Topography Image. Recent advancements in refractive surgery have accelerated the development of imaging techniques for the cornea. The pertinent principles of corneal optics are addressed in order to comprehend the significance of novel imaging techniques. Placido disc patterns or mires, which are reflected off the anterior cornea's tear film and converted to colour scales, are used to assess topography. Since the image is derived from the tear film, tear film imperfections can have a considerable impact on the accuracy and quality of a Placido disc topography. Second, poor patient fixation may degrade the topographic image's quality. Finally, posterior elevation results are less accurate, particularly following refractive surgery [2–6].

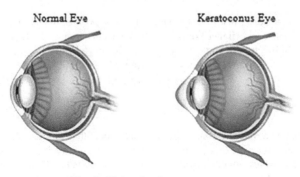

Fig. 1. Normal vs keratoconus eye

The keratoconus has been identified and categorised using several topographical indices. However, due to the sheer volume of indices, manual identification is challenging. Choosing more pertinent indices is also necessary for computerised diagnosis in order to cut down on computation time and error. Because it is so simple to gather data in a hospital clinic, the majority of prevalence studies have been done there. These results provide an approximation of prevalence, but they are probably to understate the true incidence of the disease because hospital patients are frequently symptomatic, making early stages of the condition difficult to detect [4].

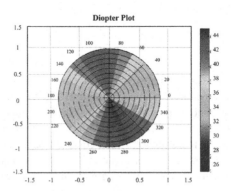

Fig. 2. Corneal Topography Image

The frequency and prognosis of keratoconus vary widely around the world, according to epidemiological research, with Middle Eastern and Asian ethnic groups and those in their 20s and 30s often experiencing the highest rates. The use of novel imaging techniques for the human cornea has improved our knowledge of the condition [5]. The severe stages of keratoconus can be distinctly seen and recognizable as Munson's sign, Vogt's striae, Fleischer's Ring, etc. [6]. Observation of corneal topography and continuous monitoring of its thickness are therefore essential for the early diagnosis of keratoconus. A novel diagnostic method and device should be developed to improve life quality and save lives in children with keratoconus since it affects children so young. The effectiveness of categorization will be impacted by the capabilities that various models bring to the table when classifying data. To achieve the best accuracy, several feature selection techniques are also applied. To a certain extent, dimensionality reduction approaches have been used to cut down on the number of features or indices. The development of deep learning and machine learning architectures has aided in keratoconus diagnosis [13, 14].

The following is a summary of this study's significant contributions. First, the most important parameters are extracted from the examination of other parameters, particularly for the analysis of categorization data. The second step is a comparison of various machine learning models, including the Support Vector Machine (SVM), Ensemble Network (EN), and Neural Network based Classifier (NN). The rest of the paper is outlined as follows, Sect. 2 reviews the existing and current methods involved in the detection of KC. Section 3 provides detailed description of the dataset, feature selection methods and classifiers. Section 4 discusses the outcomes of the study and Sect. 5 concludes the research.

2   Related Works

Over the past few years, machine and deep learning analysis has drawn a lot of attention in a variety of medical fields, including ophthalmology. Using machine learning to analyse clinical and topographical data from 124 KC patients. With reference to the current Amsler-Krumeich (A-K) classification method, supervised multilayer perceptron and unsupervised variational autoencoder models were both employed to categorise KC patients. High accuracy was achieved by both techniques, albeit the unsupervised technique performs better. The outcome demonstrated that the unsupervised method using a choice of 29 variables might be an effective tool to give clinicians an automatic classification tool [1]. Ensemble Deep Transfer Learning (EDTL) technique along with Pentacam Indices (PI) was used in the classification of KC along with four pre-trained models. An improved accuracy of 98.3% was achieved with AlexNet. The imbalance in the PI was corrected using Synthetic Minority Over-Sampling Technique (SMOTE). In the pre-processing stage, the topographic map and the colour code were extracted [4].

PSO was considered for the optimisation of the segmented image. PSO, DPSO (Discrete Particle Swarm Optimization) and FPSO (Fraction order Particle Swarm Optimization). Pre-trained Convolutional Neural Network (CNN) – VGG16 was used for the training and testing. Three distinct classes of images were considered, Normal, Subclinical and Keratoconus. When optimization was performed, as well as when compared to the results from the literature with three different classifications of keratoconus, the results revealed increased performance in terms of accuracy, sensitivity, and specificity [6]. Keratoconus Harvard dataset was used in the study for the classification of KC. Eleven different feature selection techniques were used along with seven different classifiers. The authors experimented that Sequential forward selection algorithm along with

RF yielded best outcomes. Considering the execution time, the SFS algorithm showed promising results in the performance. This work aimed at the identification of KC through corneal topographic maps [7]. The anterior and lateral portion of the eye was captured by the smartphone camera and was used to identify KC. A total of 280 images were considered in the study. The automated contour model and semiautomatic spline model were used to extract the geometric features from the segmented portion of the image. The feature selection was done using an infinite latent feature selection method and three different classification techniques were utilised in the study. The method proved to be efficient in the identification of KC based on fusion features [8]. SVM was used for the classification of the early stage of KC using topographic, pachymetry and aberrometry features. Two different classes of classification were one: former is KC with normal and latter is early KC with subclinical KC [9]. 25 different machine learning algorithms were used for the prediction of KC. The algorithms were tested based on real-time data which includes, corneal elevation, topography, and parameters of pachymetry. The dataset was split and the performance was evaluated on 2 class and 3 class techniques. In both the predictions, Support Vector Machine (SVM) achieved maximum accuracy of 94% [10].

A hybrid deep learning model was proposed for detecting KC using corneal maps. An average of 5024 images were collected from 280 subjects (540 eyes). Seven deep learning models were developed based on the extracted features. The available dataset was split into three classes, the developmental dataset with 542 eyes, independent test dataset with 150 eyes, and Merged dataset consisting of 692 eye images. 2 class prediction and 3 class prediction were done for the identification of KC [11]. Table 1 describes the different features extracted and the methods used for the extraction by various researchers, along with their performance metrics.

Table 1. Comparative Study

Reference	Number of Images	Features Extracted	Feature Selection Method	Classification	Inference
Al-timemy et al., 2021	5024	• Anterior and Posterior Eccentricity • Anterior and Posterior elevation • Anterior and Posterior sagittal curvature • Corneal thickness	EfficientNet-b0	EfficientNet-b0	AUC-0.99 F1 – 0.99 Accuracy – 98.8%

(*continued*)

Table 1. (*continued*)

Reference	Number of Images	Features Extracted	Feature Selection Method	Classification	Inference
Lavric A et al., 2020	3151	• Higher Order irregular astigmatism • Maximum keratometric power • Best fit sphere • Standard deviation of pachymetry • Higher-order aberrations • Aberrations parameters in coma orders 5 • Aberrations parameters in Sphere orders 5	-	25 - ML	SVM Accuracy – 94%
Shanthi. S et al., 2021	205	• Corneal Topography of the anterior face -6 features • Corneal Topography of the posterior face -21 features	Recursive Feature Elimination	SVM	Accuracy-91.8%, sensitivity-94.2%, specificity-97.5%
Daud.M et al., 2020	280 images (140 KC and 140 normal)	• Horizontal Visible Iris Diameter • Vertical Visible Iris Diameter • Eccentricity • Asphericity • Major Line • Minor Line • Orientation	Infinite Latent Feature Selection	Random Forest with n = 50 SVM-Linear, Quad, Cubic, RBF KNN	Accuracy – 96.5%, Sensitivity-98.4%, Specificity-93.6%

(*continued*)

Table 1. (*continued*)

Reference	Number of Images	Features Extracted	Feature Selection Method	Classification	Inference
Aatila M et al., 2021	3162 observations	446 features from.csv file	Wrapper Embedded Filter and Hybrid	LR LDA KNN CART NB SVM RF	RF – 98%
Subramanian. P, Ramesh.G 2022	1500 images	-	PSO, DPSO, FPSO	CNN – VGG16	Accuracy-95.9%
Al-timemy et al., 2022	444 (226 right eye, 218 left eye cases)	-	SMOTE	EDTL, SqueezeNet, AlexNet, Shuffle Net, Mobile Net-v2, PI	-
Hallet N et al., 2020	124	29 Features collected from Questionnaire, PI, Clinical, Medical records	-	MLP VAE	Accurcy-73% and 80%

3   Methodology

The work model of the proposed study is shown in Fig. 3. The dataset description, the feature selection models and classifiers are discussed in this section. Based on the previous research studies, the feature selection algorithms are chosen. Three algorithms are chosen to identify and classify KC. The work is implemented using MATLAB R2021a.

3.1   Dataset

The dataset used in this study is taken from [12]. This dataset, which is organized as a csv file, contains 446 features across 3162 rows. According to Table 2 as shown below, there are four categories for eyes [7].

3.2   Feature Selection

The representation and appropriateness of the data that a machine learning system uses are two aspects that have an impact on how well that system performs. In general, not all learning information is always pertinent to the system. However, the learning system places a high value on the selection of pertinent features by removing less useful, pointless, or even irrelevant factors.

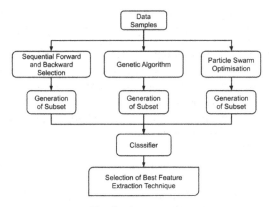

Fig. 3. Work Model

Table 2. Description of the Dataset

Size of the original dataset		Class	Number of rows
Number of features	Number of rows		
446	3162	1	264
		2	2595
		3	221
		4	82

3.2.1 Sequential Forward and Backward Selection

An iterative algorithm called sequential forward selection (SFS) begins with an empty subset of variables. The FFS algorithm assesses each variable separately for each iteration, keeping just the one that has the greatest impact on the model's performance. When a new variable no longer improves the system's performance, the selection process comes to an end. An iterative approach called sequential backward selection (SBS) uses all the dataset's attributes at the beginning of the process. Each round of BFE eliminates the least important variable until no performance gain is seen [7].

3.2.2 Genetic Algorithm

Iterative algorithms based on the genetic evolution process are known as genetic algorithms (GA). GA creates chromosomes from a starting population by suggesting potential answers to the topic being researched. To arrive at the optimal solution, this initial population of solutions evolves utilizing three operators (selection, crossing, and mutation operators) [7].

3.2.3 Particle Swarm Optimisation

Particle Swarm Optimisation (PSO) is used for the linearization of the database. With fewer parameters to alter, PSO is simple to use and faster. The particle swarm optimization can reach a solution more quickly and uses only fundamental mathematical operations rather than difficult-to-implement derivatives. A swarm or cluster of particles used in particle swarm optimization each represents a potential solution. Here, each particle's intensity N is compared to each particle's intensity L from the input image [6].

Condition 1: $L > N$, variable α is incremented by 1, and the corresponding intensity is added to β.

Condition 2: $L < N$, variable f is incremented by 1, and the corresponding intensity is added to g.

The fitness function of the optimised network is calculated as follows in Eq. 1,

$$Fitness\ Fn = f * \alpha * ((g/f) - (\beta/\alpha))^2 \tag{1}$$

3.3 Classification

3.3.1 Negative Correlation Based Deep Ensemble Network (NC-DEN)

Multiple separate models are combined using ensemble learning to improve generalization performance. Deep learning architectures are currently outperforming shallow or standard models in terms of performance. Deep ensemble learning models combine the benefits of both deep learning models and ensemble learning, improving the generalization performance of the resulting model. An essential method for educating the learning algorithms is Negative Correlation Learning (NCL). The NCL's basic idea is to promote variation among the individual models in the ensemble in order to help them understand the many facets of the training set. By minimizing the error functions of the individual networks, NCL minimizes the empirical risk function of the ensemble model. Both classification and regression tasks include evaluating NCL. On classification tasks, simple averaging, and winner-takes-all measures, as well as simple average combination approaches for regression issues, were utilized in the evaluation [15]. Figure 4 shows the flowchart of NC-DEN network.

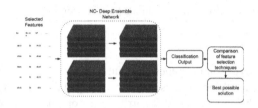

Fig. 4. Flowchart of NC-DEN

3.3.2 Neural Network-Based Classifier

Complex models called neural networks aim to replicate how the human brain creates classification rules. A neural network is made up of several different layers of neurons, each of which receives input from the layers below it and sends output to the layers above it [14]. Every output serves as an input for a subsequent function, and the neurons within the network communicate with the neurons in the layer below. Every function, including the starting neuron, uses an internalized function that incorporates the addition of a bias term that is specific to each neuron to produce a numeric output. The output is then multiplied by the appropriate weight to create the numeric input for the function in the following layer. This continues until the network produces its result.

3.4 SVM

SVM is an algorithm for machine learning for classification and regression issues that is built on kernels. In recent years, SVM has gained a disproportionate amount of attention from researchers in the fields of data mining, pattern recognition, and machine learning due to its exceptional generalization efficiency, optimal outcome, and differentiation power. The main goal of SVM is to divide the training set's various classes into as many as possible using a surface that represents the proportion between the classes. With the objective of minimizing misclassifications, each training sample is represented by a piece of evidence in a two-dimensional region that can be divided by a line. More precisely, there are countless lines that can help create a data set that is adequately divided into acceptable parts. The goal of SVM classification is to choose the line that minimizes the maximum margin as the most suitable one [15].

4 Experimental Parameters

The best feature selection technique is tested based on the performance of the identification of KC. This method plays a vital role in the removal of redundant and irrelevant data, and increases the classification performance. The dataset is split into training and testing set. The classification performance of the classifier by using different feature selection techniques are shown in Fig. 5, 6, and 7. In feature selection technique considered, the generation of feature subset is crucial for the determination of the efficiency.

In this work, three different feature extraction techniques were implemented, of which, PSO performed well. Despite the difference in the classification network, the forward and backward selection algorithm yielded an average accuracy of 88%, GA with 90% accuracy, and finally PSO with 92% accuracy. The comparison of feature selection models with different classifiers is shown in Table 3. The NC-DEN classifier produced better results than all of the feature selection techniques used in the investigation.

Sensitivity is the ability of the network to identify the class of the disease correctly. Specificity is the ability of the network to identify people who do not have the disease class. The formula for the calculation of accuracy, sensitivity and specificity are mentioned in Eqs. 2–4.

Table 3. Classifier Vs Feature Extraction performance

Classifier	Feature selection model	Accuracy	Sensitivity	Specificity
NC-DEN	SF-SB	**0.93**	**0.93**	**0.92**
NN		0.85	0.91	0.89
SVM		0.86	0.84	0.93
NC-DEN	GA	**0.95**	**0.94**	**0.95**
NN		0.87	0.92	0.92
SVM		0.90	0.86	0.92
NC-DEN	PSO	**0.96**	**0.97**	**0.97**
NN		0.89	0.94	0.95
SVM		0.92	0.93	0.94

$$Accuracy = \frac{TP + TN}{(TP + TN + FP + FN)} * 100 \qquad (2)$$

$$Sensitivity = \frac{TP}{(TP + FN)} * 100 \qquad (3)$$

$$Specificity = \frac{TN}{(TN + FP)} * 100 \qquad (4)$$

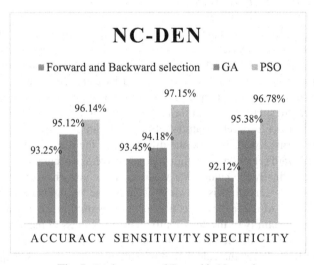

Fig. 5. Performance of Ensemble Network

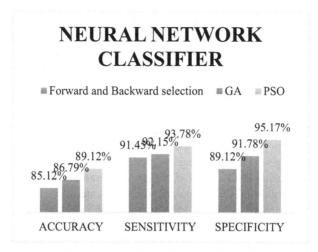

Fig. 6. Performance of Neural Network based Classifier

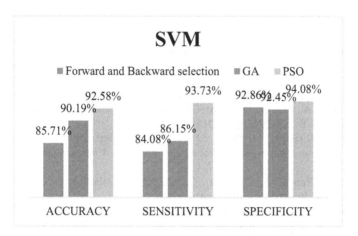

Fig. 7. Performance of SVM

From the Table 3 and Fig. 5 it is inferred that the NC-DEN classifier showed better results for all the feature selection methods utilized in the study. However, of all the feature extraction methods, PSO performed well for the entire classification network. This work highlights that PSO in combination with NC-DEN works efficiently in the identification of classes of KC.

5   Conclusion

It is hard to categorize the severity of keratoconus since the duration for the onset of the illness's signs and symptoms and their correlation with pathogenicity are highly diverse. The precision of the created algorithm enables the proper treatment to be administered when the sickness is still in its early stages, considerably improving quality of life. The acquired results indicate the validation as well as performance assessment of the created algorithm, which may be simply integrated in an ophthalmologist's instrument and help with the early detection of keratoconus. The proposed method is efficient in the identification of the severity of KC using the implemented feature selection and classification technique. PSO exhibited better performance and a higher convergence rate compared to SF-SB and GA. The execution time required for SF-SB, GA and PSO methods are 270 s, 240 s and 150 s respectively.

The feature selection technique is important in machine learning approach to obtain accurate results. They help in increasing the prediction accuracy of the classifiers. The proposed technique using PSO and NC-DEN provided promising results in the classification and identification of KC at an early stage. The network provided an average accuracy of 95%, sensitivity of 95%, and specificity of 94%. GA also showed better results compared with SF-SB technique. By employing the feature selection technique, the most redundant and the irrelevant data are removed, thus enhancing the performance in the classification of Keratoconus Disease.

References

1. Hallett, N., et al.: Deep learning based unsupervised and semi-supervised classification for keratoconus. In: 2020 International Joint Conference on Neural Networks (IJCNN), pp. 1–7 (2020)
2. Shahida, Qadir, M.: Keratoconous: an eye disease. Biomed. J. Sci. Tech. Res. (2020)
3. Gordon-Shaag, A., Millodot, M., Shneor, E., Liu, Y.: The genetic and environmental factors for keratoconus. BioMed Res. Int. (2015)
4. Al-timemy, A.H., Ghaeb, N.H., Mosa, Z.M., Escudero, J.: Deep transfer learning for improved detection of keratoconus using corneal topographic maps. Cogn. Comput. **14**, 1627–1642 (2022)
5. Santodomingo-Rubido, J., Carracedo, G., Suzaki, A., Villa-Collar, C.C., Vincent, S.J., Wolffsohn, J.S.: Keratoconus: An updated review. Contact Lens and Anterior Eye (2022)
6. Subramanian, P., Ramesh, G.P.: Keratoconus classification with convolutional neural networks using segmentation and index quantification of eye topography images by particle swarm optimisation. BioMed Res. Int. (2022)
7. Aatila, M., Lachgar, M., Hamid, H., Kartit, A.: Keratoconus severity classification using features selection and machine learning algorithms. Comput. Math. Methods Med. (2021)
8. Daud, M.M., Zaki, W.M., Hussain, A., Mutalib, H.A.: Keratoconus detection using the fusion features of anterior and lateral segment photographed images. IEEE Access **8**, 142282–142294 (2020)
9. Shanthi, S., Nirmaladevi, K., Pyingkodi, M., Dharanesh, K., Gowthaman, T., Harsavardan, B.: Machine learning approach for detection of keratoconus. IOP Conf. Ser. Mater. Sci. Eng., 1055 (2021)
10. Lavric, A., Popa, V., Takahashi, H., Yousefi, S.: Detecting keratoconus from corneal imaging data using machine learning. IEEE Access **8**, 149113–149121 (2020)
11. Tiwari, S.M., et al.: Applications of machine learning approaches to combat COVID-19: a survey. Lessons from COVID-19, 263–287 (2022)
12. Gaurav, D., Rodriguez, F.O., Tiwari, S.M., & Jabbar, M.A. (2021). Review of Machine Learning Approach for Drug Development Process. Deep Learning in Biomedical and Health Informatics

13. Al-timemy, A.H., et al.: A hybrid deep learning construct for detecting keratoconus from corneal maps. Transl. Vision Sci. Technol. **10** (2021)
14. https://dataverse.harvard.edu/dataset.xhtml?persistentId=doi:https://doi.org/10.7910/DVN/G2CRMO
15. Liu, Y., Yao, X.: Ensemble learning via negative correlation. Neural Netw. **12**, 1399–1404 (1999). https://doi.org/10.1016/S0893-6080(99)00073-8

Semantic Segmentation of the Lung to Examine the Effect of COVID-19 Using UNET Model

Oluwatobi Akinlade[1], Edlira Vakaj[1]($\boxtimes$), Amna Dridi[1] , Sanju Tiwari[2] ,
and Fernando Ortiz-Rodriguez[2]

[1] School of Computing and Digital Technology, Birmingham City University,
Birmingham B47XG, UK
edlira.vakaj@bcu.ac.uk
[2] Universidad Autonoma de Tamaulipas, Reynosa, Mexico

Abstract. The Covid-19 pandemic is a universal problem that has
caused significant outbreaks in every country and region, affecting men
and women of all ages around the world. The automatic detection of
lung infection is a major challenge that poses a limitation to the potential medical imaging offers to augment patient treatments and strategies
for tackling the impact of Covid-19. One of the best and fastest way to
diagnose this virus on a patient is to detect it on lung computed tomography (CT) scan images. Although, to find the tissues that are infected
and segmenting them on the CT scan images face many challenges. To
overcome these challenges, a method was created to enhance the slides
on the CT scans, then a region of interest in which the lung was cropped
out of the CT images to reduce the noise of the dataset before fitting it
into the model for training. Due to the small amount of data, a method
was utilized for data augmentation to overcome the problem of over-
fitting. After compiling the Unet model on the dataset and evaluating
the model metrics, the results and the output that was generated show
that the model achieved good results. The model achieved an Accuracy
of approximately 96%, Intersection over Union (IoU) of approximately
85%, Dice Similarity Coefficient of approximately 92%, Precision of 92%,
Recall of 93%, F1 score of 93%, and Loss of -85%.

Keywords: Covid-19 · Semantic Segmentation · Medical Imaging ·
Unet Model · CNN

1 Introduction

In the last month of 2019, every country in the universe experienced a disease
caused by Severe Acute Respiratory Syndrome Coronavirus 2 (SARSCoV2) that
can cause acute respiratory dysfunction, asthma, loss of taste, loss of smell and
can possibly cause permanent change to the lung of patient tested positive of the
disease, regardless of age [14]. This disease was first reported in Wuhan, China's
Hubei Province, and has become a pandemic in the world [9].

© The Author(s), under exclusive license to Springer Nature Switzerland AG 2023
M. A. Jabbar et al. (Eds.): AMLDA 2022, CCIS 1818, pp. 52–63, 2023.
https://doi.org/10.1007/978-3-031-34222-6_5

The SARSCoV2 can be classified as an ribonucleic acid (RNA) virus which belongs to a large set of viruses called coronavirus. There is a positive sense single-stranded RNA with four main structural proteins that include spike protein (S), envelope protein (E), membrane protein (M) and nucleocapsid protein (N) in this virus. Therefore, the two ways of detecting the virus from specimen are (i) detecting viral RNA nucleic acids, or (ii) detecting antibodies produced by the patient's immune system.

The new deadly disease caused by this virus has been called Coronavirus disease 2019 (COVID-19) according to the World Health Organisation (WHO) report, and this coronavirus has been named SARSCoV2 by the International Classification Committee Virus (ICTV) [1]. "Common symptoms of COVID-19 are difficulty breathing, diarrhoea, cough, sore throat, headache, fever, loss of taste, blocked nose, loss of odour, body aches, and fatigue are noticed in the patient" [16]. Some laboratory tests that were conducted are of standard procedure, such as blood gas analysis, complete blood count (CBC), the pleural in processes that requires transportation of the test from hospital to laboratory, which may take long time. Non-lab tests, on the other hand, are computer-aided image analysis techniques used to examine areas of the lungs using standard 2D chest X-ray or CT scan. Unlike conventional 2D radiography, where using a stationary X-ray tube do not give many details compare to a 3D computed tomography (CT). The CT scan is a non-destructive technology used for scanning. It has the potential of displaying a very detailed view of the lungs, bones, soft tissues, and blood vessel [3]. Some of the merits of using a CT scan is that it provides a wide range of availability, high spatial resolution that has a multislice scanner, its low cost, short scanning time, and a higher sensitivity. While its demerit includes lower soft tissue contrast comparing to Magnetic Resonance Imaging (MRI) and X-ray exposure [7].

The development of inflammation in the lungs can lead to risks to the health of humans. The frequency of those infected are increasing in the population which requires more potent treatments as well as a cost-effective strategy based on the main methods of diagnosing [4]. Fast and accurate identification of tissues infected play an important part in the effective treatment and survival of the patient [8]. Different computer vision frameworks have been presented to address different aspects of the fight against the COVID19 pandemic which include segmentation and classification methods [11]. These methods can be categorized into two basic categorises: classic machine learning and deep learning frameworks [15,19].

Overall, image segmentation is increasingly becoming an important problem to tackle in biomedical research and its medical practices. The purpose of segmentation task is to separate areas of interest from other part of the object body to make quantity measures. Specifically, collect additional diagnostic information which include the area and volume measurements of segmented regions. The main problem of the segmentation algorithm is the magnification due to the heterogeneity of the intensity, the presence of artifacts, and the proximity of gray levels of different soft tissues.

Several algorithms used for the purpose of segmentation have been explored in the past. The Current approaches used for segmentation task can be categorized into three major categories: manual segmentation, semi-automatic segmentation, and fully automated segmentation. Doing a segmentation task manually are time consuming, monotonous, and are subject to inter-observer and intra-observer variability. Semi-automated methods are common and are incorporated into available software tools that are openly available. Finally, the fully automatic segmentation approaches are completely automated with no need for human intervention. Every approach has its merits and its constraints. Nevertheless, innovators are trying to make the segmentation procedures to be easy using automated software tools. However, the problem of segmentation remains difficult for the following reasons [18]: (i) there is no universal solution that is applicable to a large and growing number of different regions of interest (ROIs); (ii) large differences in properties of ROI; (iii) different medical imaging modalities; and (iv) changes related to signal uniformity mainly the variability and noise for each subject [5].

This work will provide answers to the questions such as "how to enhance and crop the region of interest from CT scan images, then feeding those images to a segmentation model which will be helpful in the task of segmenting the regions affected in the lungs of patient tested positive for Covid-19 to help doctors giving the required dosage for quick infection recovery?". The main objectives of this work are four-fold: (i) analyse the images from CT scans, (ii) enhance and crop the region of interest of the images on CT scans for proper segmentation, (iii) build a model for the segmentation and model metrics, and (iv)evaluate the performance of the segmentation model. The rest of the paper is organised as follows: Sect. 2 reviews the literature and existing work. Section 3 presents the methodology proposed in this paper. Section 4 discusses the results and finally Sect. 5 concludes the paper.

2   Literature Review

When screening for covid-19, a reverse transcriptive polymerase chain reaction (RT-PCR) has been considered the best standard. In addition, RTPCR tests have also been reported to have a high false-negative rate, in addition, a clinical study involving 1,014 patients in Wuhan, China showed that thoracic computed tomography analysis was able to achieve a sensitivity of 0.97, specificity of 0.25, and an accuracy of 0.25. 0.68 accuracy for COVID-19 detection, with RTPCR results for reference [2].

The flow of extracting and detecting information from the texture of the lung when observing manually takes a lot of time, and it is a tedious procedure. The computer-assisted diagnosis (CAD) approach is used to solve such problems, and it relies on machine learning and artificial intelligent methods to understand the boundary difference between two objects. These processes are standardized, repeatable, and it can be useful to improve diagnosing accuracy in short time [12]. Xu et al. [17] combined CNN and ResNet models to form a COVID-19 system to screen a CT scan dataset including 110 COVID19 patients, 224 influenza patients and 175 healthy people, their model reached 86.7% accuracy to classify whether a patient is positive for Covid.

A workflow model starting from a small series of manual segmentation of CT scans, the first model is based on this batch and applies to the next batch group; the radiologist was asked to correct the segmentation; refine the model and perform another iteration, the model used was a 3D CNN machine learning model in combination with V-net with the structure of bottleneck trained 249 CT scans of 249 patients and tested over 300 CT scans of 300 patients, their active learning framework requires human experts to cut back or add 9.17% of the final output to do segmentation better [14].

The application of deep learning frameworks on chest X-rays images for detecting if a patient is Covid-19 positive was presented by Minaee et al.,(2020) in their work they used some CNN networks which include DenseNet-121, ResNet18, SqueezeNet, and ResNet50 to identify if a patient is suffering from Covid-19, transfer learning employed on a subset of 2000 radiograms so that to all the networks can overcome the problem of overfitting problem and improve the models' accuracy. Fan et al., [6] presented a deep learning framework (Inf-Net) that can be used to segment lung infection and it infected tissues on a CT scan, their model consist of a parallel partial decoder which was employed to aggregate the high-level features and create a global map, explicit edge-attention was used in their model to segment the lung boundaries, their work achieved a dice coefficient of 0.68 and sensitivity of 0.69 for segmenting the infected part of the lungs.

3   Methodology

In this paper, U-Net model will be applied to a dataset for lung CT scan segmentation.

3.1   Overview

The U-Net model is the most common convolutional neural network (CNN) architecture for solving biomedical problems (*e.g.*, segmentation of different cell types and recognition of boundaries between very dense cell structures) and other image classification problems. One of the main advantages of U-Net models in Fig. 1 is the ability to learn relatively accurate models from (very small) datasets [10]. This is very good to solve tasks with small datasets such as the Covid19 CT scan dataset.

3.2   U-Net Architecture

Figure 1 provides an illustration of the U-Net architecture, which is composed of two main paths: a shrinking path (located on the left) and an expanding path (located on the right). The contraction path is a typical architecture for convolutional networks and consists of repeated applications of two 3×3 convolutions (padless convolutions) followed by a 2×2 maximum pooling operation with a rectified linear unit (ReLU) and Stride 2 for down sampling. The number of channels is doubled at each down sampling step. The extended path involves up sampling the feature map, followed by a 2×2 convolution that halves the number of feature channels (referred to as "up convolution") and a properly tuned feature map from the reduced path. It consists of convolution and two 3×3 folds, each followed by a ReLU. Each fold loses edge pixels and needs to be trimmed. The final layer uses a 1×1 convolution to map the feature vector of each 64 components to the desired number of classes. In total, the network has 26 convolutional layers [13].

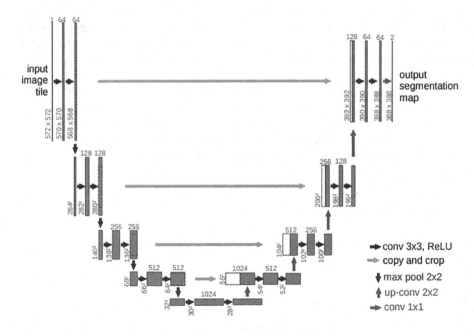

Fig. 1. Overview of U-Net [13]

3.3   Data Pre-Processing

The dataset contains of 20 CT images that are of nibbabel (.nii) files with its corresponding lung mask, infection masks, and lungs and infection mask gotten from Kaggle.

Data Enhancement. Ultrasound images often suffer from contrast issues, as demonstrated in Fig. 2. To address this, Contrast Limited Adaptive Histogram Equalization is employed to enhance the contrast of the images.

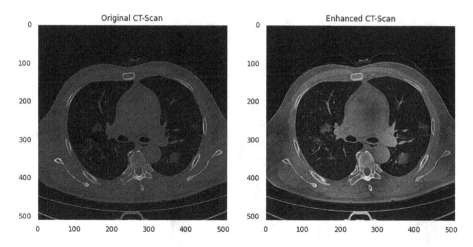

Fig. 2. Data Enhancement

Cropping Region of Interest. There are a lot of black slices that contains nothing which will take value RAM and convolutions when training the model, to solve this problem and eliminate the black slice so that the input image will be the region of interest, a method was created to some boundary in form of a rectangle for each lung (left and right) and then was concatenated together as shown in Fig. 3.

Image Normalisation. The goal of the image normalization is to help transform the features of the images to be on similar scale (0 and 1). The formular below was used to scale the images in the dataset to a range:

$$X' = (X - X_min)/(X_max - X_min) \qquad (1)$$

This will make the dataset to be uniformly distributed

Data Augmentation. In order to prevent overfitting due to small amount of data to train the model, a method to augment the dataset from the existing one. 100 augmented CT images with it corresponding masks was created by rotating the original one in different angles.

3.4   Metrics for Model Segmentation

To assess a typical machine learning model, its predictions are divided into four primary groups: true positive (TP), false positive (FP), true negative (TN), and false negative (FN). True positive reflects the number of pixels correctly identified, while true negative (TN) refers to the count of non-lung infection pixels that are accurately identified as such. False-positive (FP) outcomes indicate the

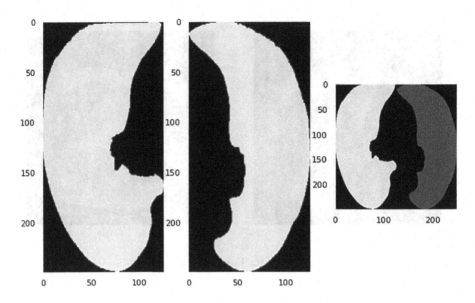

Fig. 3. Cropping Region of Interest

number of non-lung infection pixels that are mistakenly identified as lung infections, and false-negatives (FNs) occur when lung infection pixels are erroneously classified as non-lung infections.

For the semantic segmentation project, the objective is to predict the pixel class in CT images. The output shape of the model's predictions corresponds to the input resolution (width and height) and image channel. The binary mask in the input image channel labels the areas where a specific class exists.

Intersection over Union. The Jaccard index is known as Intersection over Union (IoU) metric is an essential method that can be used to measure the quantity of the percentage overlap between the target mask and our prediction results. This metric is closely related to the Dice coefficient which is often used as a function of the loss during training. The IoU metric measures the percentage of pixels shared between the target and predictive masks divided by the total number of pixels in both masks.

$$IoU = (Target \cap Prediction)/(Target \cup Prediction) \tag{2}$$

Dice Similarity Coefficient (DSC). This is the level of agreement between the segmented area and the ground truth in pixel (2D image) or voxel (3D image).

$$DSC = 2TP/((TP + FP) + (FN + TP)) \tag{3}$$

where TP = True Positive, TN = True Negative, FP = False Positive and FN = False Negative.

Accuracy. This is used to calculate the percentage of pixel of the input image that was correctly classified.

$$Accuracy = (TP + TN)/((TP + TN + FP + FN)) \qquad (4)$$

Precision. This effectively describes the purity of the model detection relatively to the ground truth.

$$Precision = TP/((TP + FP)) \qquad (5)$$

Recall. This is used to describe the completeness of model predictions relatively to the ground truth.

$$ecall = TP/((TP + FN)) \qquad (6)$$

3.5 Model Structure

The structure of the model is mainly divided into encoders and decoders. The encoder includes convolution, batch normalization (BN), normalized linear unit (ReLU), and queries that can extract and analyse features from the input image. The decoder includes oversampling, convolution, BN (batch normalization), and ReLU, whose function is to generate a segmented block map after the analysed image is received by the encoder. The highest network resolution uses 64 feature maps, and the lowest resolution uses 1024 filters. Figure 4 represents the model structure.

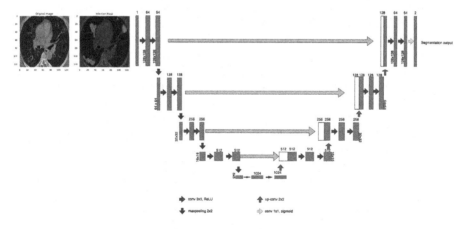

Fig. 4. Model Structure

3.6 Model Parameters

Convolution: The CNN heavily relies on the convolution layers as its primary building blocks, where the majority of the computations take place. The key elements needed for this process include input data, feature maps, and filters. A feature detector, which is also referred to as a filter, is utilized to move across the input's receptive field, searching for the presence of certain features. These operations are commonly known as convolution. Feature detectors are represented by two-dimensional (2D) arrays of weights that signify distinct parts of an image, typically a 3×3 matrix that also dictates the size of the receptive field. When the filter is applied to the image, the dot product between the input pixel and the filter is calculated, and this value is then transmitted to the output array. This procedure repeats as the filter moves across the image, with the final output being a feature map, activation map, or complex feature that is generated from the collection of point products obtained from the inputs and filters.

- Batch Normalization: This is an algorithmic technique that makes deep neural network (DNN) training faster and more stable. It consists of normalizing the activation vector from the hidden layer using the first and second statistical moments (mean and variance) of the current stack. This normalization step is applied immediately before (or immediately after) the nonlinear function.
- Max Pooling: Pooling is one of the features mostly used in CNN architectures. The Pooling layer help to gather features from the feature map generated by convolving the filter on the image. Normally the function is to reduce the spatial size of the representation gradually to reduce the number of parameters and calculations in the network. Maximum pooling is performed to overcome the problem of overfitting by providing an abstract form of representation. It also reduces computational effort by reducing the number of parameters to learn and providing the basic translational symmetry of the internal representation. Maximum pooling is done by applying a maximum filter to the (usually) non-overlapping subsections of the initial representation.
- Rectified Linear Unit (ReLU): Rectified Linear Units are the most used activation functions in deep learning models. This function returns 0 if it receives a negative input but returns that value for every x positive value. It's amazing how a model can explain non-linearity and interactions well with such a simple function (and a function consisting of two linear parts). Therefore, we can write f (x) = max (0, x).
  - Stride: It is the distance or number of pixels the kernel travels across the input matrix. It is rare for a step value to be more than one, but the larger the step, the worse the performance.
  - Filters: The number of filters affects the depth of the output.
  - Padding: The padding makes the output layer the same size as the input layer.
  - Weight: Weights are parameters in the neural network that transform the input data in the hidden layers of the network. When the input enters the node, the weight value is multiplied, and the resulting output is observed or passed to the next layer of the neural network. Neural network weights are often contained in the hidden layers of the network.

4   Results

Figue 5 shows the outcome of the model prediction in comparison to the original infected mask.

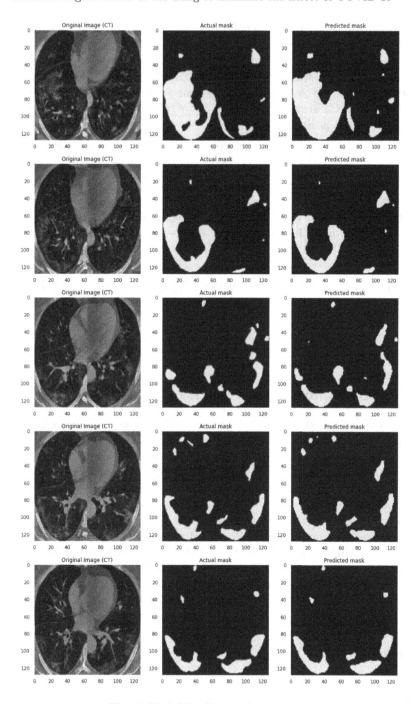

Fig. 5. Model Prediction Comparison

Dice Similarity Coefficient (DSC) has been used as an evaluation metric to evaluate the similarity between the predicted the infected regions of the lung CT scans and the original lung CT infection mask increased across the epochs, at the 100th epoch the DSC was approximately 0.92, which means that the similarity between the predicted areas of the lungs that was affected by Covid-19 to the original Covid-19 CT scans yield a similarity of 92%. The mathematical equation for DSC presented in Eq. 3 above.

IoU at the last iteration was approximately 0.85 which means that the model predicted 85% of intersected region between the predicted the infected regions of the lung CT scans and the original lung CT mask.

Accuracy for the model prediction reached approximately 0.96 by the time it reached 100 epochs which means that the predicted segmentation of the affected regions of the Covid-19 lung CT scan to it corresponding masks. The representation of the mathematical formula for calculating accuracy was presented in Eq. 1 above.

Precision helps to quantify the number of infected region of the lungs that was truly predicted, in this case at the 100th iteration the precision was 0.9234 which is approximately 0.92.

F1 score is used to evaluate the harmonic mean between the model sensitivity (Recall) and Precision. At the 100th epoch, the F1 score was approximately 0.93.

5   Conclusion and Future Work

After completing all the project objectives and evaluating the semantic segmentation metrics, it can be concluded that Unet method has the potential to segment the infected regions of the lungs of Covid-19 patients from CT scans which will help the doctors to know the amount and regions affected by Covid-19 and they will be able to give the right amount of care and medication required for the patient recovery.

However, there are some recommendations for future works which will be helpful in creating models that will exceed the current segmentation metrics. Firstly, tuning Unet hyperparameters can improve the model to get higher evaluation metrics. Secondly, more segmentation models should be created and trained on the dataset that will help to compare the evaluation metrics. Lastly, getting the right dataset was one of the challenges of this task, more datasets should be available because it may help to improve the model training.

References

1. Ahmadi, M., Sharifi, A., Dorosti, S., Ghoushchi, S.J., Ghanbari, N.: Investigation of effective climatology parameters on covid-19 outbreak in Iran. Sci. Total Environ. **729**, 138705 (2020)

2. Ai, T., et al.: Correlation of chest CT and RT-PCR testing in coronavirus disease 2019 (covid-19) in China: a report of 1014 cases. Radiology **296**, E32–E40 (2020)
3. Bhandary, A.: Deep-learning framework to detect lung abnormality-a study with chest x-ray and lung CT scan images. Pattern Recogn. Lett. **129**, 271–278 (2020)
4. Chen, Y., Sohel, F., Shah, S.A.A., Ding, S.: Deep Boltzmann machine for corrosion classification using eddy current pulsed thermography. Optik **219**, 164828 (2020)
5. Elnakib, A., Gimel'farb, G., Suri, J.S., El-Baz, A.: Medical image segmentation: a brief survey. In: El-Baz, A.S., Acharya U, R., Laine, A.F., Suri, J.S. (eds.) Multi Modality State-of-the-Art Medical Image Segmentation and Registration Methodologies, pp. 1–39. Springer, New York (2011). https://doi.org/10.1007/978-1-4419-8204-9_1
6. Fan, D.P., Zhou, T., Ji, G.P., Zhou, Y., Chen, G., Fu, H., Shen, J., Shao, L.: Inf-net: automatic covid-19 lung infection segmentation from CT images. IEEE Trans. Med. Imaging **39**(8), 2626–2637 (2020)
7. Gu, Y., et al.: Automated delineation of lung tumors from CT images using a single click ensemble segmentation approach. Pattern Recogn. **46**(3), 692–702 (2013)
8. Hamzenejad, A., Jafarzadeh Ghoushchi, S., Baradaran, V., Mardani, A.: A robust algorithm for classification and diagnosis of brain disease using local linear approximation and generalized autoregressive conditional heteroscedasticity model. Mathematics **8**(8), 1268 (2020)
9. Jaiswal, A., Gianchandani, N., Singh, D., Kumar, V., Kaur, M.: Classification of the covid-19 infected patients using densenet201 based deep transfer learning. J. Biomolecular Struct. Dyn. **39**(15), 5682–5689 (2021)
10. Lozej, J., Meden, B., Struc, V., Peer, P.: End-to-end iris segmentation using u-net. In: 2018 IEEE International Work Conference on Bioinspired Intelligence (IWOBI), pp. 1–6. IEEE (2018)
11. Oulefki, A., Agaian, S., Trongtirakul, T., Laouar, A.K.: Automatic covid-19 lung infected region segmentation and measurement using ct-scans images. Pattern Recogn. **114**, 107747 (2021)
12. Ouyang, W., Xu, B., Yuan, X.: Color segmentation in multicolor images using node-growing self-organizing map. Color Res. Appl. **44**(2), 184–193 (2019)
13. Ronneberger, O., Fischer, P., Brox, T.: U-Net: convolutional networks for biomedical image segmentation. In: Navab, N., Hornegger, J., Wells, W.M., Frangi, A.F. (eds.) MICCAI 2015. LNCS, vol. 9351, pp. 234–241. Springer, Cham (2015). https://doi.org/10.1007/978-3-319-24574-4_28
14. Shan, F., et al.: Abnormal lung quantification in chest CT images of covid-19 patients with deep learning and its application to severity prediction. Med. Phys. **48**(4), 1633–1645 (2021)
15. Tiwari, S., et al.: Applications of machine learning approaches to combat covid-19: a survey. In: Lessons from COVID-19 pp. 263–287 (2022)
16. Wang, X., et al.: A weakly-supervised framework for covid-19 classification and lesion localization from chest CT. IEEE Trans. Med. Imaging **39**(8), 2615–2625 (2020)
17. Xu, X., et al.: A deep learning system to screen novel coronavirus disease 2019 pneumonia. Engineering **6**(10), 1122–1129 (2020)
18. Yuan, X.: Segmentation of blurry object by learning from examples. In: Medical Imaging 2010: Image Processing, vol. 7623, pp. 1379–1387. SPIE (2010)
19. Yuan, X., Xie, L., Abouelenien, M.: A regularized ensemble framework of deep learning for cancer detection from multi-class, imbalanced training data. Pattern Recogn. **77**, 160–172 (2018)

SMDKGG: A Socially Aware Metadata Driven Knowledge Graph Generation for Disaster Tweets

E. Bhaveeasheshwar[1] and Gerard Deepak[2]([⊠])

[1] Department of Computer Science and Engineering, National Institute of Technology, Tiruchirappalli, India
[2] Manipal Institute of Technology Bengaluru, Manipal Academy of Higher Education, Manipal, India
gerard.deepak.christuni@gmail.com

Abstract. Knowledge Graph Generation is a requisite in the modern era, where Knowledge is scarce whereas the data is exponentially surplus and extensively high. So, in this paper Knowledge Graph Generation framework, the SMDKGG has been proposed, is a Semantically Inclined Metadata driven model for Knowledge Graph Generation, which is a text to Knowledge Graph generation strategy where the document dataset is subjected to a lateral mapping of categories and alignment of generated ontologies with that of the categories for auxiliary Knowledge enhancement. Subsequently, applying Structural Topic Modeling (STM) and harvesting entities from LOD Cloud, NELL, DBPedia, and CYC Knowledge sources ensures the cohesiveness of the auxiliary Knowledge encompassed in the framework becomes extensively high, making the density of the harvested auxiliary Knowledge high. Apart from this, the Metadata generation and its classification using Transformers ensure that many more auxiliary knowledge substrates are selectively added to the framework. Its classification by a Deep Learning Transformer classifier ensures its ease of handling. Subsequently, the classification of the dataset using the AdaBoost, the encompassment of Twitter Semantic Similarity (TSS) for intra-class similarity computation, and the integration of Normalized Google Distance (NGD) with selective thresholds at various stages of the model ensure robust relevance computation mechanism for conceiving the best-in-class Knowledge Graph. Moreover, the optimization of the initial solution set is carried out using the Chemical Reaction metaheuristic optimization algorithm with NGD as the criterion function, ensuring the most relevant entities are alone conceived in the finalized Knowledge Graph. The proposed SMDKGG yields an overall Precision of 96.19%, Recall of 98.33%, Accuracy of 97.26%, F-Measure of 97.25%, and an FNR of 0.02.

Keywords: Chemical Reaction Optimization Algorithm · Transformer · TSS

M. A. Jabbar et al. (Eds.): AMLDA 2022, CCIS 1818, pp. 64–77, 2023.
https://doi.org/10.1007/978-3-031-34222-6_6

1 Introduction

World Wide Web has an extensive amount of data, information must be derived from comparatively lesser data, and Knowledge is almost negligible compared to the amount of data. So, owing to this, there is a need for Knowledge synthesis, categorization, generation, modeling, representation, and reasoning. For all this converse transformation of data to Knowledge, there is a need for strategies because cognitively processed or preprocessed data and information will lead to Knowledge. So, therefore human-verified and contributed information leads to Knowledge or any information with some amount of human cognition can be termed as Knowledge once it is verified and accepted by the community at large, or there must be a semi-automatic approach, human in the middle approach or approaches without human being with a large amount of cognition or automated reasoning for transforming data to Knowledge. In this model, there is an indirect amalgamation of human cognition utilizing entities from human-contributed, verified, and community-accepted sources and introducing or imbibing semi-automatic approaches for Knowledge generation and synthesis. As Knowledge generation is particular to a domain, and the domain must be widely accepted, disaster tweets as a domain itself are important. For the recent trends, disaster tweets are required. So, there is some amount of social awareness to the model. Socially awareness ensures some amount of human cognition because human interactions among several human beings will lead to several tweets either given, viewed, commented by, as well as opposed by many, or accepted by many. So, therefore Twitter is one of the best sources for generating indirect cognitive Knowledge, and that is why the tweets for the disaster entirely as a domain are taken into consideration, and that is why social awareness in Knowledge management, Knowledge Graph generation, synthesis, and derivation is one of the most intuitive mechanisms. In this framework, a tweet-driven, cognitively re-arranged Knowledge Graph generation framework, Semantically Inclined, and aligned, has been proposed with the incorporation of Machine Intelligence.

Motivation: The Worldwide internet is flooded with unstructured data which needs to be examined, and not several techniques are compliant with the semantic Web for Knowledge Graph Generation for Socially Disaster Tweets due to the structural complexness of internet 3.0. Due to the absence of Socially driven frameworks for Knowledge Graph generation by assimilating Machine Intelligence into the model, there is a need for Semantically Inclined, driven, socially aware, cognitively accepted model for Knowledge Graph generation by integrating several hybrid Knowledge derivations and Semantically regulated Knowledge Graph synthesis is the need of ours.

Contribution: The proposed SMDKGG has the following novel contributions. First, the classification of the dataset using the AdaBoost, and the generation of Metadata and its classification using a Deep Learning Transformer classifier. Lateral Mapping of generated ontologies along with topic modeling using STM and harvesting Knowledge from traditional sources like LOD Cloud, NELL, DBPedia, and CYC to increase the heterogeneity of auxiliary Knowledge. Semantic Similarity is computed using the Twitter Semantic Similarity, NGD at several stages with differential thresholds. Metaheuristic optimization uses the Chemical Reaction Optimization algorithm to filter out the initial solution to the most optimal solution set with differential thresholds by setting NGD as the criterion function. Hence, Precision, Recall, Accuracy, and F-Measure are increased, and the overall FNR is decreased.

Organization: This paper's section is organized as Related Works are included in Sect. 2. An overview of the Proposed System Architecture is given in Sect. 3, whereas Sect. 4 with Results and Performance evaluation. Section 5, the final section, concludes the paper.

2   Related Works

An approach called COVID-KG was presented by Wang et al. [1]. Utilize the multi-media (KGs) produced for question-answering and report preparation utilizing the case study of drug repurposing. A method for generating and evaluating assembly processes for complex components is proposed by Zhou et al. in [2]. The development of an APKG framework with SKGCN is intended to produce process planning. The dual-driven strategy with knowledge assessment approach for assembling various sequences is described. Feng et al. [3] introduced a strategic-model that involves Knowledge Graph that incorporates dependencies based on extended graphs. For each query, Fan et al. [4] have illustrated the mechanisms that will encode representations of graphs in a conventional end-to-end sequential scenario. Luan et al. in [5] developed SciIE, a unified framework with shared span representations, and SciERC, a dataset with annotations for all three tasks. Through coreference links, the multi-task configuration minimizes cascading errors between tasks.

Binary relations developed by an OpenIE methodology are recommended by Martinez-Rodriguez et al. [6] in their method for developing KGs. Additionally, offer choices for choosing the information elements extracted to produce RDF triples that the KG might find helpful. Li et al. [8] (TMKGE) Bayesian nonparametric method extracts more coherent subjects by utilizing (KG) embedding in the context of TM. In order to address the pervasive sparsity in KGs with graph context and contrastive learning, Tan et al. [8] present the novel framework KRACL. First, by projecting nearby triples to various latent spaces and jointly aggregating messages with the attention mechanism, they propose the Knowledge Relational Attention Network (KRAT) to take advantage of the graph context. In knowledge graphs, KRAT can use multi-hop information and capture the essential and subtle semantic information of various context triples. The contrastive knowledge loss they propose in the second place is created by fusing the contrastive loss with cross-entropy loss. This provides more negative samples and improves the feedback to sparse entities. Tang et al. [9] present a novel translational distance-based method for predicting knowledge graph links. Using two directed context representations, the graph context is secondarily explicitly described. Instead of using the traditional KG triplet structure to describe medical knowledge, Li et al. [10] propose using a unique quadruplet structure. Probability, specificity, and dependability are considered in a unique related-entity ranking mechanism (PSR). Additionally, the PrTransH algorithm teaches the created KG how to embed graphs using probabilistic translation on hyperplanes.

Yu et al. [11] present the relationship extraction method for constructing domain KGs. Fan et al. [12] introduced the CRF driven BiGRU framework with multiple branches for facilitating NER using Deep Learning. This model combines a (CRF) model with a (BiGRU) layer. With a focus on Chinese-language papers, Wang et al. [13] in order to train the Conditional Random Fields model's Chinese word segmentation rules, they first created a hybrid corpus that combines general and geological terms from geology dictionaries. Second, parsed documents into individual words using word segmentation techniques. Third, examined the semantic relationships between content words using statistical analysis. A unique, three-layer representation of SciKG is put forth by Jiang et al. [14]. Concept nodes, attribute nodes, and connections connecting attributes to concepts are all in the top layer. Fact and condition tuples are both represented in the second layer. Unambiguous sentence nodes linked to the authors and original paper are included in the third layer. The knowledge graph's creation, maintenance process, and application are all thoroughly described by Haussmann et al. [15]. One of these applications is a cognitive assistant that can respond to questions in plain language using the knowledge graph. A SPARQL-based service enables users to choose a recipe based on the ingredients they currently have on hand while considering restrictions like allergies. In [16–18] Knowledge Graphs have been considered as the centrifugal force in empowering recommendations. Knowledge models when fed into a recommendation environment, empower learning paradigms and scheme provisioning background knowledge for inferencing which help in solving the serendipity problem and ensure diversity in the results and facilitate a higher degree of recommendation by enhancing the overall efficacy of recommendation. Patience Usip et al., [19, 20] have used Ontologies as a means of conceptualization and conception of Knowledge and used NLP based approaches in extracting meaningful text from unstructured data.

3   Proposed Architecture

Figure 1 depicts the proposed system architecture for the Meta Data Driven Knowledge Graph Generation framework, which encompasses the extraction of categories from the documents, as it is data document, dataset driven, and these categories are extracted randomly from the documents based on the dataset of the documents, as well as the keywords on the documents set, is extracted and subjected to structural topic modeling which is a topic modeling strategy for discovering and uncovering the relevant hidden topics from the underlying structure of the World Wide Web and the external Web corpora.

Once structural topic modeling is subjected to the extracted categories, it is enriched, but for further enrichment, it is sent to the LOD Cloud through SPARQL querying. SPARQL querying of the LOD Cloud for extracting the entities and further discovery of the entities from NELL, DBpedia, and the CYC Knowledge stores. So, an array of Knowledge stores, including LOD Cloud, NELL, DBPedia, and Yahoo, are used. For DBPedia, SPARQL querying is used; however, for NELL, and CYC, the respective APIs are used to yield and retrieve entities from the standard Knowledge stores to enrich the categories subjected to STM further to add more entities to it. To populate with entities, relevant Knowledge is to be embarked as Knowledge Graphs. The reason to use four different heterogeneous Knowledge stores is to enrich the entities exponentially so auxiliary Knowledge can be added without deviating from the relevance and high quality,

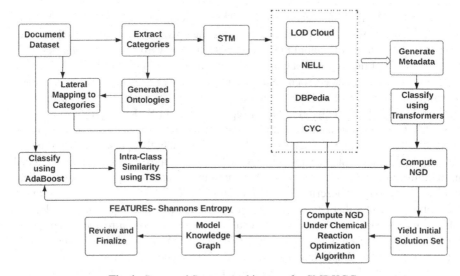

Fig. 1. Proposed System Architecture for SMDKGG

which would be a basis for the high-quality Knowledge Graph generation. Further using the entities discovered from the STM, LOD Cloud, NELL, DBPedia, and CYC, these entities are fed as features where the feature selection is made using the Shannons Entropy and classification of the dataset using the AdaBoost classifier.

Structural Topic Modeling (STM) is computed for achieving discovery of hidden and yet relevant topics from the external text corpora into the localized framework. Topic prevalence within documents is influenced by covariate data, including document metadata. In order to describe word use distributions within a topic, STM also employs covariate data. STM permits topical correlations. Furthermore, STM is a generalization of the more popular correlated topic models and latent Dirichlet allocation (LDA).

The Relation for STM is depicted in the Eq. (1). Here, m_v, the baseline log frequency for words v, v is used to index specific words within the pertinent vocabulary of potential words. The κ terms in the following equation capture modifications depending on the pertinent topic and covariate data.

$$\beta_{d,\kappa,v} \alpha \exp(m_v + \kappa_v^{\cdot,\kappa} + \kappa_v^{\cdot,\kappa} + \kappa_v^{y,\kappa}) \tag{1}$$

Using the AdaBoost classifier, the classified document dataset is classified. However, the extracted categories from the extracted dataset are subjected to the generation of Ontology using the OntoCollab as the tool. The dataset is mapped with the categories of the Ontology generated to increase the lateral subspace and visibility of the dataset and is done by computing the Concept Similarity. Concept Similarity with a threshold of 0.5, the reason to keep the threshold very fluid and relaxed to 0.5 is that many numbers of categories need to be mapped. Then the mapped categories of the documents are used to compute the intra-class similarity with that of the classes discovered from the document dataset, which is done by Twitter Semantic Similarity (TSS) with a threshold of 0.75. The TSS is kept at 0.75 because it ensures that many classes are anchored at this stage, which is the final step for making the relevance highly strong. Twitter Semantic Similarity is a robust semantic similarity computation. So subsequently, the entities discovered from STM, LOD Cloud, NELL, DBPedia, and NYC are used to generate the Metadata using the tools called Data Fountains as well as the Editor-Converter Dublin Core Metadata frameworks are used, and the generated Metadata is exponentially large volumes because two different tools are used. They are integrated and classified using the Transformers as a classifier.

Several weak classifiers are combined into a robust classifier using the iterative learning technique known as the AdaBoost method to get an incredibly accurate classification. The fundamental idea behind Adaboost is to train a data sample and establish classifier weights for each iteration to deliver exact predictions of uncommon observations. Consider using our training data to train a Decision Tree algorithm to produce predictions as the first stage in creating an AdaBoost classifier. The weight of misclassified training instances is now increased using AdaBoost's methodology. Iteratively repeating the process after accepting the updated weights, the second classifier is trained. Following each model prediction, we increase the weights of the erroneously classified cases to enhance the performance of the following model on those examples. By gradually adding predictions, AdaBoost enhances the ensemble. The primary limitation of this method is that it cannot be parallelized because each predictor can only be learned after the previous one has been trained and evaluated.

AdaBoost must adhere to two requirements. First, it is necessary to train the classifier using different weighted training instances interactively. Second, to provide these instances with the best possible match, it works to reduce training error as much as feasible. The corresponding classification error rate ε_m is calculated when the data are classified using a weak classifier, y_m. The weights of each sample are updated in the subsequent iteration using ε_m, and the weak classifier y_m's weight α_m determined. Iterative processes are repeated over and over. Equation (2) depicts the weak classifier's classification error rate for the training set.

$$\varepsilon_m = \sum_{n=1}^{N} \omega_n^{(m)} I(y_m(x_n) \neq t_n) \tag{2}$$

The current weak classifier is weighted as $\omega_n^{(m)}$, where t_n is the actual label, I is the weight coefficient optimization function, and $y_m(x_n)$ is the weak classifier's prediction result. Weak classifier weights are merged to produce a robust classifier, as shown in Eq. (3).

$$\alpha_m = \frac{1}{2}\ln\left(\frac{1 - \varepsilon_m}{\varepsilon_m}\right) \tag{3}$$

The prediction outcome of each weak classifier is expressed as $Y_M(x)$ in Eq. (4), where N is the number of weak classifiers.

$$Y_M(x) = sign\left(\Sigma_{m=1}^{N}\alpha_m y_m(x)\right) \tag{4}$$

The classified entities are further used to compute the intra-class similarity outcome. NGD (Normalized Google Distance) is used. NGD is set to a threshold of 0.6. It is increased to yield the initial solution set because NGD is a stringent Semantic Similarity measure. As we try to reach relevancy, the threshold needs to be increased. However, because it is already computed using intra-class similar instances, a threshold of 0.6 is computed as refinement in the first step. Henceforth, it is set as 0.6. Further, the initial feasible solution set is yielded, which is self-optimization. The entities discovered from the STM, LOD Cloud, NELL, DBPedia, and CYC are used for optimization. Again, NGD is computed with a threshold of 0.6 under the Chemical Reaction Optimization Algorithm, which is a metaheuristic optimization algorithm in which the objective function or the criterion function is set as the NGD with a threshold of 0.6. Again the same threshold point is because the Chemical Reaction Optimization Algorithm is a robust optimization mechanism. Apart from the NGD, which is also stringent, thresholding is kept as 0.6. So, the algorithm optimizes or transforms the initial feasible solution set to a much more optimum solution set to yield the most optimal entities. These entities are re-ordered in the increasing order of NGD and aligned based on the NGD measures; a link is created for the Knowledge Graph, and further, the modeled Knowledge Graph is subjected to review and finalization. Once finalized, instantiation is done by adding more instances from the respective participant Knowledge stores LOD Cloud, NELL, DBPedia, and CYC.

Transformer, a Deep Learning model, uses the self-attention strategy to determine the relative relevance of each incoming data element. The encoder-decoder technique was utilized in the Transformer model. Each encoder layer's purpose is to generate encodings that indicate which input items are connected. It sends its encodings as inputs to the following encoder layer. The reverse is done by each decoder layer, which takes all the encodings and creates an output sequence utilizing the contextual information they have absorbed. To accomplish this, an attention mechanism is used in each encoder and decoder layer. Every token in context receives embeddings from the attention unit that provide information on the token and a weighted combination of additional pertinent tokens, each of which is weighted by its attention weight.

The softmax function can represent each token's attention computation as a single enormous matrix calculation. Due to its ability to swiftly perform matrix operations using computational matrix operation optimizations, the softmax function is helpful for training. The i_{th} rows of the matrices Q, K, and V are the vectors q_i, k_i, and v_i. Before running the attention weights through a softmax to normalize them, $\sqrt{d}_k$, which stabilizes gradients during training. The Attention function is represented by Eq. (5).

$$Attention(Q, K, V) = softmax(\frac{QK^T}{\sqrt{d_k}})V \qquad (5)$$

Language models frequently interpret the input sequence from one end to another, either constituting from left to right or from right to left to strategically implement BERT. BERT encompasses training which is bi-directional to have a more profound interpretation of context of the language. The term "non-directional" is also used occasionally to describe it. Therefore, it simultaneously considers the previous and next tokens. Language modeling is done by BERT using Transformer's bidirectional training while it also picks up on text representations. An encoder is all that BERT is. There is no decoder on it. Reading and processing text input fall under the purview of the encoder.

Twitter Semantic Similarity (TSS) is depicted by Eqs. (6) and (7) is employed for computation of semantic similarity at several points in the framework. High-resolution temporal precision is employed by TSS to estimate word similarity. Through the Twitter API, Twitter offers a limited-time service that allows users to crawl tweets automatically at a rate of about 180 requests every 15 min. It estimates the rate at which tweets containing the word are being produced using the time stamps of the tweets that have been provided. Consequently, one may determine a word's frequency on Twitter based on how frequently it appears.

When taking the word ω into consideration, the time stamp-sequence $\{\tau_i(X)\}$ of the tweets, the frequency $\Phi(X)$ by Eq. (6) can be derived as the mean amount of time taken between several tweets in a sequence to compute the total count of occurrences of word in a tweet.

$$\Phi(X) = \left(\frac{\sum_{i=1}^{N-1}(\tau_{i+1}(X) - \tau_i(X))}{N-1} \right)^{-1} \tag{6}$$

Irrespective of the chronology of occurrence of a term within a tweet, the frequency of cooccurrence of a pair of words A and B depicted by $\Phi(\omega_1 \wedge \omega_2)$ from creating tweets containing both. The TSS between terms A and B is defined by the Eq. (7).

$$Sim(A, B) = \left(\frac{\Phi(A \wedge B)}{\max(\Phi(A), \Phi(B))} \right)^{\alpha} \tag{7}$$

The semantic similarity is also computed using Normalized Google Distance (NGD), is depicted by Eq. (8). It is calculated based on hits on a specific set of phrases generated in the Google search engine.

$$NGD(a, b) = \frac{\max\{logf(a), logf(b)\} - logf(a, b)}{logN - \min\{logf(a), logf(b)\}} \tag{8}$$

The information content similarity (ics) of two terms x_1, x_2 is given by Eqs. (9) and (10),

If $x_1 = x_2$,

$$ics(x_1, x_2) = 1 \tag{9}$$

Otherwise,

$$ics(x_1, x_2) = \frac{2logp(x')}{logp(x_1) + logp(x_2)} \tag{10}$$

where, x' is a provides the maximum information content shared by x_1 and x_2.

For a pair of concepts (E_1, I_1) and (E_2, I_2), sum of the ics of the pairs of attributes is given by $M(I_1, I_2)$. The concept similarity between (E_1, I_1) and (E_2, I_2) is depicted by the Eq. (11).

$$Sim((E_1, I_1), (E_2, I_2)) = \frac{|(E_1 \cap E_2)|}{r} * w + \frac{M(I_1, I_2)}{m} * (1 - w) \tag{11}$$

where, r and m are the greatest between the cardinalities of the sets E_1, E_2, and I_1, I_2, respectively. w is a weight lying between 0 and 1 to enrich flexibility.

3.1 Performance Evaluation and Result

The proposed SMDKGG framework was developed and successfully implemented using Python 3.10.0 for the architecture. The Integrated Development Engine (IDE) was Google's Colaboratory, Python's NLTK libraries have been used for carrying out the language processing tasks, Tokenization was done using the customized Blankspace special character tokenizer, the Lemmatization was done using the WordNet lemmatizer, and the implementation was done utilizing an Intel Core i7 CPU with a processing speed of 1.8–3.6 GHz and 16 GB of RAM to facilitate powerful processing activities. The Dataset was used for the experimentations for the proposed SMDKGG framework, a disaster tweets-driven model for Knowledge Graph generation focusing on natural disasters as the primary domain of choice. They are seven different disaster-based datasets, namely the CrowdFlower (2022). Disasters on Social Media [Dataset] [21] from Data.World, the Disaster Tweet Corpus 2020 [Dataset] [22] by Matti Wiegmann et al., Harvard Dataverse (2017). Hurricanes Harvey and Irma Tweet ids [Dataset] [23], Tweets on Super-typhoon Haiyan that hit the Philippines [Dataset] [24], Nepal_2015_earthquake_tweet_dataset [Dataset] [25] by Kaggle, and the Statista.com - Damage caused by natural disasters worldwide by type of catastrophe 2020 [Dataset] [26], and the Statista (2021). Most natural disasters by country 2020 [Dataset] [27].

These datasets were extensively large and quite variable because of their heterogeneity; each has a common content on the disasters. Each of the datasets was curated for different purposes at different points in time. However, most of these datasets were text-oriented, which is the only commonality apart from the context of the disaster. So, these datasets were annotated at a common platform by crawling contents from Wikidata, LOD Cloud, and LSI used for annotating the datasets. Once the datasets were annotated, all the records were re-arranged based on common annotations, if present and the rest of the entries in the datasets were retained as they are. However, this alone was not sufficient, based on the annotations generated for each of the datasets and also based on the keywords present in every record of the dataset. Nearly 23,846 documents were crawled for each of the datasets, and the most relevant dataset was alone by setting the crawler to a very high restriction of relevance rate, which was curated together to generate a single large dataset for which the experimentations were conducted. The performance of the proposed Semantically Metadata Driven framework for Knowledge Graph Generation focusing on social disaster tweets is evaluated using Precision, Recall, Accuracy, F-Measure percentages, and False Negative Rate (FNR) as potential metrics. Precision, Recall, Accuracy, and F-Measure quantify the relevance of results, whereas the FNR quantifies the number of false negatives discovered by the model. To evaluate the performance of SMDKGG, it is baselined with AKGCF, AliMeKG, EAKG, and KGCLTF, respectively. The performance of the baseline models is estimated for comparison and benchmarking using the same dataset in the same environment as the proposed SMDKGG. The exact number of trials and experiments have been conducted.

From Table 1, it is evident that the AKGCF yields 86.22% of Average Precision, 88.61% of Average Recall, 87.41% of Average Accuracy, 87.40% of Average F-Measure, and FNR of 0.12. The AliMeKG yields 90.12% of Average Precision, 91.18% of Average Recall, 90.65% of Average Accuracy, 90.64% of Average F-Measure, and FNR of 0.09. The EAKG yields 91.14% of Average Precision, 93.13% of Average Recall, 92.13% of

Table 1. Comparison of Performance of the proposed SMDKGG with other approaches

Search Technique	Average Precision %	Average Recall %	Accuracy %	F-Measure %	FNR
AKGCF [28]	86.22	88.61	87.41	87.40	0.12
AliMeKG [29]	90.12	91.18	90.65	90.64	0.09
EAKG [30]	91.14	93.13	92.13	92.12	0.07
KGCLTF [31]	92.13	94.18	93.15	93.14	0.06
Proposed SMDKGG	**96.19**	**98.33**	**97.26**	**97.25**	**0.02**

Average Accuracy, 92.12% of Average F-Measure, and FNR of 0.07. The AKGCLTF yields 92.13% of Average Precision, 94.18% of Average Recall, 93.15% of Average Accuracy, 93.14% of Average F-Measure, and FNR of 0.06.

It is evident that the proposed SMDKGG model yields the highest Average Precision of 96.19%, highest Average Recall of 98.33%, highest Average Accuracy of 97.26%, and highest Average F-Measure of 97.25%, and the lowest FNR of 0.02. The reason why the proposed SMDKGG yields the highest Average Precision, Recall, Accuracy, and F-Measure percentages and the lowest value of FNR is because it is empowered with socially aware Knowledge and moreover, it is Metadata-driven which ensures amalgamation of a large amount of Auxiliary Knowledge from the real world external Web to be imbibed into the localized framework. Moreover, the proposed SMDKGG framework is based on categories extraction from the document dataset, which is a document-centric (i.e., text-centric), text-driven framework for knowledge Graph Generation, but the dataset dependence alone is not done; instead, it is mapped to lateral categories utilizing ontology generation, Structural Topic Modeling (STM) for topic discovery and modeling which is a probabilistic topic discovery framework in order to aggregate the relevant real-world topics from external texts or the web corpora into the localized model which ensures diversity in terms of categories. So, apart from this, the auxiliary knowledge addition is carried out by depending on four different heterogenous knowledge stores LOD Cloud, NELL, DBPedia, and CYC, ensuring a large number of cognitive Knowledge which is a community contributed, verified from traditional Knowledge sources to imbibe variational heterogeneity in terms of entities and topics and also reduces the cognitive gap between the Knowledge and the external World to the Knowledge imbibed to the localized framework.

The Metadata is also generated, which exponentially enhances the probability of augmented auxiliary Knowledge from the external real-world Web. So, this generated Metadata is again classified using the Transformer, which is a multiclass Deep Learning driven classification model which preprocesses, trains, and predicts with BERT, which is a robust classifier model to automatically discover the classes from the Metadata and ensure that the enormous volumes of Metadata are enabled for classification. Furthermore, incorporating the document classification by employing the feature-controlled AdaBoost Machine Learning classifier, a robust classifier, ensures that the features are selected from the yielded Knowledge. Therefore, the deviance from the dataset and its relevancy is maintained and does not deviate (i.e., its deviance is controlled). The computation of intra-class similarity using Twitter Semantic Similarity (TSS), feature selection using Shannons Entropy, and NGD for computing the most relevant term in the framework at different stages ensures strong relevance computation measures in terms of Semantic Similarity and information measure. Owing to all these hybridizations, a collective Knowledge Centric model to reduce the cognitive gap between the Knowledge and the external World Wide Web and the localized framework is proposed to generate and conceive the best-in-class, most relevant Knowledge Graphs.

So, the reason the EAKG model does not perform as expected compared to the proposed model is mainly due to the reason that EAKG is an end-to-end augmentation Knowledge Graph construction framework. This framework only helps in anchoring the readily available instances. However, there is no transformation of data to Knowledge in this model. Wherein text is directly anchored to the model, the relevance computation mechanism is not robust, and the Knowledge derivation mechanism is absent. Due to these factors, the EAKG model does not perform as well as the proposed model. The reason why the AliMeKG, which is domain KG construction and application for the e-commerce domain, also does not perform as expected when compared to the proposed model is due to the reason and the fact that it is highly dependent on business scenarios and prosperous domain relevant features are required for this model. So, the feature settings must be readily available and highly domain-specific, and the relevance computation mechanism is almost absent. This model does not augment auxiliary Knowledge but directly requires features that should be properly extracted from the Knowledge. So, owing to these limitations, this model does not perform as expected compared to the proposed SMDKGG.

The AKGCF model framework does not perform as expected compared to the proposed model because it only has a single source of Knowledge from DBPedia and is rule-based with a Semantic Similarity based approach. Predicate mapping is followed, which is a robust relevance computation mechanism. However, the strength of the mechanism should be expanded by augmenting a large amount of Knowledge from several heterogeneous sources and derivation of Knowledge from Metadata. So that a large-scale expansive Knowledge Graph with high relevancy should be discovered, this method has a limitation of discovering a very small-scale Knowledge Graph. So, therefore increasing the strength of the similarity computation models or relevance computation models increasing the number of sources of Knowledge apart from the derivation of Knowledge from Metadata is absent in the model and does not perform as expected compared to the proposed model.

The KGCLTF model, which is building KG using a cross-lingual method and distributed MinIE Algorithm on a spark, is a Big Data-driven model based on a spark; distributed processing is required. So, therefore the processing power is immense, and the problem can be solved by inferencing and aggregating inferred Knowledge. Here, the data has to be processed computationally. It is highly expensive to process. However, Knowledge sources are nodded from Google Knowledge Graph, Yahoo, DBLP, DBPedia, etc., but the relevance computation mechanism is not very strong compared to this model. It is based on a solid MinIE algorithm for computing the relevance, which is a recreator model. However, the Big Data model does not extensively compute the Knowledge because no amount of learning is involved. So, therefore the Data which is augmented as Knowledge is approximate, and there will be deviations and out layers. The relevance of the Knowledge Graph will be affected as the scale and the number of instances and concepts in the Knowledge Graph increase. So, therefore this model is not very good because there is no learning, no robust relevance computation mechanism, only depending upon the spark-based framework, which is a Big Data model, approximates data as Knowledge into the model.

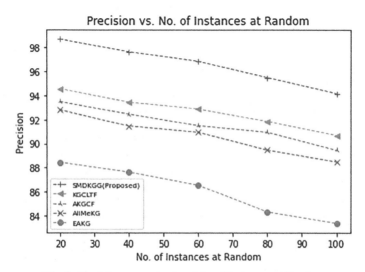

Fig. 2. Precision percentage vs. No. of Instances at Random

The Precision vs. No. of Instances at Random is depicted in Fig. 2. To evaluate the snippets of the large KG, the instances are taken for every 20, 40, 60, 80, and 100 at random, and their Average Precision is computed. The proposed SMDKGG framework occupies the highest in the hierarchy, which is followed by the KGCLTF. The third in the hierarchy is the AKGCF, and the fourth is the AliMeKG. The EAKG is last in the hierarchy.

4 Conclusion

The proposed SMDKGG model outperforms the compared baseline models in all categories, with the highest average Precision of 96.19%, Recall of 98.33%, Accuracy of 97.26%, F-Measure of 97.25%, and lowest FNR of 0.02., indicating that it is by far the best option. The model's high performance is due to the empowerment of socially aware

Knowledge, Metadata driven. The document dataset underwent lateral category mapping and ontology generation alignment to enhance auxiliary Knowledge. The density of the harvested auxiliary Knowledge is then increased by applying (STM) and extracting entities from the LOD Cloud, NELL, DBPedia, and CYC Knowledge sources. This increases the cohesion of the auxiliary Knowledge included in the framework. Additionally, the framework is selectively expanded with additional auxiliary knowledge substrates owing to the metadata generation and its classification utilizing transformers. Subsequently, the classification of the dataset using the AdaBoost, the encompassment of (TSS) for intra-class similarity computation, and the integration of (NGD) with selective thresholds at various stages. In the integrated customized dataset, nearly 23,846 documents were crawled from each dataset used for the experiment. The viable solution set is refined to an optimal one using the Chemical Reaction metaheuristic optimization algorithm with NGD as the criterion function to complete the optimization.

References

1. Wang, Q., et al.: COVID-19 literature knowledge graph construction and drug repurposing report generation (2020)
2. Zhou, B., Bao, J., Chen, Z., Liu, Y.: KGAssembly: knowledge graph-driven assembly process generation and evaluation for complex components. Int. J. Comput. Integr. Manuf. **35**, 1–21 (2021)
3. Feng, Z., et al.: A schema-driven synthetic knowledge graph generation approach with extended graph differential dependencies (GDD x s). IEEE Access **9**, 5609–5639 (2020)
4. Fan, A., Gardent, C., Braud, C., Bordes, A.: Using local knowledge graph construction to scale seq2seq models to multi-document inputs (2019). arXiv preprint arXiv:1910.08435
5. Luan, Y., He, L., Ostendorf, M., Hajishirzi, H.: Multi-task identification of entities, relations, and coreference for scientific knowledge graph construction (2018). arXiv preprint arXiv:1808.09602
6. Martinez-Rodriguez, J.L., López-Arévalo, I., Rios-Alvarado, A.B.: Openie-based approach for knowledge graph construction from text. Expert Syst. Appl. **113**, 339–355 (2018)
7. Li, D., Zamani, S., Zhang, J., Li, P.: Integration of knowledge graph embedding into topic modeling with hierarchical dirichlet process. In: Proceedings of the 2019 Conference of the North American Chapter of the Association for Computational Linguistics: Human Language Technologies, vol. 1, pp. 940–950 (2019)
8. Tan, Z., et al.: KRACL: contrastive learning with graph context modeling for sparse knowledge graph completion (2022)
9. Tang, Y., Huang, J., Wang, G., He, X., Zhou, B.: Orthogonal relation transforms with graph context modeling for knowledge graph embedding (2019). arXiv preprint arXiv:1911.04910
10. Li, L., et al.: Real-world data medical knowledge graph: construction and applications. Artif. Intell. Med. **103**, 101817 (2020)
11. Yu, H., Li, H., Mao, D., Cai, Q.: A relationship extraction method for domain knowledge graph construction. World Wide Web **23**(2), 735–753 (2020). https://doi.org/10.1007/s11280-019-00765-y
12. Fan, R., Wang, L., Yan, J., Song, W., Zhu, Y., Chen, X.: Deep learning-based named entity recognition and knowledge graph construction for geological hazards. ISPRS Int. J. Geo Inf. **9**(1), 15 (2019)
13. Wang, C., Ma, X., Chen, J., Chen, J.: Information extraction and knowledge graph construction from geoscience literature. Comput. Geosci. **112**, 112–120 (2018)

14. Jiang, T., Zhao, T., Qin, B., Liu, T., Chawla, N.V., Jiang, M.: The role of "condition" a novel scientific knowledge graph representation and construction model. In: Proceedings of the 25th ACM SIGKDD International Conference on Knowledge Discovery & Data Mining, pp. 1634–1642 (2019)

15. Haussmann, S., et al.: FoodKG: a semantics-driven knowledge graph for food recommendation. In: Ghidini, C., et al. (eds.) ISWC 2019. LNCS, vol. 11779, pp. 146–162. Springer, Cham (2019). https://doi.org/10.1007/978-3-030-30796-7_10

16. Tiwari, S., Al-Aswadi, F.N., Gaurav, D.: Recent trends in knowledge graphs: theory and practice. Soft. Comput. **25**(13), 8337–8355 (2021). https://doi.org/10.1007/s00500-021-057 56-8

17. Abhishek, K., Pratihar, V., Shandilya, S.K., Tiwari, S., Ranjan, V.K., Tripathi, S.: An intelligent approach for mining knowledge graphs of online news. Int. J. Comput. Appl. **44**(9), 838–846 (2022)

18. Gupta, S., Tiwari, S., Ortiz-Rodriguez, F., Panchal, R.: KG4ASTRA: question answering over Indian missiles knowledge graph. Soft. Comput. **25**, 13841–13855 (2021)

19. Usip, P.U., Udo, E.N., Umoeka, I.J.: An enhanced personal profile ontology for software requirements engineering tasks allocation. In: Villazón-Terrazas, B., Ortiz-Rodríguez, F., Tiwari, S., Goyal, A., Jabbar, M.A. (eds.) KGSWC 2021. CCIS, vol. 1459, pp. 197–208. Springer, Cham (2021). https://doi.org/10.1007/978-3-030-91305-2_15

20. Usip, P.U., Ekpenyong, M.E., Nwachukwu, J.: A secured preposition-enabled natural language parser for extracting spatial context from unstructured data. In: Odumuyiwa, V., Adegboyega, O., Uwadia, C. (eds.) AFRICOMM 2017. LNICSSITE, vol. 250, pp. 163–168. Springer, Cham (2018). https://doi.org/10.1007/978-3-319-98827-6_14

21. CrowdFlower. Disasters on Social Media (2022)

22. Wiegmann, M., Kersten, J., Klan, F., Potthast, M., Stein, B.: Disaster Tweet Corpus 2020 (1.0.0). Zenodo (2020)

23. Littman, J.: Hurricanes Harvey and Irma Tweet ids. Harvard Dataverse, V1 (2017)

24. Legara, E.F.: Tweets on Super-typhoon Haiyan that hit the Philippines (2017)

25. kaggle datasets download -d rishabh6377/nepal-2015-earthquake-tweet-dataset

26. Damage caused by natural disasters worldwide by type of catastrophe 2020 (2021)

27. Statista. Most natural disasters by country 2020 (2021)

28. Kertkeidkachorn, N., Ichise, R.: An automatic knowledge graph creation framework from natural language text. IEICE Trans. Inf. Syst. **101**(1), 90–98 (2018)

29. Li, F.L., et al.: AliMeKG: domain knowledge graph construction and application in e-commerce. In: Proceedings of the 29th ACM International Conference on Information & Knowledge Management, pp. 2581–2588 (2020)

30. Al-Khatib, K., Hou, Y., Wachsmuth, H., Jochim, C., Bonin, F., Stein, B.: End-to-end argumentation knowledge graph construction. In: Proceedings of the AAAI Conference on Artificial Intelligence, vol. 34, no. 05, pp. 7367–7374 (2020)

31. Do, P., Phan, T., Le, H., Gupta, B.B.: Building a knowledge graph by using cross-lingual transfer method and distributed MinIE algorithm on apache spark. Neural Comput. Appl. **34**, 1–17 (2020). https://doi.org/10.1007/s00521-020-05495-1

Brain MRI Image Classification Using Deep Learning

Anand Meti$^{(\boxtimes)}$, Akanksha Rao , and Pratyush Jha

KLE Technological University Hubballi, Hubballi, India
{anandsmeti,01fe19bcs135,01fe19bcs134}@kletech.ac.in

Abstract. Brain Tumors can be lethal if not diagnosed or misdiagnosed. Seeing the mortality because of this is high there's a need to find a solution to detect, classify and diagnose this problem effectively and help medical professionals save precious lives. Brain MRI [1] images help in detection of these tumors. Though there are classification techniques the most common limitation is low accuracy. In this paper we use Deep Learning Architectures to perform these tasks. Architectures like VGG19, ResNet50 [2], DenseNet201 [4] and Xception [5] which are Convolutional Neural Networks [6] are analysed and compared and a novel model is built. We used the BraTS2020 [3] dataset which consists of images of four types Pituitary tumor, Meningioma tumor, Glioma tumor and no tumor we next performed resizing, re-scaling, preprocessing techniques on them. Following which we deployed the architecture to obtain our first set of results i.e, VGG19 gave accuracy of 70%, ResNet gave 72%, Xception gave 75% and DensetNet201 gave 76%. To make our accuracies better we performed image enhancement. [7]the process where adjusting of digital images takes place to ensure that the results are more suitable to display or for doing further image analysis is called image enhancement. Three types of Image enhancement techniques have been used: Adaptive Thresholding [8], Brightening [9], Contrasting [10] and we found that with contrasting we got the best results and VGG19 architecture gave highest accuracy of 83% proving the importance of image enhancement.

Keywords: Data Collection · Preprocessing · Deep Learning · MRI ·
CNN · Convolutional Neural Networks · Image Enhancement ·
Brightening · DL · Contrasting · Adaptive Thresholding · Accuracy ·
VGG19 · DenseNet201 · Xception · ResNet50

1 Introduction

Humans are affected by various kinds of diseases in their lifetime. The types of diseases involve- infectious, deficiency, genetic and non-genetic hereditary diseases. [11] and physiological diseases. Though advancements are made to find

KLE Technological University Hubballi, India.

treatment to these kinds of diseases, the treatment for genetic disorders like cancer still poses a big question on the medical health professionals. When it comes to neurological cancers is difficult. MRI or Magnetic Resonance Imaging has always been vital in detecting cancers. Brain Tumors are dangerous, they put a pressure on healthy living tissues and hamper their functioning. These tumors can be present in meninges, glial cells and pituitary gland. Some can even be present in a single neuron or nerve cell and travel throughout the body which is called metastasis. Tumors can be of two types, one is benign(not harmful) one is malignant(harmful). They may appear as lumps or an aggregation of cells but what makes them different is their ability to move, grow and affect other organs. Benign Tumors are generally fixed in one place, they don't move, whereas Malignant Tumors move throughout the body and grow in size with time, their cells multiply and damage healthy cells around it and wherever they move. There are chances, that a benign tumor can turn malignant. [12] Medical Image Processing [13] has helped in detection of cancers since 30 years and evolving to detecting more efficiently with the help of new emerging AI techniques. The appearance of the tumor, shape, size are important and they help in making efficient bio-markers. [23] In India there are around 40000 to 50000 people diagnosed with brain cancer every year. Children account to 20% of the numbers. In rural areas there are several cases go undetected and unreported as well. In 2018, Brain Tumors were the one of the most common diseases among Indians, ranking 10. India is a country with massive population which mostly youth and children and if they suffer from deadly diseases like these and aren't treated it may be fatal. This motivates us to find a solution for this problem which will facilitate medical health professionals in better detection and diagnosis of the tumor. The loss of lives of youth and children due to brain tumors is a big loss for the country in turn. Hence, a classification for these MRI images, of brain tumors is crucial. Deep Learning Technologies are a way to device the solution for this problem and achieve our desired goal. Previous works have been done in this field but most is observed by image segmentation but, here we have implemented image enhancement and employed deep learning architectures involving CNNs. The old architectures like U-Net [16], AlexNet [15], LeNet [14] were used in the works done before but here new architectures are used. The number of convolutional layers and their impact on the performance is also taken into consideration while analysing the performance. In medical image processing image enhancement makes it easy for professionals to have a quality view of the image. It makes the image more distinct for the human eye and removal of unwanted features makes it easy to compute for the model. Three different image enhancement techniques have been employed: Adaptive Thresholding, Brightening, Contrast Adjustment. Adaptive Thresholding is a where the threshold value is calculated for smaller sections, every section may have varying values for threshold. Brightening implies the simple addition of images. Contrast is a difference in the intensity values of the pixels of an image. It is multiplication of the images in terms of pixel values. There is a possibility that similarity in the dataset can pose an issue and can lead to under-performance of the model. Here we hence have chosen two light-weight architectures and two large architectures with a thought that the more the convolutional layers the better the accuracy and enhancement of images making more features evident the model will identify them and make itself sensitive and perform better

This paper contains our Abstract, Intrduction and Related work followed by Methodology which is subdivided into Flow Diagram and working, Data Preprocessing, Architecture Study, Architecture Deployment, Result analysis and Reiteration for improvement, Experimental Result Analysis, Conclusions and lastly References

2 Related Work

In Multiscale CNNs for Brain Tumor Segmentation and Diagnosis [31] by Kevin Jia et al. focuses on diagnosis of brain tumor mainly by segmentaion and CNN used here is multiscale CNN. Here they intended to reduce the time taken but there was lack of preprocessing observed. In Brain Tumor Segmentation by Cascaded Deep Neural Networks Using Multiple Scales [32] by Ali Emami et. al. their focus extends mainly in improving segmentation over the whole dataset and use multiscale input but a draw back seen was low accuracy. In Brain Magnetic Image Resonance Classification using Deep Learning Architectures with Gender and Age [33] by Maji AK et. al. contrary to segmentation classification is used though the overall accuracy was good but the time taken was high. In Inception [34] Architecture for Brain MRI Images by S. Gopinathan et. al, Inception architecture usage is done to overcome over-fitting in classification but the time taken was high. Abdelhakim El Boustani et al, in MRI Brain Images Classification Using Convolutional Neural Networks [17], this paper intends to build an automatic system for extraction and classification of brain tumor in medical images. The system uses MRI images with high detection rates. Here they have taken care of performing computations in less time. Indeed, based on Convolutional Neural Network (CNN) method for classification along with image segmentation have been used here there were various optimizers employed too whereas Weddad Sallam et. al, in the paper, A Review on Brain MRI Image Segmentation [18], Brain image segmentation is regarded as one of the important parts of clinical diagnostic tools. It is stated that brain images generally contain noise, when it comes to homogeneity and deviation and hence accurate segmentation of brain MRI images is a very difficult task. Accurate segmentation is crucial in clinical diagnosis of the cancer. The author in the review covers a classification of several segmentation algorithms like simple threshold methods, high level segmentation approaches as deformable methods, classifier methods and graph based approaches. Here it can be concluded that Thresholding methods are the simplest and fastest to implement. Yunliang Qi, et al, in A Comprehensive Overview of Image Enhancement Techniques, [19] Image enhancement plays an important role in improving image quality in the field of image processing, which is achieved by highlighting useful information and suppressing redundant information in the image. In contrast to segmentaion where a lot of work has already been proposed, image enhancement is different to observe. In this paper, the development of image enhancement algorithms is surveyed. Image enhancement techniques when applied to medial image processing can yield better results and if optimized, they can be computationally less expensive and less complex than image segmentation. J. Thirumaran et al. [20] talk about image enhancement and its importance in biomedical image processing. It states that analysing and enhancing a volume of images can significantly help in gathering high quality information which will help in treatment of diseases efficiently. This will enhance the accuracy of the state of the art methods. In various techniques of enhancement used the author V. S Padmavathy et al. In Image contrast enhancement techniques-a survey, [21] talks about vaious new age image enhancement techniques. The basis of all this research is Image Processing so Rash Dubey, et al. in A review on MRI image segmentation techniques [22], mentions that image processing is the most important in medical science and is the most sought after methods to perform non-invasive diagnosis [26] but the foremost motivation was when we read the article, "Brain Tumor might become the second most common Cancer by 2030: Where does India Stand?" CNBCTV18 [23]. The high numbers are alarming. Besides all the papers that we read we could find that focus was on enhancing accuracy but along with that several gaps were also identified here. Where in most of the papers we observed the limitation was computation time there were a few papers we significantly observed which gave us a broader scope to identify more gaps. The gap which is crucial to address is higher accuracy without over-fitting and taking less computation time (Figs. 1 and 2).

No	Paper	Focus	Objectives	Methodology	Gaps
1	Multiscale CNNs for Brain Tumor Segmentation and Diagnosis[31]	Segmentation	Reduce time taken	Use 2D CNN	Lack of Preprocessing
2	Brain Tumor Segmentation by Cascaded Deep Neural Networks Using Multiple Scales[32]	Segmentation	Improve Segmentation	Use Multiscale Input	Low in Accuracy
3	Brain Magnetic Image Resonance Classification using Deep Learning Architectures with Gender and Age[33]	Classification	Accuracy Enhancement	Use CNN	High Time Taken
4	Inception of architecture for Brain MRI images[34]	Classification	Effective Classification	Use Inception V3	Slight Over-fitting In some areas

Fig. 1. Comparison and Identification of Gaps

3   Methodology

3.1   Flow Diagram and Working

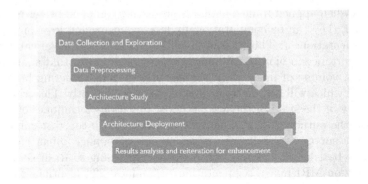

Fig. 2. System Overview

In this section we shall discuss the flow of our project, the steps defined and the processes involved in our system. We began with Data collection out of many datasets which were mostly binary classification, we found out a multiclass classification dataset Brats2020 which had 4 classes. Next step involved Data Preprocessing [24] where we fine tuned our images. Architecture study involved understanding architectures like ResNet50, Xception, VGG19, DenseNet201. We then deployed the architectures for obtaining the results. We analysed the results and reiterated for better results, this time we employed image enhancement techniques.

3.2   Data Collection

The dataset collected is the BraTS2020 dataset. BraTS2020 dataset has 4 classes Meningioma, Glioma, Pituitary, No tumor. These are x-ray images, grey-scale in nature and are 3000+ images.

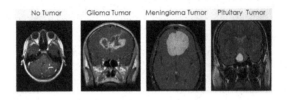

Fig. 3. Brain Tumor Dataset

3.3   Data Pre-processing

Removal of corrupt images, broken images, applying sheer, tilt, resizing to 224*224 and re-scaling was applied, images were put in a numpy array.

3.4   Architecture Study

Architectures like VGG19, DenseNet201, Xception, ResNet50 were studied for tumor classification. Figures 3, 4, 5, 6 contain their architecture diagran. VGG19 Fig. 3. VGG19 Architecture is a type of VGG model having of 19 layers which here are 16 convolutional layers,3 Fully connected layers, 5 MaxPool layers and 1 SoftMax [29] layer. It is a very widely used model in VGG group of models for image processing tasks. While a, lot of research is being done on optimizing its performance, its still is popular. It has 19.6billion FLOPs. Input image size is(224*224)which has RGB channels it's, matrix shape is (224,224,3), the kernel size here is(3*3). Here it uses a stride size of 1 pixel, this enabled them to cover the whole notion of the image. Xception or"extreme inception"is on deep convolutional neural network architecture that involves Depthwise Separable Convolutions it performs rigorous inception to say to an extreme. In Inception [25], 1×1 convolutions compress the initial image size, (original input) or does image compression. In each of those spaces there used are filters on each of the depthspace. ResNet50 architecture, a ResNet Model herein consists of 48 convolutional layers with 1 MaxPooling, 1 Average Pool layers with a total of 50. It has 38000000000FLOPS [28]. An extensively used ResNet architecture fornew model making. DenseNet (Dense Convolutional Network) architecture is involved in making the deep learning networks become more detailed and simultaneously, making them robust to train by the usage of relatively short connections between layers. DenseNet has a basic convolution and pooling layer. Further, followed by a dense block and transition layers [30], lastly a dense block followed by a classification block.

3.5   Architecture Deployment

After the detailed study of the architectures we chose, we deployed it over our dataset. We used Google Colab Platform, and the run-time was set to GPU for fast processing. Dataset was train-test split in ratio 80:20

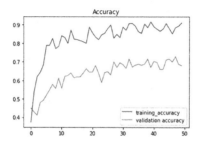

Fig. 4. VGG19 Accuracy before image enhancement

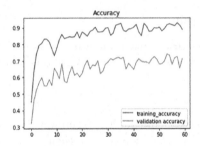

Fig. 5. ResNet50 Accuracy before image enhancement

In the Figs. 8 and 9 the train versus validation accuracy graphs of VGG19 and ResNet50 architectures are shown. The convergence is not seen here the same can be observed in Fig. 10 where the train versus validation accuracy of Xception architecture is shown but in Fig. 11 the train versus validation accuracy of DenseNet201 accuracy shows interesting initial convergence (Fig. 7).

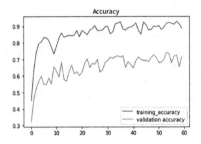

Fig. 6. Xception accuracy before image enhancement

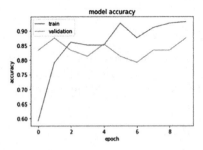

Fig. 7. DenseNet Accuracy before image enhancement

3.6   Result Analysis and Re-Iteration for Improvement

We observed the results after first iteration and we decided to perform the second iteration but with Image Enhancement Technique. Here we enhanced the feature of the images. We applied Adaptive Thresholding, Brightening, Constrasting. Adaptive Thresholding is a method where the threshold value is calculated for smaller regions and therefore there will be different threshold values for different regions. In Open CV we can perform adaptive threshold operation using the method adaptiveThreshold() of the Imgproc class. It is used to separate desirable foreground image objectives from the background based on the difference in pixel intensity of each region. Brightening implies simple addition of images. This results in increasing or decreasing the brightness of the image since we are eventually increasing or decreasing the intensity values of each pixel by same amount. This will result in a global increase or decrease in brightness. Contrasting implies multiplication of images This can be used to improve the contrast of the image. Contrast is a difference in the intensity values of the pixels of an image. Multiplying the intensity values with a constant can make the difference larger or smaller (if multiplying factor ¡1). The accuracies obtained after the image enhancements using the architectures VGG19, ResNet50, Xception and DenseNet201 are: 83 percent, 81 percent, 63 percent and 53 percent respectively.

Figures 8 shows images before and after adaptive thresholding, Fig. 9 shows images before and after brigtening and Fig. 10 shows images before and after contrasting. These three images show results of the image appearance before and after image enhancement. Followed by accuracy graphs of architectures post image enhancement. Figure 11 shows train versus validation accuracy of VGG19 architectures, here there is a convergence seen unlike the previous results, similar behaviour is observed in Fig. 12 which contains train vs validation acccuracy of Fig. 12. In Fig. 13 where train versus test accuracy of Xception architecture is shown followed by Fig. 14 where DenseNet201's train versus validation accuracy is displayed.

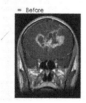
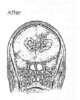

Fig. 8. Adaptive Thresholding

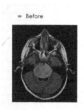
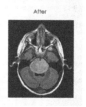

Fig. 9. Brightening

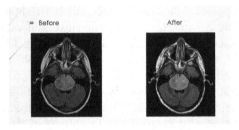

Fig. 10. Contrasting

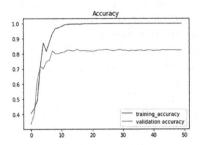

Fig. 11. VGG19 Accuracy after image enhancement.

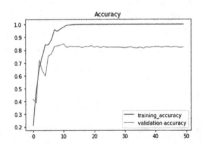

Fig. 12. ResNet50 Accuracy after image enhancement.

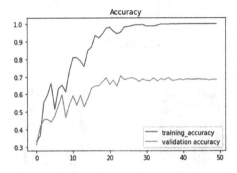

Fig. 13. Xception Accuracy after image enhancement.

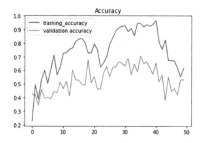

Fig. 14. DenseNet201 Accuracy after image enhancement.

Table 1. Accuracies of Architectures before and after image enhancement in %

Architectures	Accuracy(before)	Accuracy(after)
VGG19	70	83
ResNet50	72	81
Xception	75	63
DenseNet201	76	53

4   Experimental Result Analysis

We can observe that accuracies varied drastically after enhancement. It is evident from Table 1, which shows accuracies of each architecture before and after image enhancement. The architectures like VGG19 had a significant increase in acuuracy that is upto 13% which in MRI images is important for classification. Similar thing can be observed with ResNet50. But interestingly the accuracies of Xception and DenseNet201 dropped. One of the reasons is that these two architectures have a lot of convolution layers which will lead to high variance in turn leading to over-fitting [27]. This will result in mis-classification of a lot of images. Contrasting makes the features of the images very distinguishable and hence to fit to accommodate every feature, over-fitting occurs. Contrasting brings out more features, and hence to fit to accommodate every feature, over-fitting occurs. Here it can be seen that Xception and DenseNet201 showed this kind of behaviour. The more the features and the more the number of convolutional layers, the model will try to fit every feature that is present. As a result the variance will be very high. Though our prior assumption was the more the architecture can go deep and be sensitive to features the better it will perform. If the variance is high, there is a possible chance of over-fitting which will lead to under-performance of the model and if there's a similarity in the dataset, the risk becomes even higher.

5   Conclusions

Image Enhancement can be a way to increase accuracy of the model. Contrasting can give better results in image enhancement Large architectures like DenseNet201, Xception show low accuracies to enhancement whereas lightweight ones like VGG19 show greater accuracies, one of the reasoning being the difference in the number of convolutional layers. Though ResNet50 gave similar results but VGG19 is lightweight as compared ResNet50 so VGG19 shows the best performance here. Here we can see that accuracy post image enhancement is affected by number of features and the convolutional layers in the architecture being deployed. Our findings here pave way in making of a robust model which classifies tumors with better accuracy without overfitting and demonstrates the importance and advantages of image enhancement in brain MRI image classification.

References

1. Grover, V.P., Tognarelli, J.M., Crossey, M.M., Cox, I.J., Taylor-Robinson, S.D., McPhail, M.J.: Magnetic resonance imaging: principles and techniques: lessons for clinicians. J. Clin. Exp. Hepatol. **5**(3), 246–255 (2015). https://doi.org/10.1016/j.jceh.2015.08.001
2. Mo, N., Yan, L., Zhu, R., Xie, H.: Class-specific anchor based and context-guided multi-class object detection in high resolution remote sensing imagery with a convolutional neural network. Remote Sens. **11**, 272 (2019). https://doi.org/10.3390/rs11030272
3. https://www.med.upenn.edu/cbica/brats2020/data.html
4. Wang, S., Zhang, Y.-D.: DenseNet-201-based deep neural network with composite learning factor and precomputation for multiple sclerosis classification. ACM Trans. Multimedia Comput. Commun. Appl. **16**, 1–19 (2020). https://doi.org/10.1145/3341095
5. arXiv:1610.02357 [cs.CV]
6. Albawi, S., Mohammed, T.A., Al-Zawi, S.: Understanding of a convolutional neural network. Int. Conf. Eng. Technol. (ICET) **2017**, 1–6 (2017). https://doi.org/10.1109/ICEngTechnol.2017.8308186
7. https://www.lawinsider.com/dictionary/image-enhancement
8. Roy, P., Dutta, S., Dey, N., Dey, G., Chakraborty, S., Ray, R.: Adaptive thresholding: a comparative study. In: 2014 International Conference on Control, Instrumentation, Communication and Computational Technologies (ICCICCT), pp. 1182–1186 (2014). https://doi.org/10.1109/ICCICCT.2014.6993140
9. Maurya, L., Lohchab, V., Kumar Mahapatra, P., Abonyi, J.: Contrast and brightness balance in image enhancement using Cuckoo Search-optimized image fusion. J. King Saud Univ. Comput. Inf. Sci. **34**(9), pp. 7247–7258 (2022)
10. Roomi, M., Maragatham, G.G.: A review of image contrast enhancement methods and techniques. Res. J. Appl. Sci. Eng. Technol. **9**, 309–326 (2015). https://doi.org/10.19026/rjaset.9.1409
11. https://www.hopkinsmedicine.org/health/genetic-disorders
12. Patel, A.: Benign vs Malignant tumors. JAMA Oncol. **6**(9), 1488 (2020). https://doi.org/10.1001/jamaoncol.2020.2592

13. McAuliffe, M.J., Lalonde, F.M., McGarry, D., Gandler, W., Csaky, K., Trus, B.L.: medical image processing, analysis and visualization in clinical research. In: Proceedings 14th IEEE Symposium on Computer-Based Medical Systems. CBMS 2001, pp. 381–386 (2001). https://doi.org/10.1109/CBMS.2001.941749

14. Rawat, W., Wang, Z.: Deep convolutional neural networks for image classification: a comprehensive review. Neural Comput. **29**, 1–98 (2017). https://doi.org/10.1162/NECO_a_00990

15. Thalagala, S., Chamila, W.: Application of AlexNet convolutional neural network architecture-based transfer learning for automated recognition of casting surface defects. pp. 129–136 (2021). https://doi.org/10.1109/SCSE53661.2021.9568315

16. Ronneberger, O., Fischer, P., Brox, T.: U-Net: convolutional networks for biomedical image segmentation. In: Navab, N., Hornegger, J., Wells, W.M., Frangi, A.F. (eds.) MICCAI 2015. LNCS, vol. 9351, pp. 234–241. Springer, Cham (2015). https://doi.org/10.1007/978-3-319-24574-4_28

17. Boustani, A., Aatila, M., El Bachari, E., Ahmed, E.O.: MRI brain images classification using convolutional neural networks, pp. 308–320 (2020)

18. Sallam, W., Seddik, A., Ali, H.: A review on brain MRI image segmentation (2013)

19. Qi, Y., et al.: A comprehensive overview of image enhancement techniques. Archives of Computational Methods in Engineering (2021)

20. Thirumaran, J., Shylaja, S.: Medical image processing-an introduction. Comput. Graph. Image Process. **4**, 5–611 (2014)

21. Padmavathy, V.S., Priya, R.: Image contrast enhancement techniques-a survey. Int. J. Eng. Technol. (UAE) **7**, 466–469 (2018)

22. Dubey, R.: A review on MRI image segmentation techniques (2015)

23. https://www.cnbctv18.com/healthcare/brain-tumour-might-become-the-second-most-common-cancer-by-2030-13741422.htm

24. Agarwal, V.: Research on data preprocessing and categorization technique for smartphone review analysis. Int. J. Comput. Appl. **131**, 30–36 (2015). https://doi.org/10.5120/ijca2015907309

25. Tejas, P., Akshay, K., Rishi, S., Rushi, B.: UNDERSTANDING INCEPTION NETWORK ARCHITECTURE FOR IMAGE CLASSIFICATION (2020). https://doi.org/10.13140/RG.2.2.16212.35204

26. https://www.hindawi.com/journals/mis/

27. Ying, X.: An overview of overfitting and its solutions. J. Phys. Conf. Ser. **1168**, 022022 (2019). https://doi.org/10.1088/1742-6596/1168/2/022022

28. https://developer.arm.com/documentation/ka004288/latest

29. Binghui, C., Weihong, D., Junping, D.: Noisy Softmax: improving the generalization ability of DCNN via Postponing the Early Softmax Saturation (2017). https://doi.org/10.1109/CVPR.2017.428

30. Zhou, T., Ye, X., Lu, H., Zheng, X., Qiu, S., Liu, Y.: Dense convolutional network and its application in medical image analysis. Biomed. Res. Int. **2022**, 2384830 (2022). https://doi.org/10.1155/2022/2384830

31. Zhao, L., Jia, K.: Multiscale CNNs for brain tumor segmentation and diagnosis. Comput. Math. Methods Med. **2016**, 1–7 (2016). https://doi.org/10.1155/2016/8356294

32. Sobhaninia, Z., Rezaei, S., Karimi, N., Emami, A., Samavi, S.: Brain tumor segmentation by cascaded deep neural networks using multiple image scales. In: 2020 28th Iranian Conference on Electrical Engineering (ICEE), pp. 1–4 (2020). https://doi.org/10.1109/ICEE50131.2020.9260876

33. Wahlang, I., Maji, A.K., Saha, G., et al.: Brain magnetic resonance imaging classification using deep learning architectures with gender and age. Sensors (Basel). **22**(5), 1766 (2022). https://doi.org/10.3390/s22051766
34. Tamilarasi, R., Gopinathan, S.: Journal of Physics: Conference Series. **1964**, 072022 (2021). https://doi.org/10.1088/1742-6596/1964/7/072022

A Real-Time Face Recognition Attendance Using Machine Learning

Umurerwa Marie Adeline[1] , Hararimana Gaspard[2] ,
and Kabandana Innocent[2(✉)]

[1] The African Center of Excellence in Internet of Things (ACEIoT),
College of Science and Technology, University of Rwanda, Kigali, Rwanda
rerwad26@gmail.com
[2] College of Science and Technology, University of Rwanda, Kigali, Rwanda
gharelim@alumni.cmu.edu

Abstract. Systems for managing attendance are crucial for all organizations. One of the most often utilized biometrics for verifying human identity is the face. Most businesses in Rwanda utilize logbooks, cards, or fingerprints to track employees' attendance at work. However, because of COVID-19, which is an infectious disease, attendance has been discontinued due to concerns over its spread. This study describes real-time Face recognition attendance using Machine Learning, an Internet of Things (IoT)-based biometric face recognition solution. To capture the live streaming video, a high-quality camera with a Sony IMX477 sensor and a 16mm 10MP Telephoto lens connected to a Raspberry Pi 4 Model B, can send frames at a time to the cloud. The pre-trained FaceNet model is employed by the system to extract features from a face image after using MTCNN (Multi-Task Cascaded Convolutional Neural Networks) to recognize facial landmarks on images. Real-time image processing is done in the cloud, and attendance is recorded on a dashboard that is accessible from anywhere. The system sends the email to the employee using SMTP Protocol in case of arriving late /absent without permission. The result reveals that the system is safe, dependable, trustworthy, and does not require physical touch.

Keywords: Machine Learning · IoT · Face recognition · Face detection · MTCNN · FaceNet

1 Introduction

1.1 General Introduction

In the '70s, fingerprint research technology began which proved reliable over 50 years. In 89 the research of face recognition technology began in case of enforcing security and the launching of fingerprint recognition products and widespread

The African Center of Excellence in Internet of Things (ACEIoT), College of Science and Technology, University of Rwanda.

M. A. Jabbar et al. (Eds.): AMLDA 2022, CCIS 1818, pp. 91–107, 2023.
https://doi.org/10.1007/978-3-031-34222-6_8

usage of it in most countries around the world in the 1990 s s [1]. Around 160 countries use facial recognition for security and collection of information technology [2]. Artificial intelligence (AI) plays its role in enhancing the performance the basic daily tasks automatically like health factors etc. One of the techniques that can verify attendance due to the pandemic to stop the virus from spreading is machine learning, a subset of artificial intelligence that focuses on using data and algorithms to simulate human learning.

The world is suffering from Coronavirus diseaseVID-19) which is an infectious disease caused by the SARS-CoV-2 virus as announced by The World Health Organization (WHO) on December 31, 2019 [3]. Most people infected with the virus will experience mild to moderate respiratory illness and recover without requiring special treatment. The virus can spread from an infected person's mouth or nose in small liquid particles when they cough, sneeze, speak, touch, sing or breathe, or breathe, The virus spreads more easily indoors and in crowded settings [4,5]. Several governments have implemented a new policy to combat the spread of Covid-19 illness by implementing Covid-19 Self-quarantine (Self-isolation at home) [6]. The virus spreads more easily indoors and in crowded settings. Statistics show since the pandemic began that 600M have been infected, and 6.4M are dead worldwide [7]. In our country Rwanda, 130 k cases have been infected and 1.45K are dead [8]. This loss shows that COVID-19 is a serious pandemic that needs to be considered a priority to be prevented even if high numbers of the population have been able to take vaccines but if you are fully vaccinated (which requires more than one dose), you can transmit the virus easily. That is why the transmission of this virus must be prevented at any cost.

Attendance plays a vital role in institutions/(companies) management to determine the key performance indicator of employees [9]. It is the technique used to keep track of the time your employees put in and the time they spend on vacation. Using a biometric method, is one of the best potential options to avoid the spread of disease within a company [10].

A biometric is the use of distinctive biological/behavioral characteristics to identify people by using a device that helps an organization record the attendance of its employees systematically. Businesses attempting to limit time theft and save expenses associated with lost productivity are now turning to biometric attendance systems as their weapon of choice. Face recognition is one of the methods developed to tackle these challenges and can help organizations to be able to stand on and increase productivity in this revealed unpredictable global pandemic. Therefore, institutions/organization needs to enhance the safety and health of the employees to struggle with it. It is a security mechanism used for providing access to an individual based on face recognition, which is pre-stored in a biometric security system. It is more precise in terms of data collection and verification.

The Internet of Things (IoT) allows device interconnection by centralizing data and connecting both physical and virtual objects. IoT has shown to be very important in the healthcare industry, especially now that the COVID-19 pandemic has changed the situation and social distancing is promoted globally.

A real-time Face recognition attendance with ML is an IoT-based approach that combines sensors, actuators, and software, which collect frames through live streaming videos and sends them to the cloud, and records attendance in the dashboard in real-time. It takes automatic attendance without the intervention of the employees.

Many researchers use a large number of IoT-based frameworks to track employee attendance carried out in developed countries and not in favor of the poor population in developing countries. My research uses IoT devices with machine learning, which use the MTCNN to detect faces and a pre-trained FaceNet model to extract features from frames.

The overall contributions of this research can be summarized as follows:

i. A framework based on machine learning for detecting and recognizing faces through live-streamed videos from cameras.

ii. Designing the dashboard to record attendance and generate statistics

iii. To incorporate a notification system that informs employees of their attendance status into the prototype that has been developed.

2   Problem Statement

Traditionally, manual attendance is done by signing in and out in a register, which increases the chances of human error and is time-consuming which normally affects the productivity and the key performance of the employees. The data recorded manually is easier to be manipulated or falsified and this can significantly affect business activities and can be a costly affair.

In addition, most companies use fingerprints for staff attendance, which is a biometric solution that requires an exact match. Inexact matching can lead to two different forms of errors: false acceptance rate (FAR) and false rejection rate (FRR) [11]. False Acceptance: If an imposter's template is similar enough to the intra-user variation of the real user, they can be mistaken for one another. False Reject: If the biometric signal collected during authentication is of poor quality, even a legitimate user may be rejected. The technical term for this error is "false reject." If your submission does not fit your template, you have been unfairly rejected. Other attendance methods of the employees like RFID Cards which can be stolen, or misused by other employees to record fake attendance by asking a friend to punch their card for them when they are running late. Another method is comprised of a card NFC-based smartphone, backend server, and reporting equipment [12,13]. Because NFC technology often includes a suite of associated devices, equipment, and upgrade-dependent standards, it may be too costly. This technique is not entirely risk-free. Hackers have devised creative methods of getting illegal access to personal data held on phones, and the battle to protect that data is never-ending and can be a way of spreading the pandemic.

Due to the rise of different diseases like COVID 19 can be spread by touching each other or the material touched by an infected person. Thus, fingerprints, registers, and cards are using human intervention, which increases errors, which is not a good idea in the case there is a break-out disease as the disease can be transmitted or spread easily in the companies that use the above-said methods. Adopting this facial recognition attendance system can alleviate the aforementioned problems because it uses high-accuracy algorithms that do not rely on physical touch to identify personnel.

3   Related Work

This paper presents earlier work on facial recognition attendance systems, as well as the algorithms and methods utilized to implement those systems. More researchers had implemented different systems with different technologies using the facial recognition approach. This section discusses the existing solutions, existing open prototypes, and their limitations and finally shows the contribution of the research.

E. Jose et al(2019), This paper presents the implementation of an intelligent multicamera Face Recognition based surveillance system using FaceNet and MTCNN algorithm on Jetson TX2. The proposed portable system tracks the subject or the suspect with the camera ID/location together with the timestamp and logs his presence in the database, using multiple camera installation. This standalone system detects the person which was already given in the dataset to track and an embedding being created was successfully detected with an accuracy of 97 percent and help in surveillance and tracking suspects system [13]. G. Anitha et al(2020), Face Recognition based attendance using MTCNN and FACENET, use MTCNN to detect faces and FACENET to recognize the individual faces and generates the attendance sheet and share the report through mail to the respective departments and staff members. the facial recognition turns out to be a viable option because of its high accuracy along with minimum human intervention.This system is aimed at providing a significant level of security and reducing manual errors. [14] In this research, Z. Yang at al(2020) propose an enhanced model of face recognition which is based on MTCNN and integrated application of FaceNet and LBP method. The work that described in this article using LBP parallel FaceNet to improve the illumination robustness of the model only consists of MTCNN and FaceNet. Experiments show that the enhanced model is very effective in improving the illumination robustness [15].

K. Sanath et al(2021), RFID and Face Recognition based Smart Attendance System, proposes a model which marks the attendance of an employee using RFID and facial recognition along with a temperature check. Also, it captures the facial express installations employee to detect the emotion for counseling if required. Some limitations encountered in this proposed system include: if the whole face of the employee captured for facial recognition is not clearly visible, then the facial recognition will work successfully because the training set contains all such images but emotion classification will fail because detection of the entire face is necessary for emotion recognition. [16]. S. Kangwanwatana et al(2022), presents Improve Face Verification Rate Using Image Pre-Processing and FaceNet, a method that does not require retraining each time there is a new person not in the da tabase using a pre-trained FaceNet model. Improvement of the face verification rate is done, in this research paper using image pre-processing on the inputted images, such as using MTCNN to select out the face, face alignment, and brightness adjustment. From the dataset, the proposedod shows an improvement in accuracy [18].

My contribution research focuses on designing and prototyping a system to monitor the attendance of the employees without contact and real-time using a machine learning approach and able to attain more improvement by using devices with high quality and performance which will be a less expensive system with more accuracy.

4   Methodology

4.1   Background Knowledge

Transfer Learning. Transfer learning is a machine learning method where a model developed for a task is reused as the starting point for a model on a second task. The primary idea behind transfer learning is to use what has been learned in one task to enhance generalization in another. It is mostly employed in computer vision. It can be used for classification, regression, and clustering problems.

Recently, convolutional neural networks (CNNs) achieve remarkable progress in a variety of computer vision tasks, such as image classification [19] and face recognition [20]. Inspired performance of CNNs in computer vision tasks, some of the CNN-based face detection approaches have been proposed in recent years. Li et al.(Li et al. 2015) [21] use cascaded CNNs for face detection, but it requires bounding box calibration from face detection with the extra computational expense and ignores the inherent correlation between facial landmarks localization and bounding box regression.

Convolutional neural networks (CNNs), a subclass of artificial neural networks that have gained prominence in several computer vision applications, are gaining popularity in several fields, including image processing. Using a variety of building pieces, including convolution layers, pooling layers, and fully connected layers, CNN is designed to automatically and adaptively learn spatial hierarchies of features through backpropagation. The CNN model of stringed neural networks proposed by LeCun et al. in 1989 [22] opened up a new research direction in detecting patterns in images as well as in videos. A convolution neural network consists of an input and an output layer, as well as multiple hidden layers. CNN's hidden layers usually consist of a series of complex layers that can vary with convolution [24]. The trigger function is usually ReLU layers, and then following by additional convolutional parts such as layers of convolution, pooling, and fully connected layers. Therefore, they are called hidden layers because of their inputs, and the active functions and final convolution operators obscure the output.

4.2   Face Detection

Numerous author teams have studied face detection algorithms. MTCNN, short for multi-tasking, deeply layered model, was proposed by Zhang et al. in 2016 [25], proposed a multi-tasking, deep layered model called MTCNN [26]. Firstly, the candidate window is created through the quick proposal network (P-Net). Secondly, the candidate areas in the next phase are refined through network refinement (R-Net). Thirdly, the output network (O-Net) creates the final bounding box and the position of the main landmarks of the face as shown in Fig. 1. As a result, the accuracy is approximately 82.1% high, perhaps 95.9%, and the maximum FPS with GPU is 100.

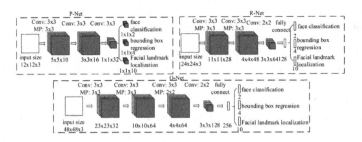

Fig. 1. The architectures of P-Net, R-Net, and O-Net, where "MP" means max pooling and "Conv" means convolution. The steps real-timenvolution and pooling is 1 and 2, respectively. [25]

1. Stage1: The proposal Network(P-Net) This Proposal Network is used to obtain candidate windows and their bounding box regression vectors. Bounding box regression is a popular technique to predict the localization of boxes when the goal is detecting an object of some pre-defined class, in this case faces. After obtaining the bounding box vectors, some refinement is done to combine overlapping regions. The final output of this stage is all candidate windows after refinement to downsize the volume of candidates.
2. Stage2: The Refine Network(R-Net) All candidates from the P-Net are fed into the Refine Network. The R-Net reduces the number of candidates, performs calibration with bounding box regression and employs non-maximum suppression (NMS) to merge overlapping candidates. The R-Net outputs whether the input is a face or not, a 4 element vector which is the bounding box for the face, and a 10 element vector for facial landmark localization.
3. Stage3: The Output Network(O-Net) This stage is similar to the R-Net, but this Output Network aims to describe the face in more detail and output the five facial landmarks' positions for eyes, nose and mouth.

The multi-task cascaded convolutional neural networks (MTCNN) is used to achieve rapid face detection and face alignment while keeping real time performance. Pre-processing is performed during the training phase, after the detection of faces in employees images. It is a procedure for improving the image's features. The suggested approach crops and resizes recognized faces from dataset photos before converting them to grayscale images. The processed photos are saved in a separate folder for each person. During the testing phase, the discovered faces from the live capture are fed into the FaceNet model for face recognition. Experimental results had always been demonstrated that while keeping the reliability of real-time performance, MTCNN consistently outperforms the sophisticated conventional methods across the most challenging benchmarks.

The Three Tasks of MTCNN The Network's task is to output three things: face/non-face classification, bounding box regression, and facial landmark localization.

4.3 Face Recognition

FaceNet is a deep neural network used for extracting features from an image of a person's face. It was published in 2015 by Google researchers Schroff et al. paper titled "FaceNet: A Unified Embedding for Face Recognition and Clustering" [27]..FaceNet uses a deep convolutional network trained to precisely optimize the embedding itself, instead of intermediate bottleneck layers as in previous deep learning approaches. It is a robust and efficient face recognition system, and the general nature of the extracted face embeddings provides the approach to the range of applications [17]. FaceNet takes an image of the person's face as input and outputs a vector of 128 numbers which represent the most important features of a face.

In machine learning, this vector is called embedding. Basically, FaceNet takes a person's face and compresses it into a vector of 128 numbers. Ideally, embeddings of similar faces are also similar. FaceNet Keras is a one-shot learning model. It fetches 128 vector embeddings as a feature extractor. It is even preferable in cases where we have a scarcity of datasets. It consists of high accuracy even for such situations [28]. So, I used the pre-trained Keras FaceNet model (88 megabytes) provided by Hiroki Taniai which is the best for the deep learning model and ready for use is around 0.994 of LFW [29]. It was trained on the MS-Celeb-1M dataset and expects input images to be color, to have their pixel values whitened (standardized across all three channels), and to have a square shape of 160×160 pixels (Fig. 2)

4.4 System Architecture

System architecture is the conceptual design that defines the structure and/or behavior of a system. Figure 3, system architecture, the sensing unit, and the microcontroller connected to the cloud system are the main components of the

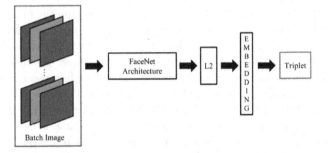

Fig. 2. FaceNet model structure [27]

architecture, via the internet. The HQ camera with a 16 mm lens, buzzer, LED, cooling fan, and servo motor connected to the raspberry pi 4 model B is from the camera, then transfer to the cloud. The processed data is accessed via a web server (Fig. 4).

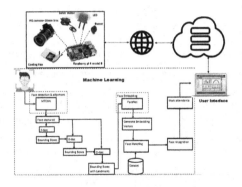

Fig. 3. The proposed system Architecture

4.5   Working Principle of the System

1. **Employee Registration**

   The admin registered the new employees with the photo via a dashboard. The MTCNN detect images, FaceNet process the images, and store extracted features of the employees. Here in the dashboard, the admin can be adding multiple images from different angles, environments and conditions, orientations, locations, and brightness into the system to be able to increase accuracy.

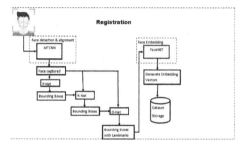

Fig. 4. The Registration Phase

2. **Frame Capturing Phase**
   this phase Raspberry pi, a High-Quality Camera with a lens of 16mm 10MP telephoto connected to the Raspberry pi 4 Model B captures real-time video and then splits it into frames with the software OpenCV library.
3. **Face detection and recognition Phase**
   The system uses the MTCNN to detect the face area in the frame; it detects as many faces as present in the given live-streaming videos and delivers their bounding-box coordinates. After getting the bounding box of a face in an image, it is easier to crop the face part of the image and use it. I use a pre-trained FaceNet model to build the database of embeddings corresponding to the existing face image dataset.
   Mainly 2 functions are used in the face recognition approach:
   (a) face_encoding: retrieves all images stored at a person's images locations, resizes and normalizes them. It then uses MTCNN to detect the face in each image and crops the image where the face is located the image is then encoded using the FaceNet model nd stored in the encodings.json file.
   (b) face _comparison when an image is passed from the picamera, the face_comparison takes the image, in addition, passes it into MTCNN to detect every face in it. For every face in it, the function crops the face section and encodes it using FaceNet. The encoding of each face is then compared to all the encodings in encodings.json using the cosine rule with a tolerance of 0.3, the function returns the image which holds the highest similarities in the encodings.json. Using cv2, the name is then added to the image and returned.
4. **Marking attendance phase**
   In this phase the attendance is marked, if the person in the uploaded frame matches the encoding stored in the database, then the attendance is marked present and saved in the database. However, if any employees do not attend during the morning time, the system will check, generate, and send the email to the employee. Then in the time set the camera will rotate 180 0 to take the afternoon attendance after a certain time also the system will send the email to those who didn't sign out. The system administrator has the ability to edit via the dashboard in the event of an informed leave or absence in order to avoid confusing the system (Figs. 5, 6, and 7).

4.6   Proposed System Requirements

This section contains the main hardware components based on their functions in the prototype system.

1. **Raspberry Pi4 Model B**
   it is the latest product in the popular Raspberry Pi range of computers and is the sixth generation of Pi, is a series of small single-board computers (SBCs) developed in the United Kingdom by the Raspberry Pi Foundation in association with Broadcom [30]. It offers a high-performance 64-bit quad-core processor, dual-display support at resolutions up to 4K via a pair of micro-HDMI ports, hardware video decode at up to 4Kp60, with 2GB of RAM, dual-band 2.4/5.0 GHz wireless LAN, Bluetooth 5.0, Gigabit Ethernet, USB 3.0, and PoE capability (via a separate PoE HAT add-on. It used to process the image captured by the raspberry pi HQ camera and transfers data to the web server for analysis.

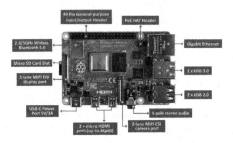

Fig. 5. Raspberry pi 4 Model

2. **Raspberry Pi High-quality Camera Sony IMX477**
   It is a sensor released in 2020 used for data acquisition. It has 12.3 megapixels with 7.9mm diagonal image size, 7.9 mm sensor diagonal and 1.55μm × 1.55 μm pixel size with videos up to 1980×1080 pixels [31]. It used a Hoya CM500 infrared filter, which blocks visible light, and only allows infrared light to pass through into the lens and camera. By adding a 16mm C-mount telephoto lens on it, provide superior low-light performance. This HQ Camera with lens will help to build a CCTV Camera, which captures videos up to 4056 × 3040 pixels through live streaming.

Fig. 6. Raspberry pi High-quality camera with the ribbon used to connect to the Raspberry pi

3. **16 mm 10MP Telephoto Lens** It has a resolution of 10 MP and uses a 16mm ultra-wide angle focal length high definition telephoto lens [32]. It captures every tiny detail and multi-field angle option which brings the beautiful world into your vision and has a wide field of view (FoV),°and a variety of uses, like CCTV applications. It takes a High-quality picture with a more zoomed-in view making it perfect for close-up capture.

Fig. 7. 16 mm 10 MP Telephoto Lens

4. **Other devices**
   There are other devices that helped to accomplish the project like an SD card to store the operating system, buzzer, MG90 micro servo engine/motor servo to rotate the camera, Cooling fan to keep your system from overheating,300ohm of the resistor, LED(Light emitting diode)to get the necessary light that indicates the powered system with Raspberry pi power charger, Buzzer that gives the sound in case the camera rotates in the time set, and wire jumpers etc.

5   System Analysis and Design

A system's architecture is a high-level description of the entire system that specifies its essential pieces and functions, as well as the rules that each element must follow to communicate and collaborate. A real-time face recognition system was developed using the IoT architecture paradigm. Figure 8, IoT architecture, this is how the real-time face recognition attendance works accordingly as per it has been designed/developed. It describes hardware or software systems as well as represents the workflows and processes. This 4 layers components/layers Device connectivity/physical layer, Network layer, Data processing, management layer, and application layer.

1. Device connectivity/Physical Layer: this part consists of different IoT components with different technologies, which are interconnected together to perform the main goal of this research. Raspberry pi 4 Model B is used as a control unit, raspberry pi HQ camera, LED, and fan which are connected and controlled by a raspberry pi.
2. Network layer: used WIFI as a communication network to link the Control unit with the cloud server
3. Data processing and management Layer: this is the data engine of the system from cloud services such as data storage, security, machine learning, and execution of the instruction.
4. Application layer: This Layer consists of a web application interface that helps the admin to manage and monitor the system for data analysis. It allows the admin to manage and monitor the attendance of the employees and generate reports. This is Web App and a personal computer or smartphone. In this layer, the SMTP protocol is used to send your email.

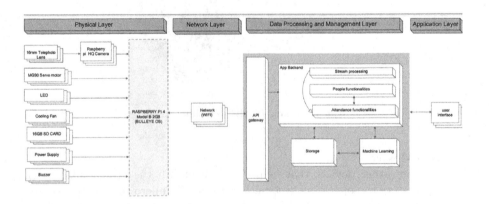

Fig. 8. IoT Layered architecture

6 Experiment and Result Analysis

6.1 Machine Learning Approach

The images is added into a file called images; every person you want to recognize must have a dedicated directory with the image in it and its corresponding names. MTCNN help us to detect the face in frames and locate it by drawing the bounding box around their extent and FaceNet to extract features from the image. Thus, it compares the new faces with other encoded images, adds a rectangle-bounding box to the frame, and sends the results to the web for marking the attendance into the dashboard (Table 1).

Table 1. Describes the functions used in the proposed system and its executed results.

Test image	Expected Result	Observed Result	Pass / Fail
Cv2.imread() Cv2.imwrite()	Use the CV2 function to read and write the images to corresponding files	Read and write images	pass
PiCamera()	use the capture() function from the camera object to take a Videos	Camera started	pass
face_encoding()	Retrieves all images stored at a person's images locations, resizes, and normalizes. Then using MTCNN detects the face in the frame and crops where the face of a person is located, then extracts features using the FaceNet Pre-trained model	Detected and extracted images features, then stored them in encodings.json file	pass
Face_comparison()	A new image with a person is then turned to its encoding, using FaceNet, and compared to other encodings stored in encoding.json using the cosine rule with a tolerance of 0.3	Face matching	pass

The results show that the system was successfully implemented with the expected results. The figure below is the face encoded from the saved photos in the file.Json which is a plain text written in JavaScript object notation (Fig. 9).

Fig. 9. Image encoded with 128 vector embeddings

6.2   Results

After designing the full circuit, I implemented the circuit. I did a test of my prototype to check if it is working. This is a prototype of the system which consists of a raspberry pi HQ camera with a 16 mm telephoto 10 MP lens, LED, Servo motor, and buzzer connected to the Raspberry pi 4 Model B with 2 GB of RAM (Fig. 10).

Fig. 10. the First picture is an Embedded system, the Center picture shows the login page of the system, and the left picture shows a web interface created to display data in the dashboard. By clicking on add employee button; the admin will be able to register the new employees with full details using a computer or a smartphone.

After saving the new employees, the new face will be compared with other encoded images and then display if the images captured are known with corresponding names or unknown on them via the dashboard (Fig. 11).

Fig. 11. Image comparison /matching with encoded images through live streaming and attendance is recorded automatically

Figure 12, shows the dashboard which graphically groups together all the information concerning the attendance made.

Fig. 12. Dashboard is automatically updated after recording and also the system is capable of sending an email to the employee if he or she is absent or late for work.

7   Conclusions and Future Works

The article presents a simple yet efficient approach to calculating attendance in any institution /organization by employing facial recognition techniques to avoid the propagation/ mitigation of Transmission of disease in general. The project was implemented using IoT tools with Machine Learning, which leads me to the success of the project, The system also successfully recognizes and marks the attendance of the detected employees, and sends the emails to the corresponding employee successfully. After carrying out the necessary test, it was observed that the aim of the work was achieved with an efficient, time-saving, and easy-to-operate system, which will in turn benefit both institutions and employees at the same time. The goal of this study is to eliminate errors and human intervention in spreading COVID-19 during attendance records by using real-time face recognition using machine Learning to protect the well-being of society. The outcome demonstrates our system's ability to address the issues raised in Chap. 2.

Future studies could improve on the operational paradigm, which collects videos and sends them to the cloud for further processing, decision-making, and data storage via an IoT-enabled system. This project could benefit from edge data processing rather than cloud processing to reduce latency time between raw data transmission, data processing, and decision-making. It will also be linked to the payroll management system to automatically record financial transactions.

References

1. Recfaces. The History of Biometrics. https://recfaces.com/articles/history-of-biometrics. (Accessed 09 Sept 2022)
2. Collection of biometric data and facial recognition (2022) eReader, https://www.mediadefence.org/ereader/publications/advanced-modules-on-digital-rights-and-freedom-of-expression-online/module-4-privacy-and-security-online/collection-ofbiometric-data-and-facial-recognition. (Accessed 21 Dec 2022)
3. Karthickraja, R., et al.: Covid-19 Prediction and symptom analysis using wearable sensors and IOT. Int. J. Pervasive Comput. Commun. **18**(5), 499–507 (2020). https://doi.org/10.1108/ijpcc-09-2020-0146

4. Swaroop, K.N., et al.: A health monitoring system for vital signs using IoT. Internet of Things **5**, 116–129 (2019). https://doi.org/10.1016/j.iot.2019.01.004
5. Coronavirus WHO(World Health Organization) (2022). https://www.who.int/health_topics/coronavirus#tab=tab_3. (Accessed 06 Sept 2022)
6. Al Bassam, N., Hussain, S.A., Khan, J., Al Arguli, A., Sumesh, E.P., Lavanya, V.: Iot based wearable device to monitor the signs of quarantined remote patients of covid-19. Infor. Med .Unlocked **24**, 100588 (2021). https://doi.org/10.1016/j.imu.2021.100588
7. Who coronavirus (COVID-19) dashboard (2022). https://covid19.who.int. (accessed 06 Sept 2022)
8. Rwanda: Who coronavirus disease (covid-19) dashboard with vaccination data, World Health Organization (2022). https://covid19.who.int/region/afro/country/rw. (Accessed 06 Sept 2022)
9. Arjun Raj, A., Shoheb, M., Arvind, K., Chethan, K.S.: Face recognition-based smart attendance system. In: IEEE 2020 International Conference on Intelligent Engineering and Management (ICIEM), pp. 354–357 (2020). https://doi.org/10.1109/iciem48762.2020.9160184
10. Patiland, M.A., Parane, K., Sivaprasad, D.D., Poojara, S., Lamani, M.R.: Smart attendance management system using iot, pp. 1–6 (2022). https://doi.org/10.1109/iccsea54677.2022.9936433
11. Chew, C.B.: Sensors-enabled smart attendance systems using nfc and rfid technologies. Int. J. New Comput. Archit. their Appl., 19–28 (2015)
12. OzcanCengiz Özcan, C., Ilhan, I., Saray, F., Mustafa, T.: Student attendance system appli- cation with nfc label in mobile devices. In: 2nd International Conference on Networking and Computer Application, ResearchGate, pp. 138–142 (2016)
13. Jose, E., Greeshma, M., Haridas, M.T.P., Supriya, M.H.: Face recognition based surveillance system using facenet and mtcnn on jetson tx2. In: IEEE, 2019 5th International Conference on Advanced Computing Communication Systems (ICACCS), pp. 608–613 (2019)
14. Anitha, G., Devi, P.S., Sri, J.V., Priyanka, D.: Face recognition based attendance system using mtcnn and facenet. Zeichen J. 189–195 (2020)
15. Yang, Z., Ge, W., Zhang, Z.: Face recognition based on mtcnn and integrated application of facenet and lbp method. In: IEEE, 2020 2nd International Conference on Artificial Intelligence and Advanced Manufacture (AIAM), pp. 95–98 (2020)
16. Sanath, K., Meenakshi, K., Rajan M., Balamurugan, V., Harikumar, M.E.: Face recognition based smart at- tendance system. In: IEEE, 5th International Conference on Computing Methodologies and Communication (ICCMC), pp. 492–499 (2021)
17. Mehmood, R.G.I., Ugail, H.: Facenet: A unified embedding for face recognition and clustering. In: A Study of Deep Learning-Based Face Recognition Models for Sibling Identification, Sensors (2021)
18. Kangwanwatana, S., Sucontphunt, T.: Improve face verification rate using image pre-processing and facenet. In: IEEE, 2022 7th International Conference on Business and Industrial Research (ICBIR), pp. 426–429 (2022)
19. Krizhevsky, A., Sutskever, I., Hinton, G.E.: Imagenet classification with deep convolutional neural networks. In: Advances in Neural Information Processing Systems, pp. 1097–1105 (20120
20. Sun, Y., Chen, Y., Wang, X., Tang, X.: Deep learning face representation by joint identification- verification. In: Advances in Neural Information Processing Systems, pp. 1988–1996 (2014)

21. Li, H., Lin, Z., Shen, X., Brandt, J., Hua, G.: A convolutional neural network cascade for face detection. In: The 2015 IEEE Conference on Computer Vision and Pattern Recognition (CVPR), pp. 5325–5334
22. Lecun, Y., Bottou, L., Bengio, Y., Haffner, P.: Gradient-based learning applied to document recognition. Proc. IEEE **86**(11), 2278–2324 (1998)
23. MK GurucharanBasic. CNN Architecture: Explaining 5 Layers of Convolutional Neural Network. https://www.upgrad.com/blog/basic-cnn-architecture. (Accessed 08 Oct 2022)
24. Yamashita, R., Nishio, M., Do, R.K.G., Togashi, K.: Convolutional neural networks: an overview and application in radiology. Insights Imaging **9**(4), 611–629 (2018)
25. Zhang, K., Zhang, Z., Li, Z., Qiao, Y.: Joint face detection and alignment using multitask cascaded convolutional networks. IEEE Signal Process. Lett. **23**(10), 1499–1503 (2016)
26. Jin, R., LiHao, P.J., Ma, W., Lin, J.: Face recognition based on mtcnn and facenet (2021)
27. Schroff, F., Kalenichenko, D., Philbin, J.: Facenet: A unified embedding for face recognition and clustering. In: 2015 IEEE Conference on Computer Vision and Pattern Recognition (CVPR), pp. 815–823 (2015)
28. Ghosh, S.: How to create a Face Recognition Model using FaceNet Keras?. https://medium.com/clique-org/how-to-create-a-face-recognition-model-using-facenet-keras-fd65c0b092f1. (Accessed 16 Sept 2022)
29. Taniai, H.: How to create a Face Recognition Model using FaceNet KerasFacenet implementation by Keras 2?. https://github.co/nyoki-mtl. (Accessed 16 Oct 2022)
30. Combined Precision Component(CPC). Raspberry Pi 4 4GB Official Desktop Kit. https://cpc.farnell.com/raspberry-pi/sc0400uk/official-raspberry-pi-4-4gb-desktop/dp/SC15586?ost=raspberry+pi+4+desktop+kit&ICID=I-RS-STM7REC-2&cfm=true. (Accessed 11 Nov 2022)
31. Combined Precision Component(CPC). 12MP Raspberry Pi High Quality Camera. https://cpc.farnell.com/raspberry-pi/rpi-hq-camera/rpi-high-quality-camera/dp/SC15616?ost=raspberry+pi+HQ++camera&ICID=I-RS-STM7REC-19&cfm=true. (Accessed 11 Nov 2022)
32. Combined Precision Component(CPC). 16mm Telephoto Lens for Raspberry Pi High Quality Camera. https://cpc.farnell.com/raspberry-pi/rpi-16mm-lens/rpi-16mm-telephotolens/dp/SC15617?ost=16mm+camera+lens&cfm=true. (Accessed 11 Nov 2022)

Towards Abalone Differentiation Through Machine Learning

Ruben Barrera-Hernandez[1], Viridiana Barrera-Soto[1],
Jose L. Martinez-Rodriguez[1(✉)], Ana B. Rios-Alvarado[2],
and Fernando Ortiz-Rodriguez[1]

[1] Multidisciplinary Academic Unit Reynosa-Rodhe,
Autonomous University of Tamaulipas, Reynosa, Mexico
{a2113245102,a2213728001}@alumnos.uat.edu.mx,
{lazaro.martinez,ferortiz}@uat.edu.mx
[2] Faculty of Engineering and Science, Autonomous University of Tamaulipas,
Victoria, Mexico
arios@docentes.uat.edu.mx

Abstract. Abalone is a marine species of mollusks of a great lineage with different properties for human consumption. Abalone farming is supported by productive and industrial infrastructure in several countries, including Mexico, where polyculture is being experimented with to optimize operating costs. One of the tasks of the producers is to identify the sex of each abalone to apply certain measures for its growth or to take steps for its preservation. However, this task can be challenging for those just starting the process. This paper presents a case study for classifying abalone sex using machine learning algorithms. A methodology is presented that involves the analysis and processing of information to train and configure four different classification algorithms to recognize three types of classes: male, female, and immature. The results demonstrate the impact of using linear classifiers for this task.

Keywords: Abalone classification · Machine learning · Data mining

1 Introduction

The abalone is a single-shelled, edible, snail-like gastropod mollusk found in coastal waters worldwide. Many of the abalone species are considered endangered. There are two leading causes for this: poaching and over-exploitation and the slow development and maturation process of abalones, which can take 3 to 5 years depending on the species [6]. Globally, total fishing landings have decreased from 14,830 tonnes in 1989 to 4,351 tonnes in 2019. Thus, the vast majority of commercially available abalone (95 percent) comes from farms. In Mexico, abalone is one of the most commercially important mollusks; it is only produced in Baja California. The red abalone has the highest production with approximately 22,458 tons with a value of 4,677,499 pesos (over 235 dollars) for the year 2007 [12]. Successful farming of abalone on farms depends to a

M. A. Jabbar et al. (Eds.): AMLDA 2022, CCIS 1818, pp. 108–118, 2023.
https://doi.org/10.1007/978-3-031-34222-6_9

large extent on selective breeding and knowledge of the reproductive aspects of these systems, one of which is sex. In this sense, sex identification methods vary depending on the abalone species. Three common identification methods are known for the red abalone: a) Visual method: It is a common way to determine the sex of an abalone at a mature age. When the abalones have a gonad, the sex can be differentiated by observing their color. In males, it is white-yellow to cream-beige. In females, olive-green to dark brown, and for immature organisms, the gonad is grayish brown [5]. b) Histological method: Through histology, the sex is determined by observing the presence of the specific germ cells of each sex. c) Biochemical method: Sex is identified by detecting the differential in the lipid reserves of the conical appendix (digestive gland-gonad) existing between undifferentiated individuals, females and males [4].

It is known that environmental factors can affect the sexual anatomy of mollusks in different ways, for example, reduction in the size of the penis in males in laboratory environments or, in the case of females, development of the vas deferens and penis when there are some chemicals in the water. Therefore, determining the sex of these animals may sometimes not be a simple task, where specific knowledge is required from an expert and that the abalone is at a certain stage of maturity. Thus, it is important to have alternatives to perform such analysis, where different characteristics could be exploited in order to predict the correct value. Therefore, this paper proposes an initial data analysis through machine learning algorithms to determine the sex of abalones. We present a methodology for preparing data and configuring the parameters of four supervised algorithms: KNN, Naive Bayes, SVM, and MLP. Although some work has been proposed to predict age and species of abalone [8,11,13], this paper attempts to provide insight into the prediction of abalone sex. The results demonstrate the performance and appropriate parameters at which the algorithms work better under the current scenario. Note that a new tool based on a machine learning model for sex identification could be very useful for farming practices and preserving the species.

The remainder of this paper is organized as follows: Sect. 2 presents brief concepts of machine learning and its importance for this scenario. Section 3 present the proposed methodology for abalone classification. The experiments and results are shown in Sect. 4. Finally, Sect. 5 presents the conclusions and further work.

2   Using Machine Learning

Machine learning is a sub-field of artificial intelligence that offers various methods that can be applied in marine science to identify marine species, migration, and other features. It has significant advantages compared with manual analyses that are labor intensive and require considerable time [3]. It supports data-driven learning, which can result in automated decision-making.

Researchers use different techniques to determine various aspects of the abalone. For example, machine learning scientists apply classification and regression techniques using the physical characteristics of abalone to determine age and sex. These techniques are known as supervised learning algorithms [9]. Supervised learning algorithms are characterized by learning by example. The machine learning model is provided with a previously prepared data set that contains the characteristics or predictors and the labels, predictions, or expected values. The algorithm trains the model to determine a method to arrive at the expected values. This is performed by identifying patterns in the data, then the algorithm makes predictions and then applies corrections. This process is repeated until an acceptable level of accuracy is reached [2].

Some common supervised machine learning [7,16] algorithms are briefly described as follows:

- k-nearest neighbors (KNN). KNN is an instance-based algorithm. It's not so sensitive to noise data but heavily relies on the distance function. If some features are mixed together in a space, their performance will drop sharply [17].
- Naïve Bayes is a simple learning algorithm that utilizes Bayes' rule and strongly assumes that the attributes are conditionally independent given the class. While this independence assumption is often violated in practice, naïve Bayes usually delivers competitive classification accuracy. Coupled with its computational efficiency and many other desirable features, this leads to naïve Bayes being widely applied in practice [18].
- Support Vector Machines (SVM). SVM is a supervised learning model with associated learning algorithms that analyze data for classification and regression analysis. In addition to performing linear classification, SVM can efficiently perform a non-linear classification, drawing margins between the classes. The margins are drawn in a form that the distance between the margin and the classes is maximum which minimizes the classification error [14].
- Artificial Neural Networks (ANN) are computational models that try to replicate the functioning of the human brain. A neural network is trained to identify the relationships and implicit processes in the data. It consists of a set of units called artificial neurons, connected to transmit signals to each other. The input information passes through the neural network (where it undergoes various operations), producing output values. The multilayer perceptron (MLP) is a popular ANN made up of multiple layers, such that it can solve problems that are not linearly separable.

3   Methodology

This section presents the proposed methodology for preparing and configuring the classification algorithms. Figure 1 presents the methodology. It is composed of the following steps:

- Data collection. This step consists of collecting the data that will be used for classification. The data may contain various characteristics ranging from the size of the abalone to the number of rings indicating the age of the specimen.

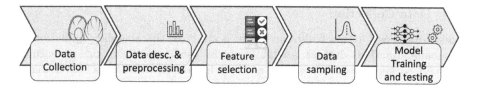

Fig. 1. Methodology for preparing and configuring the algorithms for abalone sex classification

- Data description and preprocessing. Once the data to be used are defined, the next step is to analyze them in order to know, among other things, their characteristics and domain (type and values) as well as their variability, which helps to make decisions to select certain types of techniques. In addition, it is necessary to apply some operations to the data so that the algorithms can handle them. For example, if algorithms that process numerical values are used, it is necessary to apply operations to convert textual or categorical values into a set of processable values.
- Feature selection. The goal of feature selection is to select a subset of the features from the original data set that reduces their dimensions by using a minimal feature set to represent the maximum amount of variance in the data. This subset of features is used to train the model [15].
- Data sampling. In this step, the data samples that are used for training and testing are prepared. Also, if necessary, techniques for data balancing are applied, i.e., if the number of samples of a class is predominant, techniques such as Undersampling and Oversampling are applied to have balanced data.
- Model training and testing. This is the stage where the learning takes place, it consists of feeding engineered data to a parameterized machine learning algorithm resulting in a working model that can then be validated, tested and deployed. At this point, the parameters of each algorithm are also configured and tested in order to select the combination that provides the best performance.

4   Experiments and Results

This section presents the experiments and results of the study. The experiments consist of performing the training of different classification models using different algorithms following the steps of the methodology. The objective is to correctly predict the sex of an abalone given a set of physical characteristics. Python was used for the development of the experiments. The implementation of the algorithms was performed over the online platform Google Collab and the following libraries: Pandas for the use of data frames, Numpy for matrix operations, Matplotlib for handling plots, Seaborn for graphics appearance, and Sklearn for machine learning operations. The steps taken for preparing and configuring the data are presented in the following subsections.

4.1 Data Collection

This work uses a dataset obtained from a study of the abalone population in Tasmania [10]. This dataset is intended to be used to analyze various features of abalones, such as age, shell size, and weight, among other data. A version of this data set was obtained from the Kaggle website[1].

4.2 Data Description and Preprocessing

The data set consists of nine features or columns and 4177 samples or rows. The columns are the following:

- Type: Abalone sex. It can be one of the following: Male, Female, or Immature. This column contains data of categorical type.
- Length: Measurement of the shell at its longest point.
- Diameter: Measurement perpendicular to the length.
- Height: Height of the abalone even with meat inside.
- Whole Weight: Weight of the whole abalone.
- Shucked Weight: Weight of the meat.
- Viscera Weight: Weight of the viscera after bleeding the abalone.
- Shell Weight: Weight of the shell only.
- Rings: Internal rings of the shell. Adding 1.5 to the number of rings gives you the age of the abalone.

Table 1 presents some statistics of the obtained data. The standard deviation is relatively low, so the data are clustered around the mean.

Table 1. Description values of collected abalone data

Feature	Mean	Std	Min	Max	25%	50%	75%
LongestShell	0.5239	0.1200	0.0750	0.8150	0.4500	0.5450	0.6150
Diameter	0.4078	0.0992	0.0550	0.6500	0.3500	0.4250	0.4800
Height	0.1395	0.0418	0.0000	1.1300	0.1150	0.1400	0.1650
WholeWeight	0.8287	0.4903	0.0020	2.8255	0.4415	0.7995	1.1530
ShuckedWeight	0.3593	0.2219	0.0010	1.4880	0.1860	0.3360	0.5020
VisceraWeight	0.1805	0.1096	0.0005	0.7600	0.0935	0.1710	0.2530
ShellWeight	0.2388	0.1392	0.0015	1.0050	0.1300	0.2340	0.3290
Rings	9.9336	3.2241	1.0000	29.0000	8.0000	9.0000	11.0000

Figure 2 presents an excerpt of the original dataset (ten first rows). It is worth mentioning that there are no samples with incomplete data or null values were found, and thanks to this, a few preprocessing and cleanup tasks were performed.

Regarding the preprocessing, we applied the following tasks:

---

[1] https://www.kaggle.com/datasets/rodolfomendes/abalone-dataset.

	Type	LongestShell	Diameter	Height	WholeWeight	ShuckedWeight	VisceraWeight	ShellWeight	Rings
0	M	0.455	0.365	0.095	0.5140	0.2245	0.1010	0.150	15
1	M	0.350	0.265	0.090	0.2255	0.0995	0.0485	0.070	7
2	F	0.530	0.420	0.135	0.6770	0.2565	0.1415	0.210	9
3	M	0.440	0.365	0.125	0.5160	0.2155	0.1140	0.155	10
4	I	0.330	0.255	0.080	0.2050	0.0895	0.0395	0.055	7
5	I	0.425	0.300	0.095	0.3515	0.1410	0.0775	0.120	8
6	F	0.530	0.415	0.150	0.7775	0.2370	0.1415	0.330	20
7	F	0.545	0.425	0.125	0.7680	0.2940	0.1495	0.260	16
8	M	0.475	0.370	0.125	0.5095	0.2165	0.1125	0.165	9
9	F	0.550	0.440	0.150	0.8945	0.3145	0.1510	0.320	19

Fig. 2. Sample Abalone data set

- Convert Categorical to Numeric Data. The "Type" column contains the data on the sex of the abalones. There are three possible values: "M" for male, "F" for female, and "I" for immature. In addition to grouping and graph functions, the classification algorithms only accept numerical data, so it is necessary to convert these categorical data to numerical ones. The value "M" was replaced with 1, "F" with 2, and in the case of "I" a 3 was assigned.
- Outlier removal. Outliers are data whose values are very different from the rest because they are unusually high or low. They are generally caused by: errors in the collection procedure, extraordinary events, extreme values, and unknown causes. It is important to identify them because they distort the results of the analyzes and negatively affect the predictive ability of the model [1]. Outliers were removed using the interquartile range. The upper and lower limits of the data are calculated, given by the interquartile range multiplied by 1.5 and being added or subtracted, as the case may be, from the 25th percentile and the 75th percentile. The values below or above these limits are considered atypical and are discarded.

4.3   Feature Selection

Feature selection is essential to keep those dimensions that provide the most information for classification. In this sense, we obtained the correlation matrix to summarize the data and to check possible associations. Figure 3 presents the correlation among the various features of the dataset. Only the column containing the mapping values with the "Type" feature is kept. The values of this column are averaged, and the characteristics below the average are eliminated; in this case, "Rings" and "Height".

	Type	LongestShell	Diameter	Height	WholeWeight	ShuckedWeight	VisceraWeight	ShellWeight	Rings
Type	1.000000	-0.448765	-0.458245	-0.417928	-0.461238	-0.440927	-0.454658	-0.445549	-0.351822
LongestShell	-0.448765	1.000000	0.986812	0.827554	0.925261	0.897914	0.903018	0.897706	0.556720
Diameter	-0.458245	0.986812	1.000000	0.833684	0.925452	0.893162	0.899724	0.905330	0.574660
Height	-0.417928	0.827554	0.833684	1.000000	0.819221	0.774972	0.798319	0.817338	0.557467
WholeWeight	-0.461238	0.925261	0.925452	0.819221	1.000000	0.969405	0.966375	0.955355	0.540390
ShuckedWeight	-0.440927	0.897914	0.893162	0.774972	0.969405	1.000000	0.931961	0.882617	0.420884
VisceraWeight	-0.454658	0.903018	0.899724	0.798319	0.966375	0.931961	1.000000	0.907656	0.503819
ShellWeight	-0.445549	0.897706	0.905330	0.817338	0.955355	0.882617	0.907656	1.000000	0.627574
Rings	-0.351822	0.556720	0.574660	0.557467	0.540390	0.420884	0.503819	0.627574	1.000000

Fig. 3. Correlation matrix of the abalone dataset

At the end of all preprocessing tasks, this is the state of the data set (Fig. 4). Two columns were removed, so there are only 7. Also, 120 records were removed, and only 4057 samples remain.

	Type	LongestShell	Diameter	WholeWeight	ShuckedWeight	VisceraWeight	ShellWeight
0	1	0.455	0.365	0.5140	0.2245	0.1010	0.1500
1	1	0.350	0.265	0.2255	0.0995	0.0485	0.0700
2	2	0.530	0.420	0.6770	0.2565	0.1415	0.2100
3	1	0.440	0.365	0.5160	0.2155	0.1140	0.1550
4	3	0.330	0.255	0.2050	0.0895	0.0395	0.0550
...	...	...	...	...	...	...	...
4172	2	0.565	0.450	0.8870	0.3700	0.2390	0.2490
4173	1	0.590	0.440	0.9660	0.4390	0.2145	0.2605
4174	1	0.600	0.475	1.1760	0.5255	0.2875	0.3080
4175	2	0.625	0.485	1.0945	0.5310	0.2610	0.2960
4176	1	0.710	0.555	1.9485	0.9455	0.3765	0.4950

4057 rows × 7 columns

Fig. 4. Clean dataset

4.4   Data Balancing and Sampling

We checked the data balancing of the dataset through a histogram for the "Type" values. The histogram is shown in Fig. 5. Note that this column represents the sex of the abalones, which is the class label or value that the classification algorithms will predict.

As can be seen, there is a minimal difference between the amount of data from class 1 (Male) and the rest of classes 2 and 3 (Female and Immature). The difference between classes 1 and 2 is 14.5%, while the difference between

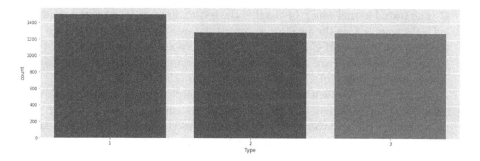

Fig. 5. Data Histogram of the Type feature

1 and 3 is 14.8%. Class 1 represents 36.94% of the samples. Class 2 represents 31.57% and class 3 31.47%, which is why the classes are considered minimally unbalanced; thus, no additional techniques are applied for balancing.

Additional Data Preparations. Two subsets were created from the original data set. The first contains only the features or predictors needed to train the model or to perform a prediction. The second subset contains only the class labels, categories, or values that are trying to be predicted based on the features.

Data Separation. Once the data for the features and class labels are organized, the following step is to separate them to form the data sets for training and testing. It is widely used to separate the data into proportions of 80% for training and 20% for testing. It is necessary to make a separation that includes proportional amounts of each label; thus, we performed a stratified sampling. As the last step, the values of the sets containing the characteristics are normalized; the objective is that all the values are within the same range (0 to 1) in order to avoid training problems.

4.5 Model Training and Testing

Different configuration values were used for testing each algorithm with the purpose of finding the best configuration. The used parameters per algorithm, are as follows:

- KNN. The k number varies from 1 to 20.
- Naive Bayes. In the implementation of a model based on Naive Bayes, the configuration is more limited within the function integrated into SKlearn; it is only possible to vary one of the following algorithms: Gaussian, Multinomial, Complement, Bernoulli and Categorical. The categorical algorithm was not used due to incompatibility with the data.
- SVM. The configuration of a classification model with SVM allows you to control different parameters, among which the following stand out: Kernel and

C. The tested kernel was "rbf" as it is the most common. The other parameter is C. Parameter C is the penalty or error tolerance in classifying samples with the support vectors. If C is equal to 0, the errors are not penalized; if C tends to infinity, no errors are allowed, and it is customary to use C equal to 100. The following values of C were tested: 1, 5, 10, 15... 95, 100.

- Artificial Neural Network. The multi-layer perceptron neural network classifier function included in SKlearn allows to configure the following used parameters: Hidden layer sizes, which indicates the number of hidden layers and the neurons in each one; Max iteration indicates the number of iterations the solver will do until convergence; Activation function of the neural network; Solver, this parameter specifies the algorithm for weight optimization between nodes; Random state, the number that always allows obtaining the same random values; Batch size, size of the batch of data that will be sent per iteration to the neural network; Tol: Tolerance for the optimization. To obtain reference values, the following configuration was used:

  - Hidden Layers: 1–10
  - Neurons per layer: 5–50 (increments of 5)
  - Maximum number of iterations: 500
  - Activation function: identity, logistic, tanh and relu
  - alpha:0.0001
  - Solver: lbfgs, sgd, and adam
  - Random state=21
  - Tol=0.000000001

Note that we performed five fold cross-validation for the experiments and then we used the test sample (20% of original data) for comparison/evaluation.

4.6 Classification Results

The classification results are presented in Table 2, where Tr. refers to training, Acc. refers to accuracy, P. is precision, and R. is recall. The best values are in bold. Moreover, we only report the best results of the tested configurations.

Table 2. Classification results

Algorithm	Tr. Acc.	Tr. P.	Tr. R.	Test Acc.	Test P.	Test R.
KNN	**0.61**	**0.61**	**0.61**	0.52	0.50	0.52
Naive Bayes	0.51	0.49	0.53	0.52	0.51	**0.54**
SVM	0.57	0.59	0.57	**0.55**	0.53	**0.54**
ANN	0.60	0.60	0.60	0.54	**0.54**	**0.54**

The best parameter configurations of the Cross Validation Results are presented in Table 3.

Table 3. Best configurations

Algorithm	Best settings
KNN	K=17
Naive Bayes	Type=Gaussian
SVM	C=40
ANN	Hidden layers=4
	Neurons=50
	Function= Tanh
	Solver= Adam

In the result values, scores close to 60% are obtained in most evaluation cases with training data. Note that training scores are considerably reduced with the test data. While KNN presents the best training results, the neural network and SVM show similar results that stand out in the test results, demonstrating that classifiers based on linear features perform better with this type of data. However, it can be noted that the consideration of several classes could be a reason for negatively impacting the performance of the classifiers. We also noted that the features present similar values for any of the three classes, which difficult the correct separation by the classifiers.

5   Conclusions

This paper presented an initial study of the analysis and classification of abalone data. The idea was to compare different classification models to predict the sex or type of the abalone according to a given set of physical characteristics. The study considered four machine learning algorithms: KNN, Naive Bayes, SVM, and MLP. By conducting tests like cross-validation and obtaining the confusion matrix, the best performing algorithm was SVM, with an accuracy of 0.55 on the test data set. Although the results could have been more encouraging, they have been helpful in providing insight into the type of analysis required to manage abalone data. While it is not a substitute for abalone experts, it provides initial classification support. In future work, we plan to exploit different data preprocessing techniques and classification algorithms that help differentiate the data from the three categories of abalones.

References

1. Valores Atípicos (2021). https://www.ibm.com/docs/es/spss-modeler/saas?topic=series-outliers
2. APD, R.: Cuáles son los tipos de algoritmos del machine learning? (2020). https://www.apd.es/algoritmos-del-machine-learning/

3. Arifin, W.A., Ariawan, I., Rosalia, A.A., Lukman, L., Tufailah, N.: Data scaling performance on various machine learning algorithms to identify abalone sex. J. Teknol. Sist. Komput. **10**(1), 26–31 (2022)
4. Basto Cuevas, A.M.: IdentificaciÓn del sexo y del desarrollo gonadal en abulÓn rojo haliotis rufescens, en cautiverio (2009)
5. Carballo, G.L., Mucino-Diaz, M.: Pesqueria de abulon. Estudio Del Potencial Pesquero Y Acuicola De Baja Cali fornia Sur. Centro de Investigaciones Biologicas del Noroeste, SC, La Paz, pp. 15–41 (1996)
6. Cook, P.A.: Worldwide abalone production statistics. J. Shellfish Res. **38**(2), 401–404 (2019)
7. Gaurav, D., Rodriguez, F.O., Tiwari, S., Jabbar, M.: Review of machine learning approach for drug development process. In: Deep Learning in Biomedical and Health Informatics, pp. 53–77. CRC Press (2021)
8. Guney, S., Kilinc, I., Hameed, A.A., Jamil, A.: Abalone age prediction using machine learning. In: Djeddi, C., Siddiqi, I., Jamil, A., Ali Hameed, A., Kucuk, İ. (eds.) MedPRAI 2021. CCIS, vol. 1543, pp. 329–338. Springer, Cham (2022). https://doi.org/10.1007/978-3-031-04112-9_25
9. Hossain, M., Chowdhury, M.N.M., et al.: Econometric ways to estimate the age and price of abalone (2019)
10. Mendes, R.: Abalone dataset (2018). https://www.kaggle.com/datasets/rodolfomendes/abalone-dataset
11. Noh, E.S., Kim, J.W., Kim, D.G.: Machine learning SNP for classification of Korean abalone species (genus haliotis). Korean J. Fisheries Aquatic Sci. **54**(4), 489–497 (2021)
12. SAGARPA: Valor de la producción acuícola en el estado de baja california en el 2007 (2007). http://www.sagarpa.gob.mx/dlg/bajacalifornia/pesca/informacion/Produccion%20acuicola%20total%202007.pdf
13. Sahin, E., Saul, C.J., Ozsarfati, E., Yilmaz, A.: Abalone life phase classification with deep learning. In: 2018 5th International Conference on Soft Computing & Machine Intelligence (ISCMI), pp. 163–167. IEEE (2018)
14. Steinwart, I., Christmann, A.: Support Vector Machines. Springer Science & Business Media (2008)
15. Tabladillo, M.: Selección de características en el proceso de ciencia de datos en equipos (tdsp)) (2022). https://learn.microsoft.com/es-es/azure/architecture/data-science-process/select-features
16. Tiwari, S., et al.: Applications of machine learning approaches to combat covid-19: a survey. In: Lessons from COVID-19, pp. 263–287 (2022)
17. Wang, Z.: Abalone age prediction employing a cascade network algorithm and conditional generative adversarial networks. Research School of Computer Science, Australian National University, Canberra (2018)
18. Webb, G.I., Keogh, E., Miikkulainen, R.: Encyclopedia of machine learning. Naïve Bayes **15**, 713–714 (2010)

Better Qualitative Searching for Effecting the Performance of Machine Translation

Anasua Banerjee[1], Vinay Kumar[1], and Debajyoty Banik[2(✉)]

[1] National Institute of Technology, Jamshedpur, Jharkhand, India
{2022rscs008,vkumar.cse}@nitjsr.ac.in
[2] Kalinga Institute of Industrial Technology, Bhubaneswar, Odisha, India
debajyoty.banik@gmail.com

Abstract. By improving a better comprehension of the human language for linguistically based human-computer communication, natural language processing (NLP) contributes to the empowerment of intelligent machines. Instead of hand-coding massive sets of rules, NLP can use machine learning to learn these rules automatically by examining a set of rules. With a view to better and clearer results in the endeavor to achieve success in the field of language translation, we have gone through some of the techniques like Machine Translation, Punctuation Restoration, Name Entity Recognition, and Sentiment Analysis. Here we mentioned different state-of-the-art methods for different techniques of NLP. This paper offers an abstract analysis of the current state of language translation techniques.

Keywords: Natural Language Processing · Deep Learning · Artificial Intelligence · Machine Learning

1 Introduction

Natural Language Processing (NLP) combines the power of Computer Science, Artificial Intelligence, and Computational Linguistics to help machines read, write and communicated by simulating the human ability to perceive language [25]. NLP not being as wide as Big Data and Machine Learning does have a huge variety of applications that are constantly helping us to perform tasks daily. Major Applications include Text Classification, Machine Translation, Automatic Summarization, Sentiment Analysis and Question Answering. Text Classification deals with categorizing documents or pieces of information, we need or search for. Machine Translation plays a vital role in conquering the language barriers which we often encounter by several translations of technical manuals. It mainly focuses on providing an understandable meaning of sentences providing a true translation. Question Answering deals with the concept of providing solutions to problems on speech or text interfaces. The emerging evolution of virtual assistants like OK Google, Echo, Siri, and Alexa is one of the biggest applications of it. Lastly, Sentiment Analysis whose goal is to identify the sentiment in each

© The Author(s), under exclusive license to Springer Nature Switzerland AG 2023
M. A. Jabbar et al. (Eds.): AMLDA 2022, CCIS 1818, pp. 119–130, 2023.
https://doi.org/10.1007/978-3-031-34222-6_10

post and also among several posts at a time. It aims to provide us with a brief of a post through a specific sentiment which may be an emoji.

NLP deal with Natural Language i.e. the High-Level language which we use in our day to day lives for communication. The world is already filled up with a variety of languages. It is thus hard even for us to understand every human language, and so making a machine understand them is obvious to be harder. Though machine can memorise faster still the method used to make them understand is difficult. Humans can easily master a language, but the imprecise and ambiguous characteristics of these languages are what makes mastering them by computers hard. Different languages have different syntax, context, phonemes, morphemes and lexemes etc. Natural Language Understanding, also known as linguistics and natural language generation, is the process through which the work of comprehending and producing the text evolves. The study of language, or linguistics, includes phonology, or the study of sound. Morphology, the development of words, Syntax, sentence structure, Semantics, syntax, and Pragmatics, which is understood. The process of creating meaningful words, sentences, and paragraphs from an internal representation is known as natural language generation, or NLG. This paper's primary goal is to provide an understanding of the many key NLP and NLG terms.

2   Related Work

Natural Language Processing (NLP) is a subset of Artificial Intelligence. It enables computers to understand natural language in the same way that humans do. Natural language processing, whether spoken or written, employs artificial intelligence to take real-world input, process it, and make sense of it in a way that a computer can understand.

Many approaches to machine translation have been proposed, including rule-based, example-based, statistical-based, and neural-based machine translation. The basic structure of RBMT systems consists of the rules, which account for syntactic knowledge, and the lexicon, which deals with morphological, syntactic, and semantic information. Lexicons and rules are both created by qualified linguists and are based on linguistic expertise [2]. For this reason, the entire process is quite costly. Examples-based machine translation (EBMT), statistical machine translation (SMT), and neural machine translation are the three corpus-based MT techniques. EBMT works well only if a similar sentence can be retrieved. With SMT, a machine may translate from one language to another from a significant amount of data rather than relying on rules, as was proposed by Brown et al. [3]. But SMT requires a large number of bilingual corpora for each language pair. Neural Machine Translation(NMT) was first proposed by Bahdanau et al. [4]. Authors in [32] create a dataset of Telangana words that come from a variety of texts, including books, plays, articles, and other literary works, as well as conversations between native speakers. Furthermore, they applied some tokenization and machine translations technique for language translation from Telugu to English.

A vital component of NLP systems for query resolution, data retrieval, relation extraction, text summarization, etc. is named entity recognition (NER). NER systems have been extensively researched and developed over the years, but accurate systems utilizing deep neural networks (NN) have only recently been made available. Statistical learning, dictionaries, and rules are the basic implementation bases for traditional named entity recognition techniques. [5]. One of the applications of NLP is Text Summarization which helps to summarize text from the large text. Sentiment analysis automates the extraction or categorization of sentiment from sentiment reviews using natural language processing (NLP), text analysis, and computational approaches. Analysis of these attitudes and opinions has appeared in a variety of publications, including websites, and social media. Sentiment analysis is becoming increasingly popular in decision-making [6]. A Query Answering System tries to determine the right response to the question posed in natural language given a set of documents. Qsuetion Answering system is mainly used to produce the response from a repository of documents [7]. In this paper [33], the authors are to analyze all currently used Knowledge Graphs in terms of their characteristics, methods, uses, issues, and difficulties. They have introduced the Multi dialect system MEXIN [34], which, despite being in its early stages, has clear objectives to support providing citizens with public administration (government) services.

3   Overview of NLP Technologies

3.1   Machine Translation

NLP includes the field of machine translation (MT). Text and speech are translated using MT from one language to another. The majority of the information is in English, but only three percent of the population speaks the language; MT solves these issues. Since 1990, numerous institutions like IIIT Hyderabad, IIT Kanpur, CDAC Pune, CDAC Mumbai, and others have been working on the development of MT systems as part of programs funded by the state governments, Department of Electronics, and other entities [8]. Figure 1 depicts MT techniques according to their classification.

- Rule-Based Machine Translation (RBMT), which is also called Knowledge-Based Machine Translation, is the traditional way to use a computer to translate between languages. In this method when source language is passed, an intermediate representation text is produced shown in Fig. 3. The intermediate representation is used to make the text in the target language. The systems are based on how the source and target languages are used. This information comes mostly from grammars and dictionaries that describe the main morphological, syntactic, and semantic patterns of each language. The primary function of RBMT is to translate the semantic and syntactic structures of the source language into those of the target language. The methodology could use a number of the strategies depicted in Fig. 2. There are some major problems faced at the time of applying the RBMT model like fails

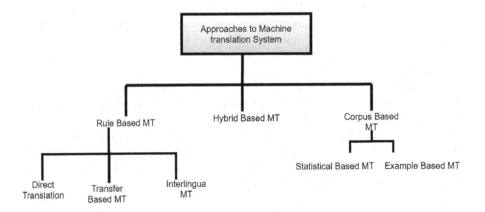

Fig. 1. Various Machine Translation Methods

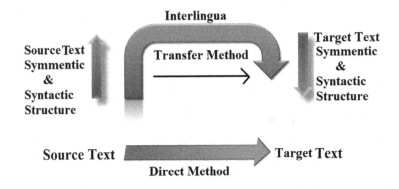

Fig. 2. Several approaches to RBMT

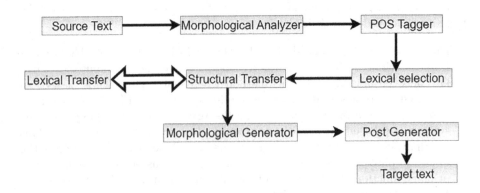

Fig. 3. The RBMT approach's architecture

to analyze dependency between the words, expensive in case of multilingual language translation and some of the meaning of the original text can be lost when it is translated.

– Corpus-based machine translation is a large collection of texts and data in both the source and target languages. The following are two additional methods for Statistical Machine Translation (SMT) and Example Based Machine Translation (EBMT). SMT consists of three models. Initially, a large number of output sentence candidates in the target language are generated. A bilingual translation lexicon is used to translate each word or phrase in the input sentence, with each translation assigned a probability. The Language Model (LM) calculates the likelihood of the target language P. (T). Following that, the decoder looks for the best output candidate using a statistical scoring function. P(T|S) is the conditional probability of target sentences given the source sentence computed using the Translation Model (TM). Although SMT systems are capable of handling local reorderings on their own, they greatly benefit from outside assistance when undergoing long-distance transformations. Figure 4 depicts schematic architecture of the SMT system.

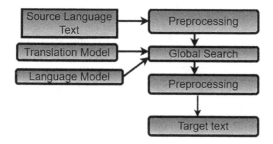

Fig. 4. Statistical Based Machine Translation Model

There are two components to an EBMT system: the retrieval module and the adaptation module. For a given source sentence, the retrieval module searches similar sentences and its translation. The adaptation module then changes the translation that was just retrieved to make the final, correct translation. In the case of the EBMT system to generate the dependency trees required for both the examples database and the sentence analysis, analysis, and generation modules are required. EBMT's computational efficiency, particularly for big databases, remains a concern.

– Neural Based Machine Translation: Since the neural translation model is trained end-to-end to maximize translation performance, this approach differs from traditional translation SMT systems. Neural machine translation (NMT) aims to develop and train a single, sizable neural network that can read a sentence and produce an accurate translation, as opposed to the conventional phrase-based statistical machine translation (PBSMT) system, which is composed of numerous small sub-components that are tweaked separately. NMT models typically use two tokens sequences-x representing a sentence in the source language and y representing its target language translation. With little training data and without spending any money on retraining the model, NMT models perform well on the target language. Even better performance may be possible with adaptation than with training on a particular subject from scratch. Some current issues with machine translation can be framed as issues with domain adaptation, which encourages the use of the tried-and-true methods discussed in the earlier portions of this article [25]. Numerous authors have already looked into the impact of sentence length on the accuracy of neural machine translation to highlight current issues with NMT. For instance, Bentivogli et al. [27] pointed out that utilizing NMT to translate longer words results in a considerably lower quality of translation based on the data that is currently available. Similar results have been reported by Toral et al. [28] who claim that PBMT performs better than NMT in sentences longer than 40 words, "with PBMT's performance remains fairly stable while NMT's decreases with sentence length." Anoop et al. [23]. presented the IIT Bombay English-Hindi Parallel Corpus as well as trained Phrase-based SMT and Neural-based machine translation. They evaluated their system by using BLEU and METEOR shown in Table 1.

Table 1. Comparing different models Using BLEU and METEOR matrix evaluation

Language	SMT		NMT	
	BLEU	METEOR	BLEU	METEOR
Eng-Hin	11.75	0.33	12.23	0.38
Hin-Eng	14.49	0.266	12.83	0.219

– Hybrid-Based Machine Translation: A new strategy known as the hybrid-based approach was created by utilizing both statistical and rule-based translation approaches, and it has proven to be more effective in the field of MT systems. This hybrid-based technique, which is based on both rules and data, is currently used by several governmental and private MT sectors to generate translation from the source language to the target language. There are several ways to apply the hybrid strategy. In other instances, rule-based translation techniques are used in the initial stage, and the result is then adjusted or corrected using statistical data. On the other hand, a statistical-based translation system uses rules to pre-process the input data as well as post-process the statistical output. This approach has more strength, adaptability, and translation control than the prior one. To select the best translation from a group of competing hypotheses (translations) produced using rule-based procedures, it integrates statistical methods into an RBMT system [26].

3.2   Sentiment Analysis

Sentiment analysis (SA) aims mainly to comprehend people's attitudes and feelings toward many types of entities, including people, organizations, issues, events, and subjects. SA provides business insights to improve brand perception and business performance. Customer-focused businesses use SA to get customer insight for corporate strategy development. Through translation APIs (Google Translation), the translation can be done manually or automatically [30]. Text is translated for the manual procedures, and for each translated term, synonyms are found. The word is then included in the lexicon along with its synonyms. For the automatic technique, a manually compiled and annotated lexicon known as the base lexicon serves as the foundation for the lexicon. Then, more synonyms and antonyms are added to expand the lexicon [31]. The process of creating lexicons manually is more accurate than automatically. However, the automatic approach needed less effort and time shown in Fig. 5. Sentiment analysis employs NLP to identify the emotional context embedded in social media material and performs a broad data analysis to produce a binary classification. Real-world social media data is comprehended by means of deep learning techniques. A deep learning network with multiple layers predicts the emotions present in data [9]. There are total five stages present for sentiment analysis (i.e. Selection of social media platforms, Data collection process, Data pre-processing, Data analysis with polarity identification and sentiment analysis or frequency analysis). Conventional sentiment analysis studies evaluate the overall sentiment polarity towards the text or document as a whole at the phrase or document level. In this context, Aspect-Based Sentiment Analysis (ABSA), often known as the requirement to recognise increasingly complicated aspect-level thoughts and attitudes, has gained growing attention over the past decade. In the ABSA dilemma, the concerned target switches from a complete sentence or text to an entity or a particular aspect of an entity. For example, in the E-commerce arena, an entity can be a specific product, and its properties or features [10].

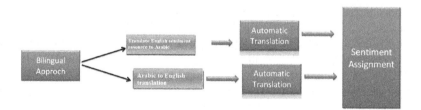

Fig. 5. Methodologies for sentiment analysis

SA is a highly domain-sensitive activity in which the ranking of sentiment is largely dependent on the domain from which the training data originates and the classifier trained on a domain's training dataset. The volume, diversity, velocity, variability, and veracity of data, which are the primary characteristics of big data, make the analysis of big data a tough operation. Sentiment analysis on large data sets is complicated by the peculiarities of large data sets [11].

Table 2 summarises some of the prior research in this field and displays various objectives, the corresponding models that were employed to achieve them, and the outcomes of experiments.

Table 2. State-of-the-art methods on Sentiment Analysis

Model	Objective	Data source	Precision	Accuracy	F1 score	Recall
Non- hierarchical clustering [16]	Assign adjectives positive or negative	WSJ corpus	78.1-92.4	N/A	N/A	N/A
SVM [17]	Assign docs sentiments using 4-point scale	Customer feedback	N/A	77.5	N/A	N/A
Assign topics sentiments [18]	NLP pattern based	Digital camera, music reviews	87	85.6	N/A	56
Assign expressions sentiments [19]	Probabilistic based	DUC corpus	N/A	75.6-77.9	N/A	97.8

3.3 Punctuation Restoration

A typical postprocessing concern with Automatic Speech Recognition (ASR) systems is punctuation restoration. It is crucial to make the transcribed text more readable for human readers and to make NLP tasks easier. The correct usage of capital letters and punctuation marks is frequently necessary for text comprehension by both humans and artificial intelligence (AI) computers.Due to the lack of punctuation in newspaper texts, for the Named Entity Recognition system, for example, there is a performance difference of more than 10% when the model is trained with newspaper texts and analyzed using transcriptions. The majority of the past attempts to resolve this issue when the process of restoring punctuation has been completed prosodic, acoustic, lexical or a mixture of these characteristics [24]. Zhang1 et al. applied some pre-trained models on the IWSLT2012-zh dataset for the punctuation restoration task. Table 3 shows F1 score on IWSLT2012-zh dataset.

Table 3. F1-scores on the IWSLT2012-zh dataset

Pretrained Model	Question	Period	Comma	Overall
ERNIELinear	0.8406	0.5447	0.5142	0.6331
BERTBiLSTM	0.8095	0.5707	0.5190	0.6330
BERTLinear	0.7400	0.427	0.4646	0.5424

3.4 Named Entity Recognition

Named Entity Recognition (NER) is a technique for retrieving various nouns that is commonly used in NLP applications such as ATS, knowledge graphs, question and answer, and machine translation. NER is used to pull out certain predefined entities from sentences and figure out what kind of thing they are. Rule-Based (RB) and Statistical-Based (SB) are the two approaches to NER methods. In a Rule-Based approach, a large number of rules are required based on a task. Different tasks require different sets of protocols which is time-consuming and limits their applicability to other fields. Rule-based approaches extract matched entities from the text based on a set of matching rules, which are primarily derived from regular expressions or dictionaries. Regular expressions are composed of specified specific characters and combinations of these specific characters to describe string or text filtering logic, whereas dictionaries composed of entities. The matching rules can be designed manually. The Statistical-Based approach needs fewer rules and is more flexible than RB. SB turns the NER task into sequence labeling. Labeling costs are cheaper than making rules [12].

Neural architectures for NER just require a modest amount of supervised training data and unlabeled corpora, with no other language-specific resources or features. A potential strategy for overcoming data scarcity recently surfaced: pre-training a large-scale language model. However, because gathered NER datasets are often small or large, pretraining for the NER work has not received much research. This is because the fundamental differences between language modelling and the NER task may limit the models' performance. [13]. Bidirectional Encoder Representations from Transformers (BERT) [15], BERT's domain-adaptive pre-training (DAPT) [15], NER-BERT$_{4type}$ [15], NER-BERT$_{212types}$ [15] and NER [14] pretrainred model F1 score are shown in this Table 4. Authors in [29] demonstrate that MT systems can be used to project information from languages with abundant resources to those with limited resources. In the categorization issue, these projections can be exploited as cross-lingual features. They have demonstrated how a Hindi-to-English MT system and English NER can improve NER for Hindi, a language with limited resources.

Table 4. F1-score on the CrossNER dataset

Pretrained Models	CrossNER									
	Science	Music	Politics	AI	Twitter	Literature	Defence	BTwi	Finance	Avg
BERT	63.33	66.59	66.56	50.37	83.34	59.95	68.42	75.61	76.23	70.19
NER- BERT	71.90	76.23	73.69	60.39	83.59	67.85	70.79	77.30	78.72	75.06
DAPT	67.59	73.39	70.45	56.36	–	64.96	–	–	–	–
NER- BERT$_{4type}$	68.31	71.02	70.76	57.03	83.40	63.91	69.22	77.26	77.55	72.83
NER- BERT$_{212type}$	71.09	75.98	73.81	58.58	83.46	68.13	70.28	77.06	77.85	74.60

4   Conclusion

The primary purpose of this paper is to investigate various aspects of the NLP technique. NLP is a subfield of computer science and artificial intelligence concerned with computer-human interaction. Any language that people pick up from their surroundings and use to communicate with one another is referred to as a natural language. Natural languages are employed regardless of the medium of communication to convey our knowledge, feelings, and reactions to other people and our environment. This paper will be helpful for any researcher who wishes to conduct research work in this field to do so easily. Here we compared many state-of-the-art methods. We attempted to investigate some of the NLP techniques such as text sentiment analysis, named entity recognition, and punctuation restoration in order to boost up langugae translation. In the future, we want to explore the pre-trained models on different NLP tasks.

Declarations

– The authors declare no conflict of interest for this manuscript.

References

1. Reshamwala, A., Mishra, D., Pawar, P.: Review on natural language processing. IRACST Eng. Sci. Technol. Int. J. (ESTIJ) **3**(1), 113–116 (2013)
2. Bennett, W.S., Slocum, J.: The LRC machine translation system. Comput. Linguist. **11**(2–3), 111–121 (1985)
3. Brown, P.F., et al.: A statistical approach to machine translation. Comput. Linguist. **16**(2), 79–85 (1990)
4. Dzmitry, B., Cho, K., Bengio, Y.: Neural machine translation by jointly learning to align and translate. arXiv preprint arXiv:1409.0473 (2014)
5. Wen, Y., Fan, C., Chen, G., Chen, X., Chen, M.: A survey on named entity recognition. In: Liang, Q., Wang, W., Liu, X., Na, Z., Jia, M., Zhang, B. (eds.) CSPS 2019. LNEE, vol. 571, pp. 1803–1810. Springer, Singapore (2020). https://doi.org/10.1007/978-981-13-9409-6_218
6. Basant, A., Mittal, N., Bansal, P., Garg, S.: Sentiment analysis using commonsense and context information. Comput. Intell. Neurosci. **2015**(6), 715730 (2015)
7. Das, B., Majumder, M., Phadikar, S., Sekh, A.A.: Automatic question generation and answer assessment: a survey. Res. Pract. Technol. Enhanced Learn. **16**(1), 1–15 (2021). https://doi.org/10.1186/s41039-021-00151-1
8. Murthy, B.K., Deshpande, W.R.: Language technology in India: past, present and future, 1998 (2011)
9. Sanjeev, V.: Sentiment analysis of public services for smart society: literature review and future research directions. Gov. Inf. Q. **39**(3), 101708 (2022)
10. Wenxuan, Z., Li X., Deng Y., Bing L., Lam W.: A survey on aspect-based sentiment analysis: tasks, methods, and challenges. arXiv preprint arXiv:2203.01054 (2022)
11. Gouthami, S., Hegde, N.P.: A survey on challenges and techniques of sentiment analysis. Turkish J. Comput. Math. Educ. (TURCOMAT) **12**(6), 4510–4515 (2021)

12. Liu, P., Guo, Y., Wang, F., Li, G.: Chinese named entity recognition: the state of the art. Neurocomputing **473**, 37–53 (2022)
13. Zihan, L., Jiang, F., Hu, Y., Shi, C., Fung, P.: NER-BERT: a pre-trained model for low-resource entity tagging. arXiv preprint arXiv:2112.00405 (2021)
14. Zihan, L., Jiang, F., Hu, Y., Shi, C., Fung, P.: NER-BERT: a pre-trained model for low-resource entity tagging. arXiv preprint arXiv:2112.00405 (2021)
15. Liu, Z., et al.: CrossNER: evaluating cross-domain named entity recognition. In: Proceedings of the AAAI Conference on Artificial Intelligence **35**(15), pp. 13452–13460 (2021)
16. Vasileios, H., McKeown, K.: Predicting the semantic orientation of adjectives. In: 35th Annual Meeting of the Association for Computational Linguistics and 8th Conference of the European Chapter of the Association for Computational Linguistics, pp. 174–181 (1997)
17. Michael, G.: Sentiment classification on customer feedback data: noisy data, large feature vectors, and the role of linguistic analysis. In: COLING 2004: Proceedings of the 20th International Conference on Computational Linguistics, pp. 841–847 (2004)
18. Bo, P., Lee, L.: A sentimental education: sentiment analysis using subjectivity summarization based on minimum cuts. arXiv preprint cs/0409058 (2004)
19. Soo-Min, K., Hovy, E.: Determining the sentiment of opinions. In: COLING 2004: Proceedings of the 20th International Conference on Computational Linguistics, pp. 1367–1373 (2004)
20. Xiangyu, D., Yu, H., Yin, M., Zhang, M., Luo, W., Zhang, Y.: Contrastive attention mechanism for abstractive sentence summarization. arXiv preprint arXiv:1910.13114 (2019)
21. Abigail, S., Liu, P.J., Manning, C.D.: Get to the point: summarization with pointer-generator networks. arXiv preprint arXiv:1704.04368 (2017)
22. Sebastian, G., Deng, Y., Rush, A.M.: Bottom-up abstractive summarization. arXiv preprint arXiv:1808.10792 (2018)
23. Anoop, K., Mehta, P., Bhattacharyya, P.: The IIT Bombay English-Hindi parallel corpus." arXiv preprint arXiv:1710.02855 (2017)
24. Agustin, G., Jansche, M., Bacchiani, M.: Restoring punctuation and capitalization in transcribed speech. In: 2009 IEEE International Conference on Acoustics, Speech and Signal Processing, pp. 4741–4744. IEEE (2009)
25. Saunders, D.: Domain adaptation and multi-domain adaptation for neural machine translation: a survey. J. Artif. Intell. Res. **75**, 351–424 (2022)
26. Okpor, M.D.: Machine translation approaches: issues and challenges. Int. J. Comput. Sci. Issues (IJCSI) **11**(5), 159 (2014)
27. Luisa, B., Bisazza, A., Cettolo, M., Federico, M.: Neural versus phrase-based machine translation quality: a case study. arXiv preprint arXiv:1608.04631 (2016)
28. Antonio, T., Cartagena, V.M.S.: A multifaceted evaluation of neural versus phrase-based machine translation for 9 language directions. arXiv preprint arXiv:1701.02901 (2017)
29. Dandapat, S., Way, A.: Improved named entity recognition using machine translation-based cross-lingual information. Computación y Sistemas **20**(3), 495–504 (2016)
30. Matīss, R.: Multi-system machine translation using online APIs for English-Latvian. In: Proceedings of the Fourth Workshop on Hybrid Approaches to Translation (HyTra), pp. 6–10 (2015)

31. Oumaima, O., Cambria, E., HajHmida, M.B., Ounelli, H.: A review of sentiment analysis research in Arabic language. Future Gener. Comput. Syst. **112**, 408–430 (2020)

32. Hashwanth, S., Duggal, A., Tiwari, S., Chaurasia, N., Ortiz-Rodriguez, F.: Dialect translation of english language to telangana. In: Proceedings http://ceur-ws.org ISSN 1613 (2022): 0073

33. Tiwari, S., Al-Aswadi, F.N., Gaurav, D.: Recent trends in knowledge graphs: theory and practice. Soft Comput. **25**(13), 8337–8355 (2021). https://doi.org/10.1007/s00500-021-05756-8

34. Fernando, R.O., Tiwari, S., Panchal, R., Quintero, J.M.M., Barrera, R.: MEXIN: multidialectal ontology supporting NLP approach to improve government electronic communication with the Mexican Ethnic Groups. In: DG. O 2022: The 23rd Annual International Conference on Digital Government Research, pp. 461–463 (2022)

RU-Net: A Novel Approach for Gastro-Intestinal Tract Image Segmentation Using Convolutional Neural Network

Shankru Guggari[(✉)], B. Chandan Srivastava, Vivek Kumar, Halli Harshita, Vishal Farande, Uday Kulkarni, and S. M. Meena

KLE Technological University, Hubballi, Karnataka, India
{shankru.guggari,uday_kulkarni,msm}@kletech.ac.in

Abstract. The Gastro-Intestinal (GI) tract is a tunnel of the digestive system that goes right through the body from the mouth to the anus. The nutrients which are present in the food are absorbed by the walls of the GI tract. The GI tract consists of the mouth, esophagus, stomach, intestine, and anus in the human digestive system. Many people get affected by GI tract cancer leading to the development of tumors in the tract. To treat these tumors, gastroenterologists use X-ray beams to avoid the stomach and intestine. There is a need to segment the stomach and intestine so that gastroenterologists recognize and avoid them while treating tumors using X-rays. In this work, the ResNet34 - U-Net (RU-Net) model is used to segment the stomach, small bowel, and large bowel organs. The best dice score obtained by our model is 0.9049 on the validation set of the UW-Madison GI Tract Image Segmentation dataset. The model proposed in this work is also compared with other techniques such as LeViT128-UNet, Mask R-CNN, and LeViT384-UNet++.

Keywords: Gastro-Intestinal (GI) tract · Image Segmentation · Convolutional Neural Network · Magnetic Resonance Imaging

1 Introduction

Gastrointestinal cancers comprise tumors of the esophagus, gallbladder, stomach, pancreas, colon, rectum, anus, liver, and bile duct [5]. Cancers of the colorectum, stomach, and pancreas are the most common gastrointestinal cancers in the United States and much of the Western world. Radiation therapy significantly reduces cancer, where radiation oncologists deliver high doses of X-rays to the tumor. While doing so, they must manually outline the stomach and intestine so that they avoid being affected by the X-rays. Outlining the organs manually is a very tedious task. So, the challenge is to implement a model which segments the internal organs with a precision close to that of a human's analytic skills. Implementing such a model saves a lot of time for gastroenterologists to treat cancer and may even reduce errors while treatment.

M. A. Jabbar et al. (Eds.): AMLDA 2022, CCIS 1818, pp. 131–141, 2023.
https://doi.org/10.1007/978-3-031-34222-6_11

Machine learning in the medical field can be used to develop better diagnostic tools to analyze medical images. It can be used to improve the efficiency of healthcare, which could lead to cost savings, and also it can be used to improve the quality of patient care. So, recently machine learning is getting popular in the medical field [3,13] and it definitely has a bright future in the field.

Magnetic Resonance Imaging (MRI) scans [8] of patients which are used as a dataset in this work issued by UW Carbone cancer center. These MRI scans are sent as input to our model. The model includes both ResNet34 and U-Net to segment the stomach, large intestine, and small intestine in the areas of the patient's MRI scans. The segmentation of the Gastro-Intestinal tract is very crucial for tumor treatment. In this paper, a novel RU-Net is proposed to segment the Gastro-Intestinal tract.

The organization of the paper is as follows: Related work is described in Sect. 2. The proposed methodology RU-Net is discussed in Sect. 3. Experimentation & Results are demonstrated in Sect. 4. The conclusion is narrated in Sect. 5.

2   Related Works

Object detection is a major component of machine learning. It is mainly based on techniques like Region based Convolution, Dense based Convolution, and others. Some of those techniques are used in previous works on medical image segmentation. Related works such as Region-Based Convolutional Neural Networks, U-Net architectures, and Mask R-CNN are described as follows:

2.1   Region Based Convolutional Neural Networks (RCNN's)

Since 2014, many state-of-the-art methods used in the tasks of object detection and semantic segmentation have evolved, when compared to the method used in Visual Object Challenge, where the PASCAL dataset was used. In one of the approaches, high-capacity CNN's [7] was used to precisely detect objects and perform segmentation, where affluent features were extracted, ranked, and used to perform a task. In region-based CNN, the regions of the image are scanned by the model for localizing the objects of the image. These features are learned by the model, and it utilizes a domain-related calibrating technique after performing supervised pre-training for fallback tasks in cases where the label for training is meagre. This novel proposed RCNN method combines region-extracted features with CNNs and is called Regions along with CNN features or RCNN. The loss function used universally in all the methods related to medical image segmentation is the dice loss function.

The results obtained using the baseline mask average method are not better than Mask R-CNN [6]. Also, R-CNN makes use of multi-stage pipelining and is expensive both in terms of space and time, as mentioned in Fig. 1. Moreover, objection detection is very slow during the test time. The model, which needs around 46 s per image, is speed up by the VGG-16 CNN using GPU. The altered approach in the study brought a number of benefits, including single-stage training (using multi-task loss), greater detection quality during training by updating all network layers, and lastly, the elimination of the need for disc storage for the caching feature.

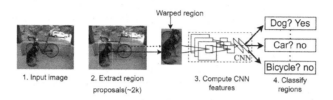

Fig. 1. R-CNN: Regions with CNN features

2.2 U-Net Type Architectures

U-Net is used to separate neuronal structure in electoral microscopic pictures, but it is also regarded as a robust network design for many other segmentation tasks in biomedical imaging.

This architecture allows for exact localization, also for every pixel, it allows the model to output a class label and results in segmentation of images. U-Net makes use of a fully convolutional network topology which substitutes the upsampling layers for typical pooling layers to improve the output resolution.

Context encoder network (CE-Net), which is based on the U-Net approach but preserves spatial information for 2-D medical image segmentation, is another significant model for this purpose [4].

Similar to U-Net, V-Net [1] has a completely convolutional design with a differentiable final Dice loss layer. It is made up of convolutional layers, with V-Net layers being 3D convolutions, to learn the volumetric structure represented by stacks of image slices. The authors of V-Net used histogram matching and non-linear adjustments on the available data to enhance the training data.

Between the convolution layer and the ReLU activation function, a batch normalisation layer is advised. The network is more stable while being trained because to the batch normalisation, which lessens internal covariance shift. Also employed at some point following the ReLU activation function is the dropout. By removing (ignoring) a few randomly chosen neurons, it compels the network to develop a new representation. It aids the network in becoming less reliant on certain neurons. As a result, the network is able to generalise more effectively and avoid overfitting.

2.3 Mask R-CNN

Mask R-CNN is a region-based convolutional neural network. It is one of the simple and flexible approaches to image segmentation, as mentioned in [2]. Since it has two phases, the Object detection part will use Faster R-CNN and semantic segmentation part will use fully connected networks. In addition to the branch already present for bounding box identification, for each region of interest (ROI), Mask RCNN adds a branch for segmentation mask prediction using Faster R-CNN. Faster RCNN carries out object detection in two steps: (1) establishing the bounding box, followed by finding the area of interest using the Region Proposal Network(RPN) protocol, and (2) establishing the class label of the item using ROI pooling. In the 2nd stage Mask R-CNN also gives the binary mark for each ROI as output.

In the ROI pooling method [12], the stride is quantized and Pooling is used for the down sampling of features and is used to introduce invariance to minor distortions and input. The major problem in Faster R-CNN is a data loss, this is due to applying max pooling on a region of interest.

During the training, on each sampled ROI, a multi-task loss is defined given by $Loss_{multi-task} = Loss_{classification} + Loss_{bounding-box} + Loss_{mask}$. In this formula, $Loss_{classification}$ represents classification loss, $Loss_{bounding-box}$ represents bounding box loss, and $Loss_{mask}$ represents average binary cross-entropy loss.

In tasks based on detection and segmentation, Region Of Interest (ROI) alignment is a better strategy for extracting a tiny feature map from each ROI. This method whose working overview is shown in Fig. 2 is used to address the problem of data loss. It does away with the strict ROI pooling quantization. By computing exact values of the input features at four regularly sampled places in each ROI boundary using the bilinear interpolation approach, ROI Align avoids ROI boundaries, and the results are then aggregated (using max or average).

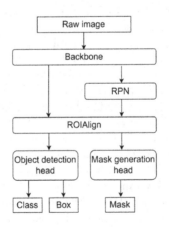

Fig. 2. Mask-RCNN

Image Pre-processing

The MRI scans are in grayscale format. To extract features from these scans, they need to be processed. The process of global contrast normalization (GCN) [15] is applied for the scans to extract the features. In computer vision, the technique in which the pixel intensity values need to be changed is called as Normalization. In fact, in most of the normalization implementations, a grayscale image is given as input and the output obtained is also grayscale. Global contrast normalization is an image enhancement technique that is used to modify the dissimilarity in an image, considering all the pixels of the image by 'stretching' the range of intensity values it contains to span all the pixels of the image.

The GCN technique is different from the histogram equalization technique, which is complicated and also it is limited to applying only linear scaling function to the image pixels. So, the enhancement is better in GCN compared to histogram equalization.

The main aim of GCN is to prevent images from having varying contrasts. It subtracts the average contrast from each image, then rescales it so that standard deviation across pixels equals constants.

Run-Length Encoding (RLE) is done on the output image. For better understanding of RLE [9]. To segment the stomach and intestine, the location of those organs needs to be known. RLE is a technique used to encode the location of foreground objects, which here is the stomach, small bowel, and large bowel, in segmentation. In other segmentation works, only a mask image is generated to segment the objects. In RLE, instead of just producing a mask for the targeted objects in an image, it gives a list of start pixels and how many pixels after each of those starts are included in the mask.

The encoding rule is based on data like, where the mask is, the Index of that mask, and how many pixels are included in the mask from the beginning.

Feature Extraction

For extracting the features, ResNet34 is used as the backbone of the model. The kernel channel of ResNet is comparatively less compared to other encoders, making the model to control the computation without reducing the receptive field of the kernel.

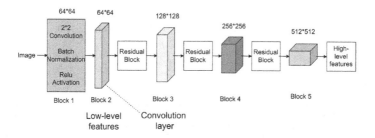

Fig. 3. Feature Extraction using ResNet34

A vanishing Gradient is a commonly occurring problem related to gradient-based learning that is encountered while training deep neural networks if the training is using the backpropagation technique. During backpropagation, the weights generated during training are updated using the gradients so as to reduce the training errors. But sometimes due to a low learning rate and limited back-propagation, the gradient becomes very (vanishingly) small, which prevents the weights to update. Due to this vanishing gradient problem, no practical work is done because, the weights are not changing during backpropagation and the same values are propagated again and again during training, keeping them constant.

To avoid the problem of backpropagation so that the proposed model works better than the visual transformers mentioned in [10], ResNet [11] is used to extract the features of the input. The architecture and functionalities of ResNet are almost similar to CNN, but with an additional skip, and connections to tackle certain problems. The skip connections present in the ResNet skip the layers during backpropagation to avoid the vanishing gradient problem. The layers description, the process of extracting the features of the MRI scans, and the structure of the encoder are shown in Fig. 3

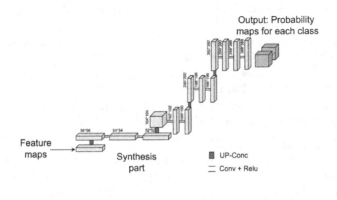

Fig. 4. Decoding the segmented output from U-Net

3   RU-Net Model

In this section, the proposed RU-Net model is described. It is the combination of ResNet as an encoder and U-Net as a decoder. The architecture of the RU-Net model is shown in Fig. 5

For extracting the features, ResNet34 is used as the backbone of the model. The kernel channel of ResNet is comparatively less compared to other encoders, making the model control the computation without reducing the receptive field of the kernel.

Segmented Image Extraction: The features extracted from the previous step are passed to the U-Net decoder to obtain the segmented output of the MRI scans. U-Net is chosen as the decoder because it computes a pixel-wise output (minus the validity margins of the convolutions), which is fitted for medical image segmentation tasks, i.e. each pixel of the image is assigned a particular class (label). The process of obtaining a segmented image from extracted features is shown diagrammatically in Fig. 4.

The energy function [14] is used to control the system while computing cross-entropy loss and combining it with the final feature map using the pixel-wise soft-max function.

The model implemented in this work is a combination of the ResNet encoder and U-Net decoder, as shown in Fig. 5. Other architectures like mask-rcnn solve the problem directly, i.e. it produces masks for each recognized object. But U-net, which is used in the proposed model can produce only one mask, hence it is used to predict the union of all masks, followed by post-processing to split the predicted mask into one mask per object.

Even though LeViT models perform with high accuracy, ResNet is used as the encoder in the RU-Net architecture to make use of skip connections so as to reduce the error and avoid the vanishing gradient problem during training.

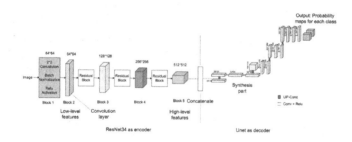

Fig. 5. RU-Net Model

The pre-processed grayscale image is passed as input to the ResNet encoder to extract the features. The skip connections in the ResNet reduce the error of locating the targeted regions. The activation function gives the output H(X), taking the input X. The input gets multiplied with weights W of the layers followed by adding a bias term B, and the features of the input are obtained. The activation function is given by, H(X) = F(WX + B).

The important pixels are given importance in the weight map.

Using these extracted features, U-Net gives a segmented image as output, where the internal organs namely, stomach, large bowel, and small bowel are segmented.

4   Experimentation and Results

In this section, the focus is on the dataset's details & exclusive experimentation with different combinations of both encoder and decoder architectures.

The UW-Madison GI Tract Image Segmentation dataset is used to segment various organs in this work. The given dataset consists of around 38000 16-bit grayscale images in the .png format and the annotations are in the form of RLE-encoded masks. Multiple sets of scan slices are used to represent each instance (each set is recognized by the scan)(each set is given an ID according to the day on which the scan was taken). Some cases are divided into time segments, while other instances are divided into case segments, with the entire case being in the train set.

Once training is done on the input data, we need to evaluate the model. There are some chances of overfitting of the test/validation set due to existing parameters. In order to overcome this overfitting, we make use of K-Fold Cross-Validation. The major focus is to split the data into K folds. We then perform training on K-1 folds whereas test/validation is done on the remaining fold which results in better performance of the model.

The training and validation loss, whose progress are given in Fig. 6 are best recorded as 0.08749 and 0.1197 respectively. This shows that with every step the model tries to improve it's performance. Training is done for 10 folds and performance is evaluated at every fold.

The learning rate tells us how effectively the model fits into the data, and finding the appropriate learning rate with each epoch is also essential. This task is performed using the CosineAnnealingLR scheduling technique. In this technique, the learning rate begins with a high value, and subsequently, it rapidly reduces the learning rate to a number close to 0 and then raises the learning rate again (similar to the cosine curve).

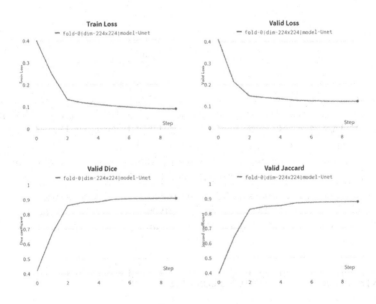

Fig. 6. Performance measures

The dice and Jaccard coefficient is calculated. The highest Validation Dice Coefficient and Validation Jaccard Coefficient, whose progress in each fold is given in Fig. 6 are found to be 0.9049 and 0.8759 respectively. It has a sudden increase in scores after 3 folds, it jumps from 0.4 to 0.8.

Table 1 shows the comparison of results of the proposed RU-Net model with other state-of-the-art models like LeViT-UNet and Mask R-CNN models. Figure 15 indicates the segmentation of the medical image of the stomach, small bowel, and large bowel.

It is inferred from the Table 1 that difference in the Validation Dice coefficient with respect to our achieved scores in comparison with LeViT128s-UNet, Mask R-CNN & LeViT384-UNet++ are 0.202, 0.132 & 0.11 respectively. And also the difference in Validation Jaccard coefficient with respect to our achieved scores in comparison with LeViT128s-UNet, Mask R-CNN & LeViT384-UNet++ are 0.243, 0.15 & 0.15.

Table 1. Comparison of performance of the Architecture

Model	Train Loss	Valid Loss	Valid Dice	Valid Jaccard
LeViT128s-UNet [10]	0.144	0.192	0.703	0.633
Mask R-CNN [2]	-	-	0.773	0.726
LeViT384-UNet++ [10]	0.089	0.134	0.795	0.726
RU-Net	**0.087**	**0.119**	**0.905**	**0.876**

Table 2 shows the key differences between the proposed RU-Net model with other previously mentioned state-of-the-art models in terms of the encoder, decoder, scheduler, optimizer & dice score.

Cosine Annealing is used as a scheduler which affects the learning rate that relatively rapidly decreases. Adam is used as an optimizer as it's the combination of gradient descent with momentum and Root Mean Square propagation algorithms.

Table 2. Comparison with State-of-Art

	LeViT-UNet++ [10]	Mask R-CNN [2]	RU-Net
Encoder	LeViT	FPN	ResNet34
		Faster	U-Net with
Decoder	U-Net++	R-CNN	Attention
	Cosine	Reduce LR	Cosine
LR-Scheduler	Annealing LP	on Plateau	Annealing LP
Optimiser	-	RMS Prop	Adam
Dice Score	0.79543	0.7266	**0.9049**

The Loss, Dice & Jaccard scores obtained during the training of each fold are given in Table 3 with respect to parameters. The model is trained for 10 folds and has achieved the results shown in following table. Parameters are updated after every fold during the training phase of the model. It is seen that the metric reaches a point wherein there isn't much change in the scores which we achieve.

Table 3. Performance Metrics of ResNet-UNet (RU-Net)

Fold	Train Loss	Valid Loss	Valid Dice	Valid Jaccard	LR
1	0.2491	0.2148	0.6763	0.6428	0.0018
3	0.1182	0.1407	0.8789	0.8481	0.0013
5	0.1018	0.1272	0.8998	0.8707	0.0006
7	0.0913	0.1212	0.9040	0.8749	0.0001
9	0.0875	0.1197	0.9049	0.8759	0.0001

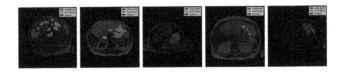

Fig. 7. Visualization results

Visualization results are shown in Fig. 7 wherein the segmentation of organs is shown for some sample images.

5   Conclusion

Even with recent successes, there is a need for scalable, robust, and computationally efficient model for MRI scan segmentation. This paper addresses the problem from the perspective of computational efficiency. In this work, a ResNet-UNet (RU-Net) model is implemented and used for the segmentation of internal organs. The RU-Net model is a hybrid combination of the ResNet encoder and U-Net decoder by which the features of both the sub-models can be used, which leads to improved model performance than other state-of-the-art models. In future, an ensemble technique is used to improve the performance of the model.

References

1. Atika, L., Nurmaini, S., Partan, R.U., Sukandi, E.: Image segmentation for mitral regurgitation with convolutional neural network based on unet, resnet, vnet, fractalnet and segnet: A preliminary study. Big Data and Cognitive Computing, **6**(4), 141 (2022)

2. Chou, A., Li, W., Roman, E.: Gi tract image segmentation with u-net and mask r-cnn
3. Gaurav, D., Rodriguez, F.O., Tiwari, S., Jabbar, M.A.: Review of machine learning approach for drug development process. In Deep Learning in Biomedical and Health Informatics, pp. 53–77. CRC Press (2021)
4. Zaiwang, G., et al.: Ce-net: context encoder network for 2d medical image segmentation. IEEE Trans. Med. Imaging **38**(10), 2281–2292 (2019)
5. Heavey P., Rowland, I.R.: Gastrointestinal cancer. Best Practice & Research Clinical Gastroenterology, **18**(2), 323–336 (2004)
6. Johnson, J.W.: Adapting mask-rcnn for automatic nucleus segmentation. arXiv preprint arXiv:1805.00500 (2018)
7. Kayalibay, B., Jensen, G., van der Smagt, P.: Cnn-based segmentation of medical imaging data. arXiv preprint arXiv:1701.03056 (2017)
8. Khalid, H., et al.: A comparative systematic literature review on knee bone reports from mri, x-rays and ct scans using deep learning and machine learning methodologies. Diagnostics, **10**(8), 518 (2020)
9. Messom, C.H., Demidenko, S., Subramaniam, K., Gupta, G.S.: Size/position identification in real-time image processing using run length encoding. In IMTC/2002. In: Proceedings of the 19th IEEE Instrumentation and Measurement Technology Conference (IEEE Cat. No. 00CH37276), vol. 2, pp. 1055–1059. IEEE (2002)
10. Nemani, P., Vollala, S.: Medical image segmentation using levit-unet++: A case study on gi tract data. arXiv preprint arXiv:2209.07515 (2022)
11. Shehab, L.H., Fahmy, O.M., Gasser, S.M., El-Mahallawy, M.S.: An efficient brain tumor image segmentation based on deep residual networks (resnets). J. King Saud Univ. -Engi. Sci. **33**(6), 404–412 (2021)
12. Su, H., Wei, S., Yan, M., Wang, C., Shi, J., Zhang, X.: Object detection and instance segmentation in remote sensing imagery based on precise mask r-cnn. In: IGARSS 2019–2019 IEEE International Geoscience and Remote Sensing Symposium, pp. 1454–1457. IEEE (2019)
13. Wernick, M.N., Yang, Y., Brankov, J.G., Yourganov, G., Strother, S.C.: Machine learning in medical imaging. IEEE Signal Process. Mag. **27**(4), 25–38 (2010)
14. Zhen, Y., Shuanhu, D., Yuqian, Z., Miao, L., Yezhan, Z.: Automatic liver tumor segmentation based on cascaded dense-unet and graph cuts. **44**, 1–11 (2022)
15. Zeiner, K., Maertens, M.: Linking luminance and lightness by global contrast normalization. J. Vis. **14**(7), 3–3 (2014)

A Credit Card Fraud Detection Model Using Machine Learning Methods with a Hybrid of Undersampling and Oversampling for Handling Imbalanced Datasets for High Scores

Omar Sinayobye$^{(\boxtimes)}$ (ID), Richard Musabe (ID), Alfred Uwitonze (ID), and Alexander Ngenzi (ID)

School of ICT, University of Rwanda, Kigali, Rwanda
sijaom2@gmail.com

Abstract. Due to recent advancements in communication technology and e-commerce systems, credit cards are currently the most popular form of payment for online as well as offline purchases. As a consequence, there is substantially more fraud involved in the transaction processes. Data mining has an issue for prediction, and data classification, therefore finding occurrences is essential. Unusual events are challenging to be identified due to their irregularity and casualness, but misclassifying unusual events can lead to large financial losses. In this study, an approach for detecting credit card fraud using machine learning methods, such as K-Nearest Neighbors, random forest, decision trees, logistic regression, and support vector machines, is proposed. The research attempts to look at the effectiveness of the classification models while applying both the Oversampling and Undersampling techniques to find instances of fraud in the dataset for fraudulent activities. The experimental study used two days of credit card transactions made by European cardholders in September 2013. To evaluate the models' performances, confusion matrix, precision, recall, f1_score, cross-validation score, and ROC_AUC score metrics were used. From different experiments of the tested model, it can be easily observed that the performance of all models was better compared with previous literature thus the KNN was the best in almost all metrics used.

Keywords: Machine learning · Sampling techniques · Credit card transactions · Fraud detection · Imbalanced datasets · Performance evaluation

1 Introduction

In the modern world, credit card fraud is expanding quickly, and fraud in businesses, government agencies, the financial sector, and various other organizations is also on the rise. Financial institutions create credit cards to help people with their daily payment transaction operations in response to the rise in internet usage. The results in detecting credit card fraud are not very accurate, despite the use of data mining methods. Utilizing effective fraud detection algorithms is the only method to reduce these losses, and doing so is a potential strategy to reduce credit card fraud.

Credit card fraud detection works to determine whether a transaction is fraudulent or not using past data. Machine learning approaches are being used to create computational algorithms that, depending on the volume and length of transactions, can identify illegitimate transactions [1]. Fraud detection for credit cards is the process of separating individual transactions. Two different kinds of transactions could take place: legitimate and fraudulent. Since real data is rarely accessible for analysis due to privacy concerns, this poses the greatest challenge when detecting credit card fraud. The fact that less than 0.03 percent of all payment transactions worldwide are fraudulent transactions presents a huge barrier to fraud detection. This ratio restrains the distribution of any dataset on credit card fraud, leading to classes that are wildly imbalanced [2]. Even though transactions involving the minority class are improperly classified, any system that correctly categorizes legal transactions would have an accuracy level of above 99 percent if this problem weren't taken into consideration.

To find credit card fraud, recorded transaction analysis is used. The majority of transaction data is made up of a set of variables, such as the credit card number, transaction date, receiver, and transaction amount. In supervised fraud detection techniques, predictive models for credit card fraud detection are frequently utilized. These models are created based on samples of valid and fraudulent transactions to determine whether future transactions are valid or fraudulent [3]. A dataset that is both extremely imbalanced and publicly available is credit card fraud, for instance. Since it contains more genuine transactions than fraudulent ones, the dataset is considerably imbalanced [4]. This means that even if a fraud transaction is not discovered, the classification will still have a very high accuracy score. One of the hardest issues in data mining is the classification of imbalanced data sets. Recent researchers in [5–7] focused a lot of attention on the issue of class imbalance.

In order to address the issues, it is preferable to balance the distribution of the classes, which includes selecting minority classes [8]. To increase the likelihood that the algorithm will make an accurate prediction in minority sampling, class training examples might be increased proportionally to the majority class [9]. For addressing the issue of class imbalance, sampling procedures change the distribution of classes in the training data. Undersampling, oversampling, and combining both of these strategies are the three basic methods for data sampling. Undersampling strategies balance the distribution of the classes by removing the majority of class sample data. Contrarily, oversampling expands the size of the minority class by producing more samples or duplicating existing ones [3, 10]. New minority class samples are produced, and oversampling techniques reduce the negative effects of the imbalanced dataset. Undersampling reduces the time required to train a model a smaller training dataset can be used. However, since samples from the majority class are eliminated, important data could be lost. Although oversampling procedures increase model training times and have the potential to lead to overfitting, they do not lose information from training samples [6]. Data points for the minority class are increased by eliminating some data points for the dominant class. These two strategies combined oversampling and undersampling to address the issue of the imbalanced class structure [9].

The research's primary objective is to improve data sampling techniques by combining oversampling to increase minority class samples and undersampling to reduce majority class samples. The second goal is to create a fraud detection model train and test it using 5 machine learning algorithms. The third goal is to evaluate the model's performance using a confusion matrix along with precision, recall, f1-score, ROC AUC score, and its plot graph. Finally, for validation, a comparison of our model's outcomes with those of earlier studies. The remaining part of the paper is structured as follows: Related research on fraud detection, approaches to imbalanced data, and performance evaluation metrics for the classification of skewed models are all covered in Sect. 2. In Sect. 3, it is described how the framework was created, the dataset, and the performance measurement techniques used in this paper. The findings of the trial are covered in Sect. 4. Section 5 then examines the paper's conclusion and prospective research.

2 Related Works

Machine learning algorithms have been implemented by numerous authors and researchers to identify different types of credit card fraud. We have summarized some of the literature's methods in this section.

2.1 Machine Learning Approaches

First, the authors built a credit card fraud detection system using a variety of ML methods, such as logistic regression (LR), decision tree (DT), support vector machine (SVM), and random forest (RF) [11]. These classifiers were evaluated using a credit card fraud detection dataset gathered in 2013 from European users. This dataset is highly imbalanced in terms of the proportion of valid to fraudulent transactions. The scholar used classification accuracy to assess each ML technique's successful implementation. The results of the experiment showed that the LR, DT, SVM, and RF all achieved accuracy scores of 97.70%, 95.50%, 97.50%, and 98.60%, respectively. Despite the excellent outcomes, the researchers hypothesized that using complex pre-processing techniques would increase the classifiers' efficacy.

A strategy for detecting credit card fraud using ML was proposed by Varmedja et al. [12]. A dataset about credit card fraud was used by the authors in [13], European credit card holders' recent activities are included in this dataset. To address the class imbalance problem in the dataset, the researcher used the Synthetic Minority Oversampling Technique (SMOTE) oversampling technique. The RF, NB, and multilayer perceptron machine learning approaches were utilized to assess the efficacy of the proposed strategy (MLP). The experimental results demonstrated that the RF algorithm performed at its peak level, identifying fraud with a 99.96% success rate. The accuracy ratings for the NB and MLP approaches were correspondingly 99.23% and 99.93%. Before applying a feature selection technique that could increase the accuracy of other ML techniques, the authors admit that more research is required.

Performance analysis of ML methods for credit card fraud detection was carried out by Khatri et al. [14]. In their work, the ML algorithms DT, KNN, LR, RF, and NB were taken into consideration. The effectiveness of each machine learning approach was assessed using a highly imbalanced dataset that the authors constructed using information gathered from European cardholders. One of the important performance metrics taken into account in the studies was the precision each classifier was able to achieve. According to the testing outcomes, DT, KNN, LR, and RF, all attained precisions of 85.11%, 91.11%, 87.5%, 89.77%, and 6.52%, respectively.

Awoyemi et al. [3] presented a comparative analysis of several ML techniques using the credit card fraud dataset for European cardholders. The authors of this study employed a hybrid sampling strategy to address the dataset's imbalance. The NB, KNN, and LR machine learning approaches were all taken into consideration. The investigations were conducted using a computational intelligence framework created in Python. Accuracy was the main performance indicator used to assess how well each ML approach performed. According to the experimental results, the accuracy values of the NB, LR, and KNN were 97.92%, 54.86%, and 97.69%, respectively. Despite the relatively outstanding results of the NB and KNN, the authors did not take into account the possibility of using a feature selection strategy.

The authors of reference [15], used a variety of ML learning-based techniques to address the problem of credit card fraud. The researchers used the European Credit Cardholder Fraud dataset for this study. The authors used the SMOTE sampling approach to address the very imbalanced nature of this dataset. The DT, LR, and Isolation Forest (IF) ML techniques were taken into consideration. Accuracy was one of the main metrics for achievement considered in the question. The findings revealed that the DT, LR, and IF possessed accuracy ratings of 97.08%, 97.18%, and 58.83%, respectively.

The performance of three machine learning algorithms RF, SVM, and Logistic Regression is compared by Ljiljana et al. in their study [16]. They employed the SMOTE sampling approach to reduce the imbalance in class sizes. Precision and recall metrics are used to assess the algorithm's performance. R. Sailusha et al. seek to concentrate mostly on machine learning techniques in their other publication [17]. Both the Random Forest and AdaBoost algorithms were used. The accuracy, precision, recall, and F1 scores of the two systems' results were contrasted. The ROC curve is drawn using the con-fusion matrix as its base. The algorithm that has the greatest accuracy, precision, recall, and F1 score when Random Forest and AdaBoost algorithms are compared is deemed to be the most effective at detecting fraud.

2.2 Sampling Methods

A method for changing the size of training sets is sampling. Oversampling alters the training samples by reusing samples from the minority training set while undersampling a bigger majority training set [8, 18]. Both strategies are projected to yield better results since the problem of class imbalance is likely to be reduced and the level of imbalance will decrease. Both sampling techniques are straightforward to use and have been shown to be successful under imbalanced settings, according to earlier studies [19, 20].

1) Oversampling: Adding extra points to an imbalanced class or example using oversampling techniques. Many researchers suggested oversampling techniques to address the

problems of the extremely imbalanced class problem in the fraud detection dataset. If the size of the training set is increased, oversampling may require more training time. Due to the repetition of minority class samples, it also has a tendency to overfit [6].

2) Undersampling: Due to the dataset's large sample size, some studies suggested using undersampling techniques for credit fraud detection. However, there is a high risk of losing data records and information when using undersampling techniques [21]. Although it requires less training time, undersampling poses the danger of missing potentially useful data [33, 22, 19].

2.3 Evaluation Performance for Imbalanced Data

It is challenging to evaluate learning algorithm performance when there is a class imbalance. For certain commonly used metrics, like as accuracy, the prevalence of more frequent classes may mask a subpar classification performance in the less frequent classes. The selection of effective measures is crucial for resolving this issue. The sensitivity or recall, precision, and F1-Score (F-Measure), as well as balanced accuracy, may all be calculated from the confusion matrix, which is generated while testing the model [8, 23]. For imbalanced datasets, these performance metrics are more important than accuracy.

Instead of using the overall classification accuracy as a single evaluation criterion, they used a set of assessment metrics associated with receiver operating characteristics (ROC) graphs to assess the success of the sampling approaches algorithm [24]. ROC-based evaluation metrics, precision, recall, and measure are used because standard overall classification accuracy may not be able to provide an accurate assessment of the observed learning algorithm under the imbalanced learning environment [3, 19–21].

The successful outcome of the suggested approach to spotting credit card fraud is assessed via a cross-validation test. The performance of the suggested strategy for credit card fraud detection is systematically and carefully evaluated using the k-fold cross-validation (CV) method. Researchers frequently use K-Fold CV, a statistical analysis method, to evaluate the effectiveness of machine learning classifiers [29]. In this study, we run a 10-fold CV test to evaluate the effectiveness of the suggested strategy. There is a class imbalance in the analyzed data sets, with more legitimate transactions than fraudulent ones.

3   Experimental Setup and Methods

The overall structure of the suggested model and the dataset used in this study were covered in this part. Along with it, it also covered the research's experimental methods and model. The final component of this section discusses the performance metrics and evaluation matrices that were utilized to assess the outcomes.

3.1   The Overall Framework Model for Credit Card Fraud Detection

The general layout of the proposed methodology for identifying credit card fraud is shown in Fig. 1. The four sections that make up the suggested method for detecting credit card fraud are each covered. The different machine learning classifiers such as Logistic Regression, Support Vector Machine, Decision Tree, KNN, and the Random Forest. All these algorithms perform different stages before generating the classifier such as data collection, data preprocessing, analysis of data, data training with different classifiers, respectively, and later testing the data. During the stage of preprocessing, the entire data are transformed into a useable format.

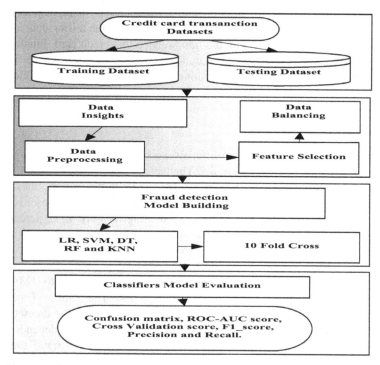

Fig. 1. The general structure of the suggested intelligent method for detecting credit card fraud.

3.2 Hybrid of Undersampling and Oversampling

In general, at data level the sampling technique is a solution to overcome imbalanced datasets. It is divided into three, namely: undersampling, oversampling and a combination of undersampling and oversampling methods [34].

Undersampling is a sampling method that requires eliminating some data from the data's majority class. This can be done randomly (random undersampling). Additionally, statistical formulas can be used to complete it. (informed undersampling). This approach further filters data in the majority class by using iteration methods and data cleaning techniques. Contrarily, the oversampling strategy involves adding a certain amount of data to minority classes in order to balance or approach the amount of data in the majority class. Oversampling via original data, such as the Random Oversampling method, and oversampling with synthetic data, such as the Synthetic Minority Oversampling Technique, are the two categories into which the idea of adding data in oversampling is split. (SMOTE). A combination of methods combines undersampling and oversampling techniques to balance data. When using the concept of undersampling, the quantity of major class data is decreased, and when using the concept of oversampling, the quantity of minor class data is increased.

The hybrid of undersampling (negative class) and oversampling (positive class) techniques were performed using two different data distribution sets. In the stage of training, the classifier algorithm is fed with preprocessed data. Later, the testing data are evaluated to find the accuracy of detecting the fraud related to a credit card. Finally, all the different models are evaluated based on accuracy and their best performance. The legal ratio with a total number of fraud transactions is a subset and used to conclude which model performs better when tested in the real-time scenario.

3.3 Data Insights and Dataset

We used real-world data sets to develop different experiments for evaluating the proposed approach and demonstrating its generality. The dataset covers credit card transactions done by European cardholders in September 2013 [13]. In this dataset, they are 492 frauds out of 284,807 transactions that occurred in two days. The dataset is heavily imbalanced, with the positive class (frauds) accounting for only 0.172 percent of all transactions. The dataset includes 31 features listed ['Time', 'V1', 'V2', 'V3', 'V4', 'V5', 'V6', 'V7', 'V8', 'V9', 'V10', 'V11', 'V12', 'V13', 'V14', 'V15', 'V16', 'V17', 'V18', 'V19', 'V20','V21', 'V22', 'V23', 'V24', 'V25', 'V26', 'V27', 'V28', 'Amount', 'Class'], the major components derived with PCA are featured V1, V2, to V28; the only features not changed with PCA are 'Time' and 'Amount.' The feature "Time" stores the number of seconds that passed between each transaction and the dataset's initial transaction. The feature "Amount," which can be used for example-dependent, cost-sensitive learning, represents the transaction Amount. When there is fraud, the answer variable, named "Class," has a value of 1, and when there isn't, it has a value of 0. It only has numerical input variables that have undergone a Principal component analysis (PCA) transformation. We are unable to get the original features and further background information about the data owing to confidentiality concerns. An Intel Core i5 processor with 8GB RAM was used in the experiment. Python v3 language setup was used to construct and test the proposed strategy as well as other machine learning approaches.

3.4 Feature Selection

For efficient credit card fraud detection when there are many features, choosing major and crucial features is essential [25]. Due to the number of features, a heatmap cannot be used in this situation. For the correlation plot, a different type of visualization was employed. Many elements from the correlation plot are useless for classifying data. We disregarded characteristics with values between [−0.1,0.1]. "v4" and "v11" have a positive correlation, while "v7," "v3," "v16," "v10," "v12," "v14," and "v17" have a negative correlation. For classification purposes, we picked the aforementioned features. The data distribution is imbalanced or skewed towards legitimate findings because there are considerably fewer fraudulent transactions overall than there are valid transactions altogether. It is well known that many machine learning algorithms perform poorly when the examined dataset is imbalanced [26]. This study used a cross-validation strategy to train and test the model in each subset of the dataset to obtain more accurate results. The average of all the previously mentioned metrics is then determined across the complete dataset [27].

3.5 Model Evaluation Using Performance Metrics

For imbalanced datasets, more significant performance metrics than accuracy can be used to evaluate the performance of the suggested technique. These metrics include Precision, Recall(sensitivity), AUC, and F1-score (F-Measure). The following terms are used in the Confusion Matrix to evaluate the effectiveness of credit card fraud detection [28]: The number of fraudulent credit card transactions that were accurately classified is referred to as TP (true positive). The number of legitimate credit card fraud transactions labeled as false positives, or FPs, is indicated. The number of fraudulent credit card transactions labeled as normal is shown by the letter FN, which stands for false negative. The number of typical credit card transactions that were accurately identified is known as TN (true negative).

The calculation for the formula is as follows:

$$Accuracy = \frac{(TP + TN)}{(TP + FP + TN + FN)} \tag{1}$$

$$Recall = \frac{TP}{(TP + FN)} \tag{2}$$

$$Precision = \frac{TP}{(TP + FP)} \tag{3}$$

$$F1 - Score = \frac{2 * (Pression * Recall)}{(Precision + Recall)} \tag{4}$$

A confusion matrix, which shows a matrix representation of predicted values in comparison to actual values, is a common measurement tool for classification models. Since the confusion matrix accuracy is meaningless for imbalanced classification, it is most advantageous to look at a model's precision and recall ability, as well as its accuracy and Area Under the Curve (AUC) [29].

The following definitions apply to various recall and accuracy combinations for a particular class [30].

- High recall and precision: The model completed the classification task.
- High Precision and Low Recall: Although the model cannot correctly categorize all the data points for a given class, it is quite reliable when it does so.
- High Recall with Low Precision: The model correctly identifies the data points of the given class, however, a large number of data points from other classes are incorrectly classified as the class under discussion.

– Low recall and precision; the model performed poorly on the categorization challenge.

The F1-Score, which is determined as the harmonic mean of precision and recall and has given a thorough definition and analysis of these measures [31], balances the precision and recall of a model. The AUC value was taken seriously in the study as a general performance indicator as well as to the aforementioned metrics. The true positive rate (TPR) and false positive rate (FPR) at different levels are expressed visibly by the AUC. As a performance metric, AUC is favored over accuracy because it is not dependent on a cutoff value. A model that works better throughout has an AUC value that is close to one.

4 Results and Discussions

In this research, the results and discussion are based on five classifier models developed; Logistic Regression (LR), Support Vector Machine(SVM), Decision tree (DT), Random Forest (RF), and KNN. For evaluating all these classifier models, training is conducted using 70% of the entire dataset, while for testing and validating, 30% of the dataset is used. The results compare the performance of our model after undergoing a Hybrid of undersampling and oversampling methods in the fraud detection dataset throughout the experiments (Table 1).

Table 1. Comparison results for confusion matrices of our proposed module prediction.

ML approaches		Actual	
LR	**Prediction**	TN 963 (65.24%)	TP 12 (0.81%)
		FN 57 (3.86%)	FP 444 (30.08%)
SVM	**Prediction**	TN 968 (66.58%)	TP 7 (0.47%)
		FN 61 (4.54%)	FP 440 (29.81%)
DT	**Prediction**	TN 969 (65.65%)	TP 6 (0.41%)
		FN 67 (4.54%)	FP 434 (29.40%)
RF	**Prediction**	TN 972 (65.85%)	TP 3 (0.20%)
		FN 62 (4.20%)	FP 439 (29.74%)
KNN	**Prediction**	TN 954 (64.63%)	TP 21 (1.42%)
		FN 15 (1.02%)	FP 486 (32.93%)

This study used the confusion matrix, roc-AUC score, and accuracy to evaluate the model. Roc-AUC gives us the relation between true positive & false positive rates. It also used the f1 score, recall, and precision. Precision describes the percentage of data points that indicate fraud when there is a fraud, whereas recall describes the capacity to find all pertinent instances in a dataset. It is immediately clear that precision refers to the model's accuracy and precision in predicting good outcomes, as well as the proportion of positive outcomes that actually occur. Precision is a useful indicator when the costs of False

Positive are high. For this dataset, a false positive indicates that a lawful transaction that isn't fraudulent (real negative) has been labeled as such (predicted fraud). If the accuracy is low for fraud detection, the user could lose significant transactions. A Recall is the model measure to employ for choosing the optimal model when a False Negative has a significant cost, according to the same concept. For instance, if a fraudulent transaction (Actual Positive) is expected to be non-fraudulent, it can be catastrophic for the bank with respect to fraud detection (Predicted Negative).

Table 2. Performance results for Non frauds and fraud detection of our proposed module.

Model / Algorithms		LR	SVM	DT	RF	KNN
Precision	NF	94%	94%	94%	94%	**98%**
	F	97%	98%	**99%**	**99%**	96%
Recall	NF	99%	99%	99%	**100%**	98%
	F	89%	88%	87%	88%	**97%**
F1_Score	NF	97%	97%	96%	97%	**98%**
	F	93%	93%	92%	93%	**96%**

From Table 2, applying the hybrid of undersampling and oversampling techniques gave a high performance in terms of precision, recall, and F1_measure. This demonstrates that the model can effectively perform classification tasks. With a precision measure of 99% for classifying frauds, DT and RF excel, while KNN comes in at 97% and 96% for recall and F1_score, respectively. On the other hand, RF is the best at classifying non-frauds with a recall of 100%, while KNN and F1_score both fared better in terms of precision. This demonstrates how accurately the model separates the data points into the appropriate class. It can be seen that the result produced by our suggested model is higher. The precision value is generally lower than the recall value.

Table 3. The overall performance results of the proposed module for ROC_AUC, CV Score, and Accuracy.

ML	CV Score	ROC_AUC	Accuracy
LR	98.16%	93.70%	95%
SVM	98.02%	93.01%	95%
DT	97.50%	93.55%	95%
RF	97.83%	93.66%	96%
KNN	99.38%	97.43%	98%

From Table 3, the overall performance of the model shows that, combining oversampling and undersampling techniques improved the ratio of data appropriate for machine learning. Specifically, the KNN outperforms well for Accuracy, CV score, and Roc_Auc score with 98%, 99.38%, and 97.43% respectively. These results show the importance of applying the hybrid of undersampling and oversampling techniques, especially when there is a class imbalance issue.

Table 4. Comparison results for the past literature accuracies with our proposed module.

ML	[11]	[12]	[14]	[3]	[16]	ours
LR	97.70%	-	87.50%	97.69%	97.18%	95%
SVM	97.50%	-	-	-	-	95%
DT	95.50%	-	85.11%	-	97.08%	95%
RF	98.60%	99.96%	-	-	-	96%
KNN	-	-	91.11%	54.86%	-	98%
NB	-	99.23%	60.52%	97.92%	-	-
MLP	-	99.93%	-	-	-	-
IF	-	-	-	-	58.83%	-

The results from Table 4 are then compared with prior research that made use of the same dataset. Based on widely used machine learning methods, a comparison is done. The approach from the Table is used since it produces the best outcomes. From the past literature, five articles' results were compared, they used 3 to 4 machine learning algorithms which performed well for their settings. For our model we used 5 machine learning algorithms with a hybrid of undersampling and oversampling techniques that performed well and the detection rates for fraud and the non-frauds transaction are high. Taking into consideration that sampling techniques are one of the crucial methods to be examined when a dataset has an imbalanced class problem. It is important to remember that the features of the data determine which techniques should be used for the dataset. Utilizing oversampling and undersampling techniques must be done to enhance the classification model in particular situations. The authors in [32] contend that the dataset used for fraud detection is thought to contain data that is considerably biased. In accordance with a study by [33], the imbalanced class issue must be solved using a combination of undersampling and oversampling methods if the data are significantly imbalanced. From the comparisons the results are convincing.

5 Conclusion and Future Work

This research aimed to propose new methods that could improve the classification performance for credit card fraud detection. We can draw the inference that the hybrid undersampling and oversampling technique can greatly boost performance. After experiments, it was shown that the proposed module performed better with precision, recall, and F1_measure metrics. This demonstrates how effectively the model can handle classification problems. For the classification of Frauds, DT and RF excel with the precision metric of 99%, KNN with 97%, and 96% for Recall and F1_score respectively. On the other hand, RF is the best at classifying non-frauds with a recall of 100%, while KNN and F1_score both fared better in terms of precision. From the past literature, five articles' results were compared, they used 3 to 4 machine learning algorithms which performed well for their settings. With a combination of undersampling and oversampling methods, we used five machine learning algorithms for our model, and both high detection rates for fraud and non-fraud transactions were obtained.

In future work, to improve further on the model, other options can be done by the researcher. Firstly, try the same model for bigger datasets, optimize the parameters, and apply different machine and deep learning techniques. Second, several classification methods, including boosting algorithms, are applicable. This is a result of the categorization model's recent widespread use of boosting methods. In order to further assess how well the strategies function with other imbalanced datasets, the model can be evaluated on more different unbalanced datasets.

References

1. Nadim, A.H., et al.: Analysis of machine learning techniques for credit card fraud detection. In: 2019 International Conference on Machine Learning and Data Engineering (iCMLDE). IEEE (2019). https://doi.org/10.1109/iCMLDE49015.2019.00019
2. Dal Pozzolo, A., et al.: Credit card fraud detection: a realistic modeling and a novel learning strategy. IEEE Trans. Neural Netw. Learn. Syst. **29**(8), 3784–3797 (2017). https://doi.org/10.1109/TNNLS.2017.2736643
3. Awoyemi, J.O., Adetunmbi, A.O., Oluwadare, S.A.: Credit card fraud detection using machine learning techniques: a comparative analysis. In: 2017 International Conference on Computing Networking and Informatics (ICCNI). IEEE (2017). https://doi.org/10.1109/ICCNI.2017.8123782
4. Dal Pozzolo, A.: Adaptive machine learning for credit card fraud detection. Unpublished doctoral dissertation, Université libre de Bruxelles, Faculte des Sciences—Informatique, Bruxelles (2015)
5. Rout, N., Mishra, D., Mallick, M.K.: Handling imbalanced data: a survey. In: Reddy, M.S., Viswanath, K., K.M., S.P. (eds.) International Proceedings on Advances in Soft Computing, Intelligent Systems and Applications. AISC, vol. 628, pp. 431–443. Springer, Singapore (2018). https://doi.org/10.1007/978-981-10-5272-9_39
6. Vandewiele, G., et al.: Overly optimistic prediction results on imbalanced data: a case study of flaws and benefits when applying over-sampling. Artif. Intell. Med. **111**, 101987 (2021). https://doi.org/10.1016/j.artmed.2020.101987
7. Sun, Z., et al.: A novel ensemble method for classifying imbalanced data. Pattern Recogn. **48**(5), 1623–1637 (2015). https://doi.org/10.1016/j.patcog.2014.11.014
8. Tyagi, S., Mittal, S.: Sampling approaches for imbalanced data classification problem in machine learning. In: Singh, P. K., Kar, A. K., Singh, Y., Kolekar, M. H., Tanwar, S. (eds.) Proceedings of ICRIC 2019. LNEE, vol. 597, pp. 209–221. Springer, Cham (2020). https://doi.org/10.1007/978-3-030-29407-6_17
9. Arun, C., Lakshmi, C.: Class imbalance in software fault prediction data set. In: Dash, S.S., Lakshmi, C., Das, S., Panigrahi, B.K. (eds.) Artificial Intelligence and Evolutionary Computations in Engineering Systems. AISC, vol. 1056, pp. 745–757. Springer, Singapore (2020). https://doi.org/10.1007/978-981-15-0199-9_64

10. Batista, G.E., Prati, R.C., Monard, M.C.: A study of the behavior of several methods for balancing machine learning training data. ACM SIGKDD Explor. Newsl. **6**(1), 20–29 (2004). https://doi.org/10.1145/1007730.1007735

11. Khare, N., Sait, S.Y.: Credit card fraud detection using machine learning models and collating machine learning models. Int. J. Pure Appl. Math. **118**(20), 825–838 (2018)

12. Varmedja, D., et al.: Credit card fraud detection-machine learning methods. In: 2019 18th International Symposium INFOTEH-JAHORINA (INFOTEH). IEEE (2019). https://doi.org/10.1109/INFOTECH.2019.8717766.

13. Credit Card Fraud Dataset. Accessed 14 June 2022. https://www.kaggle.com/datasets/mlg-ulb/creditcardfraud

14. Khatri, S., Arora, A., Agrawal, A.P.: Supervised machine learning algorithms for credit card fraud detection: a comparison. In: 2020 10th International Conference on Cloud Computing, Data Science & Engineering (Confluence). IEEE (2020). https://doi.org/10.1109/Confluence47617.2020.9057851

15. Seera, M., et al.: An intelligent payment card fraud detection system. Ann. Oper. Res., 1–23 (2021). https://doi.org/10.1007/s10479-021-04149-2

16. Puh, M., Brkić, L.: Detecting credit card fraud using selected machine learning algorithms. In: 2019 42nd International Convention on Information and Communication Technology, Electronics and Microelectronics (MIPRO). IEEE (2019). https://doi.org/10.23919/MIPRO.2019.8757212

17. Sailusha, R., et al.: Credit card fraud detection using machine learning. In: 2020 4th International Conference on Intelligent Computing and Control Systems (ICICCS). IEEE (2020). https://doi.org/10.1109/ICICCS48265.2020.9121114

18. Nguyen, H.B., Huynh, V.-N.: On sampling techniques for corporate credit scoring. J. Adv. Comput. Intell. Intell. Inf. **24**(1), 48–57 (2020). https://doi.org/10.20965/jaciii.2020.p0048

19. Mohammed, R.A., Wong, K.-W., Shiratuddin, M.F., Wang, X.: Scalable machine learning techniques for highly imbalanced credit card fraud detection: a comparative study. In: Geng, X., Kang, B.-H. (eds.) PRICAI 2018. LNCS (LNAI), vol. 11013, pp. 237–246. Springer, Cham (2018). https://doi.org/10.1007/978-3-319-97310-4_27

20. Napierala, K., Stefanowski, J.: Types of minority class examples and their influence on learning classifiers from imbalanced data. J Intell Inf Syst **46**(3), 563–597 (2015). https://doi.org/10.1007/s10844-015-0368-1

21. Kaya, A., et al.: Model analytics for defect prediction based on design-level metrics and sampling techniques. In: Model Management and Analytics for Large Scale Systems, pp. 125–139. Academic Press (2020). https://doi.org/10.1016/B978-0-12-816649-9.00015-6

22. Dhankhad, S., Mohammed, E., Far, B.: Supervised machine learning algorithms for credit card fraudulent transaction detection: a comparative study. In: 2018 IEEE International Conference on Information Reuse and Integration (IRI). IEEE (2018). https://doi.org/10.1109/IRI.2018.00025

23. Sun, Z., et al.: A novel ensemble method for classifying imbalanced data. Pattern Recogn. **48**(5), 1623–1637 (2015). https://doi.org/10.1016/j.patcog.2014.11.014

24. Kumar, R.D., et al.: Statistically identifying tumor suppressors and oncogenes from pan-cancer genome-sequencing data. Bioinformatics **31**(22), 3561–3568 (2015). https://doi.org/10.1093/bioinformatics/btv430

25. Alwan, R.H., Hamad, M.M., Dawood, O.A.: Credit card fraud detection in financial transactions using data mining techniques. In: 2021 7th International Conference on Contemporary Information Technology and Mathematics (ICCITM), pp. 160–166 (2021). https://doi.org/10.1109/ICCITM53167.2021.9677867

26. Sahithi, G.L., Roshmi, V., Sameera, Y.V., Pradeepini, G.: Credit card fraud detection using ensemble methods in machine learning. In: 2022 6th International Conference on Trends in Electronics and Informatics (ICOEI), pp. 1237–1241 (2022). https://doi.org/10.1109/ICOEI5 3556.2022.9776955

27. Illanko, K., Soleymanzadeh, R., Fernando, X.: A big data deep learning approach for credit card fraud detection. In: Pandian, A.P., Fernando, X., Haoxiang, W. (eds.) Computer Networks, Big Data, and IoT. Lecture Notes on Data Engineering and Communications Technologies, vol. 117. Springer, Singapore (2022). https://doi.org/10.1007/978-981-19-0898-9_50

28. Al-Shabi, M.A.: Credit card fraud detection using autoencoder model in unbalanced datasets. J. Adv. Math. Comput. Sci. **33**(5), 1–16 (2019). https://doi.org/10.9734/JAMCS/2019/v33i53 0192

29. Chollet, F.: Deep learning with Python. Simon and Schuster (2021). by Manning Publications Co. Printed in the United States of America. ISBN 9781617294433

30. Bej, S., Davtyan, N., Wolfien, M., Nassar, M., Wolkenhauer, O.: LoRAS: an oversampling approach for imbalanced datasets. Mach. Learn. **110**(2), 279–301 (2020). https://doi.org/10.1007/s10994-020-05913-4

31. Elrahman, A., Shaza, M., Abraham, A.: A review of the class imbalance problem. J. Network Innov. Comput. **1**, 332–340 (2013). ISSN 2160-2174, vol. 1, pp. 332–340 (2013)

32. Bhattacharyya, S., et al.: Data mining for credit card fraud: a comparative study. Decision Support Syst. **50**(3), 602–613 (2011). https://doi.org/10.1016/j.des.2010.08.008

33. Loyola-González, O., et al.: Study of the impact of resampling methods for contrast pattern-based classifiers in imbalanced databases. Neurocomputing **175**, 935–947 (2016). https://doi.org/10.1016/j.neucom.2015.04.120

34. Choirunnisa, S., Lianto, J.: Hybrid method of undersampling and oversampling for handling imbalanced data. In: 2018 International Seminar on Research of Information Technology and Intelligent Systems (ISRITI), pp. 276–280. IEEE, November 2018. https://doi.org/10.1109/ISRITI.2018.8864335

Implementation of YOLOv7 for Pest Detection

Pratibha Nayar, Shivank Chhibber, and Ashwani Kumar Dubey(✉) ⓘ

Department of Electronics and Communication, Amity School of Engineering and Technology,
Amity University Uttar Pradesh, Noida, UP, India
dubey1ak@gmail.com

Abstract. Pests have been known to destroy the yield of the crops, that would soak the nutritional value of the crops. Not only this, but some of the pests can also act as carriers to various diseases that are caused due to the transmutable nature of such bacteria. The most popular pest management technique is pesticide spraying because of how quickly it works and how easily it can be scaled up. Less pesticide use is necessary now, though, as environmental and health awareness grows. Also, existing pest visual segmentation methods are bounding, less effective and time-exhausting, which originates complexity in their marketing and use. Deep learning algorithms have come to be the major techniques to deal with the technological issues linked to pest detection. In this paper, we propose a method for pest detection using a prolific deep learning technique using the newest technology YOLOv7 model. It helps detect which type of pest it is, and if it is a pest that can cause damage, thus by allowing the person to get alert and take appropriate steps. The recommended YOLOv7 model attained the peak accuracy of 93.3% for 50 epochs.

Keywords: Deep learning · Pest · YOLOv7

1 Introduction

In agricultural field, handling of pests has been a significant issue in influencing the agricultural throughput for spans. Not only do they destroy crops, but also could weaken the quality of the future produce, by affecting the genes of the crop itself which can lead to cases of food poisoning, or hazardous diseases such as fits due the presence of a particular kind of pest in crops such as cabbage, lettuce etc.

Thus, supervision for the number of pest species is of importance to remove pests without latency also to prevent unsighted usage of pesticides which can result in harmful crops for the consumers [1]. Due to millions of kinds of pests in the ecosystem, there is a very big problem in collection of data, labelling and processing of images of such data. It is therefore very tough, for current, curators and researchers to collect images due to its high dynamic nature and be made available for algorithms to be able to detect all kinds of pests on such concise datasets. At the same time, we had only a very limited dataset which had to be modified and whose bounding boxes and labeling had to be made, due to which we have decreased the size of our dataset.

M. A. Jabbar et al. (Eds.): AMLDA 2022, CCIS 1818, pp. 156–165, 2023.
https://doi.org/10.1007/978-3-031-34222-6_13

The motive behind DL is to make use of a convolutional neural network for data analysis and feature extraction. The data elements are obtained through several hidden layers wherein every hidden layer can exist and be considered as a perceptron, which is used to obtain low-level features, and are then combined with other low-level features to get high-level features, which can substantially reduce the issue of bare minimum. Deep learning affects the difficulty that conventional procedures rely on artificially constructed features and has drawn more and more scholar's attention [2].

We are performing transfer learning on the YOLOv7 architecture, which has been derived from previous architectures of YOLO versions, which consist of over 24 convolutional layers and 2 final layers. The new feature added in the YOLOv7 is E-ELAN which helps the framework to learn better. E-ELAN significantly changed the design of the computational block, dropping the design of the transition layer completely unaffected. YOLOv7 proposed a deliberately reparametrized convolution. RepConv is able to combine 3×3 convolutions, 1×1 convolutions and identity connections into one convolution layer [3].

YOLOv7 exceeds all established object detectors in both rate and exactness ranging from 5 FPS to 160 FPS. It also has the highest exactness of 56.8% AP along with other famous real- time point detectors that has 30 FPS or has greater GPU V100 [4]. The YOLOv7 model has been able to achieve its running time for 2.8ms for the same frame rate. It henceforth has the least time consumption out of the existing YOLO versions.

In this paper, we go ahead to train the YOLOv7 model using our curated dataset, to understand the behaviour of this model on a dataset other than the standard COCO dataset.

2 Related Works

L Liu. et al. [1] proposed a multi class classification for pest detection known to be PestNet model, is based upon three segments- a novel module channel-spatial attention which has been used for extracting features, a region proposal network for detecting the positions of the pest from the first segment and position sensitive score map for classification of pests with 75.46% mAP for 80k illustrations with more than 580k pests labelled by agrarian professionals and were categorized into 16 classes. Liu. et al. [2] proposed a method combining data managing, feature blending, feature distribution, disease detection, with an mAP being modified from 71.80 to 91.83% and made a reference for usage of YOLOv3 model, to gain an accuracy of 94.5%. The challenges-big datasets aren't always applicable because most of them are limited to laboratory environment and since the plants grown are regional and seasonal, the existing results are not applied universally for plant and pest diseases also have been mentioned in this paper. Selvaraj et al. [3] proposed an AI-based banana disease and pest detection system, data from Africa and South India which consisted of 18 classes and 6 models using a DCNN to assist banana planters with accuracies of 73%, 70%, 99%, and 97% using the Resnet-50 model, Inceptionv2 had better performances. Dong et al. [5] proposed a multi-scale pest detector named YOLO-pest based on YOLOv4 has been replaced by mobileNetv3 to reduce large model size and improve the performance of pest detection included using lite but efficient backbone mobileNetv3 and lite fusion feature pyramid network, with an mAP of 62.5%. This model is efficient for realtime detection of multiple scale and objects. Roy et al. [6] proposed a model, improves the existing YOLOv4 algorithm wherein the denseNet framework is applied to preserve the important feature map and the feature information, more precisely which gets reduced in the normal YOLOv4 algorithm and they optimized discovery speed and accuracy of multiple classes for apple plant disease detection within the natural ecosystem with mAP of the recognition prototype up to 95.9%, at a detection rate of 56.9 FPS. Onler et al. [7] established an object discovery scheme to identify the thistle caterpillar (Vanessa cardui) using the YOLOv5 object detection design and attained an accuracy of 59%, the detection speed of the model was 65fps and it was discovered that the different caterpillar species can be identified with different background or plant species. Zhao et al. [8] proposed a network that included parallel interest structure module achieved by combined spatial attention, original residual structure with channel attention, which is light weight and it is possible to accurately recognize crop pests in realtime agricultural environment and residual blocks and had substantial improvements in terms of exactness and real-time working matched with other models, having achieved an accuracy up to 98.17% for crop pest illustrations. Zhang et al. [9] proposed a model capable of detecting six kinds of navel orange syndromes, based on denseNet, by adding 4 density block modules and 3 training modules as well as achieved an accuracy of 96.90%, also position and channel attention mechanisms are used. Sachan et al. resolved the issue of diseases in paddy crop wherein automation of disease classification and detection using CNN and thermal imagery techniques was made [10]. Yogesh et al. proposed a system that attained an accuracy of 99.30% with the processing time of 3.207 s for fruit nutrition detection, which was based on DL [11]. Naresh et al. discussed about various models that has been created and compared them. It also focuses on various pest diseases and how they affect the economy of the country depicting the necessity for detecting pests making use of the image processing features with deep learning capabilities [12].

3   Methodology

3.1   Dataset

To train our model, we have modified IP102 dataset [13], that was available on Github and originally consisted of over 75000 images with 102 classes of pests. One of the problems that we were able to face while working on this dataset was that this dataset was suitable for classification purposes but had to be modified since detection models need bounding boxes [14]. Because of this, we had to utilize the process of data augmentation to create individual bounding boxes for every single image and give corresponding labels on google Colab. The curated data has been modified to 3269 images with 13 classes of data with classes namely [13]-Hellula undalis, Leaf Webber, ash weevil, blister beetle, fruit fly, fruit sucking moth, helicoverpa, leucinodes, mealy bug, pieris, plutella, root grubs, schizaphis graminum. The classes were divided on the basis of the most quintessential ones i.e. the most harmful pests being given the priority since augmentation and creation of bounding boxes for so many images is a very tedious task and requires lots of time investment. The dataset has been divided for training: validation: testing in the ratio of 70:20:10, so as to ensure that the model undergoes due process of learning with standardized techniques and ensure that the model doesn't face the issue of overfitting or rather overcomes the issue to perfectly fit for the dataset. Therefore around 700 images were considered for validation and testing processes. Finally, the annotations of this dataset were then converted into YOLOv7 format for its usage in training the model.

3.2 YOLOv7 Model Architecture

We have made use of a pre-trained model, YOLOv7 which was made for running on the COCO dataset, having a 69.7% mAP for 50 epochs [14]. It consists of complete 24 convolutional tiers and 2 fully connected tiers, with subsequent pooling layers. It makes use of the Adam Optimizer, which is the most common and known to show better results in deep learning with a learning rate of 0.0001. The upsampling blocks have been given to allow an increase in the sample rate of the input vectors, for increasing the processing speed of the model and individually examine the quantity with the convolutional blocks succeeding them. The YOLO losses catered to by the heads, is a very important segment that is able to generate the weights for the next set of epochs and graphs necessary to analyze the performance parameters of the model. YOLOv7 model has 36 greater fps than YOLOv5 model and is able to achieve better accuracy results than the previous YOLO versions. The developers of this model has ensured due emphasis on the model's response to different types of datasets due to consecutive interconnection of convolutional layers and pooling layers and high end complexity, due to which larger number of images can be easily processed by this powerful model in a fraction of less time, in comparison to existing YOLO versions and at the same time is able to perform less computation with varying parameters to the previous versions. Since, it is the latest technology that has been developed, it gave us the motivation to implement this technology on a new type of dataset, that can also help us understand the variation in the model's performance with different datasets.

The model is divided into 6 phases for its sequential operation to take place. The first phase is the Backbone phase which consists of the convolutional block, which act as input to the model, that can be further converted into a vector of values for its further processing. The processed vector is then passed through an up-sample block which artificially allows an increase in the sample rate of the input treated values, which is used to ensure that the detection of the images by the algorithm for the batch size to increase and have a greater frame per second rate, thereby decreasing its running time. This upsampled vector is then fed to the FPN where the main convolutional series of operation takes place along with max pooling layers, which are the standard capabilities used in convolutional neural networks. The accumulated data is feeded to a 3 * 3 feature space for filtering purposes and making sure that the redundant values are dropped off and the required values are given to the head, whose individual dimensions are given to the head layer. The head layer consists of a pair of convolutional layers which will be sent to the individual heads of the corresponding pyramid. Each individual head's YOLO loss for the given parameters will be found that is known to update the weights of the model automatically and monitor the learning ability of our model which is reflected in due running of our model in the cfg folder of the model itself. This will be done using three key parameters that are - Cross Entropy Loss, L1 loss and Objectness Loss [15], that will be stored and be displayed in the cfg file of the model. These losses are finally available for the user to analyze and scrutinize the model's performance for optimization of weights and other parameters of the model, and thereby make adjustments to the number of epochs, batch size, weight updation mechanisms, loss functions used etc. to finally increase the accuracy of the models and gain better results (Fig. 1).

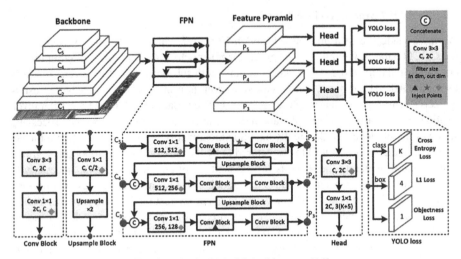

Fig. 1. YOLOv7 Model Architecture [14]

4   Results and Discussions

In Table 1. There has been a gradual increase in the mAP of the model after every 10 epochs along with a standard batch size of 16 intended for each iteration. It can also be determined that after the 30th epoch, the precision values started decreasing and started rising after the 40th epoch. It can henceforth be mentioned that the accuracy of this model can be increased with more than 50 epochs, but due to some resource allocation constraints we were able to reach correctness (mAP) of 93.3%.

Table 1. Precision, Recall and mAP values for entire model.

S. No.	No. of Epochs	Precision	Recall	mAP
1	10	0.797	0.715	0.802
2	20	0.842	0.815	0.862
3	30	0.895	0.814	0.894
4	40	0.87	0.88	0.92
5	50	0.885	0.888	0.933

Table 2. Precision, Recall and mAP values for each individual classes.

S. No.	Class	Precision	Recall	mAP
1	Hellula undalis	0.972	0.992	0.993
2	Leaf Webber	0.908	0.991	0.991
3	Ash weevil	0.942	0.728	0.854
4	Blister beetle	0.933	0.955	0.966
5	Fruit fly	0.913	0.951	0.973
6	Fruit sucking moth	0.895	0.886	0.952
7	Helicoverpa	0.773	0.621	0.766
8	Leucinodes	0.95	0.973	0.96
9	Mealy bug	0.835	0.89	0.937
10	Pieris	0.872	0.926	0.933
11	Plutella	0.928	0.896	0.917
12	Root grubs	0.739	0.929	0.944
13	Schizaphis graminum	0.843	0.8	0.857

From Table 2, it can be seen that helicoverpa was able to gain the least precision, recall and mAP values simply because the total images of this class were the least with just 22 labels for the model to learn from, while the highest precision, recall and mAP values were for Hellula undalis which consisted of 192 labels, for the constant 770 images of each class being learnt from in the entire epoch sets. This is because the model will be able to learn out from different labels for the same type of images, which will be reflected in the testing phase of the model.

Table 3. Performance of YOLOv7 Models on Different Datasets.

S. No.	Name of the Dataset	No. of Images	No. of Epochs	MAP
1	COCO Dataset	330k	50	0.697
2	PlantDoc Dataset	2598	50	0.65
3	**Our Curated Dataset**	**3269**	**50**	**0.933**

From Table 3, we can understand the behavior of the model's architecture on different datasets for constant number of epochs. The famous COCO which was developed by greater tech giants had a best responsive rate of 69.7%, wherein the MAP of the model was rising constantly, yet the number of images and epochs are disproportionate in nature and therefore the results must be monitored with larger number of epochs. The PlantDoc Dataset on which our previous research resided, was able to gain an accuracy of 65.5% after which the model started to slightly overfit. For our curated dataset, we were able to achieve an accuracy of 93.3%, which is the highest for this model on which transfer learning has been performed.

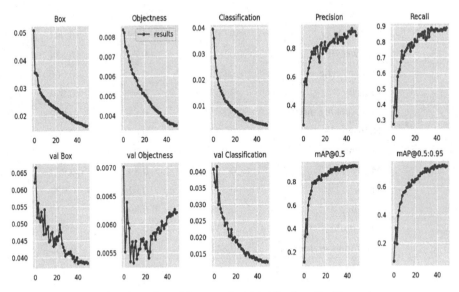

Fig. 2. Plots of precision, recall and mAP values for 50 epochs

Figure 2 shows the output plots that have been generated for 50 epochs for the YOLOv7 model and was generated in the cfg file of our clone model. Box and Val Box shows the coordinates and of the bounding boxes generated in an image. Objectness [15] is the extent of overlap to the desired values, as trained using the training set of the dataset. The three quantities- Box, Objectness and Classification have got a drop in the peak with gradual increase in the epochs i.e. it can be very well understood that as we increase the number of epochs, all of these three quantities decrease gradually after every iteration and hence highlighting that these quantities are inversely proportional to the total number of Epochs [16]. It must be also kept in mind that since the three quantities namely box, objectness and classification indicates the YOLO losses and a loss for a model's ability to identify an image must be enhanced after every iteration i.e. loss must decrease with the number of epochs therefore justifying the inverse proportionality based behavior [17]. While Precision, Recall and mAP values have the usual meanings, it can be very well seen that the precision values after reaching 20 epochs, were oscillating within 5% of their values up till the point the model was exposed to 35 epochs after which the precision values started becoming constant. A thing to note here is that even when the highest precision value i.e 0.895 was achieved at the 30th epoch wherein the corresponding mean accuracy precision was 0.894, the proposed model has shown its best accuracy at the 50th epoch itself wherein the precision score was 0.885. It can therefore be observed that as soon as we increased the total number of epochs there was a very slight trade off that can be noticed between the precision and the MAP values with 0.895 and 0.87 precision values for 30 and 40 epochs with corresponding MAPs as 0.894 and

0.92 respectively. But as soon as we reached the 45 epochs value, we were once again able to see a gradual increase in precision scores from 0.87 to 0.895. Similarly, the model recorded the highest recall value at the 36th epoch of 0.915 yet the corresponding overall MAP value was slightly less around 0.905, while the recall values oscillated the most between 0.815 and 0.885 between 30 and 40 epochs. It can therefore be highlighted that the model adjusted the most between 30 and 40 epochs which can be considered as the onset period of the model after which the model maintained consistency for all the three parameters – precision, recall and MAP and gradually reached the peak MAP of 93.3%.

It can be very well analyzed from Fig. 2. That the MAP of our model for 95% over-lapping of the curated dataset's images has been continuously rising and has maintained its consistency after 40 epochs. It can also be further mentioned that the model has shown perfect fitting for the dataset since no fall in the peak in the values of Precision, Recall and MAP have been recorded upto 50 epochs. Even if perfect fitting for the said objective of the model has been recovered, it is necessary to understand the nature of the model by increasing the number of epochs which can be done using increased iterations and different batch sizes.

Fig. 3. Sample Detection by Proposed Model

Figure 3 illustrates the detection made by the model with the corresponding accu-racies for a batch size of 16. For instance, the 1st image of the Leaf Webber is detected to be Leaf Webber itself with a certainty of 90%, at the same time the 2nd image of the

Table 4. Pre-existing YOLO models and Proposed Model for Pest Detection.

S. No	Name of the Model	Highest Achieved MAP
1	YOLO-Lite	0.517
2	YOLOv3	0.976
3	YOLOR	0.968
4	YOLOv5-n	0.84
5	YOLOv5-s	0.946
6	YOLOv5-m	0.972
7	YOLOv5-l	0.970
8	YOLOv5-x	0.983
9	Proposed YOLOv7	**0.933**

same batch, the model is 100% certain that the image detected by the model is actually Leaf Webber.

Table 4 shows the existing models for pest detection that have been proposed in [18] wherein the percentage MAPs of YOLO-Lite, YOLOv3, YOLOR, and YOLOv5 with five different scales (n, s, m, l, and x) were recorded as 51.7%, 97.6%, 96.80%, 83.85%, 94.61%, 97.18%, 97.04%, and 98.3% respectively. Our proposed model, even if has scored 93.3% has an added advantages of better running time of the algorithm due to a much better frames per second of the YOLOv7 model in comparison to previous models with 2.8ms and161fps respectively, plus the dataset that we have made use of is more realistic to natural conditions and the most common yet destructive classes being considered, will be more effective if compared to the existing models on the field.

5   Conclusions

The proposed transfer learning has been carried out on the YOLOv7 model, which was able to achieve an accuracy of 69.7% on the COCO dataset. While the same model when trained for the curated dataset was able to give us a mAP of 93.3%, which is the highest for this model. We have been able to train our model for 50 epochs and due to limited resources, we weren't able to perform the same for more epochs, to understand the variation of the curve and be able to analyze the mAP plot. Another limitation of our work is that only 3269 images were chosen and labelled, for which we wish to increase the size of our dataset to more than 10000 images and increase the classes of pests, for diversification. We also wish to expand our research work for a greater number of epochs, which will be rectified after GPU is available for more amount of time, using Google Colab + feature and expand the same for more prolific MAP values, at the same time understand the variation of precision, recall scores with MAP, as we identified the same between 30 and 40 epochs. We also wish to extend our study from texts to implementation at the ground level by adding our algorithms in a useful interface, for its easy usability and first phase testing of the proposed algorithm such as an application.

In future, we also wish to expand this project and create a mapped model, where we would be combining the features of this model, to identify which kind of a disease the corresponding pest is causing, making use of multiple object detection in a single model itself.

References

1. Liu, L., et al.: PestNet: an end-to-end deep learning approach for large-scale multi-class pest detection and classification. IEEE Access **7**, 45301–45312 (2019)
2. Liu, J., et al.: Plant diseases and pests detection based on deep learning: a review. Plant Methods **17**, 22 (2021)
3. Selvaraj, M.G., Vergara, A., Ruiz, H., et al.: AI-powered banana diseases and pest detection. Plant Methods **15**, 92 (2019)
4. Wang, C.Y., et al.: YOLOv7: trainable bag-of-freebies sets new state-of-the-art for real-time object detectors, arXiv preprint (2022)
5. Dong, S., Zhang, J., Wang, F., Wang, X.: YOLO-pest: a real-time multi-class crop pest detection model. In: International Conference on Computer Application and Information Security 12260 (2022)
6. Roy, A.M., Bhaduri, J.: A deep learning enabled multi-class plant disease detection model based on computer vision. AI **2**(3), 413–428 (2021)
7. Önler, E.: Real time pest detection using YOLOv5. Int. J. Agric. Nat. Sci. **14**(3), 232–246 (2021)
8. Zhao, S., et al.: Crop pest recognition in real agricultural environment using convolutional neural networks by a parallel attention mechanism. Frontiers Plant Sci. **13**, 839572 (2022)
9. Zhang, Y., et al.: Identification of navel orange diseases and pests based on the fusion of densenet and self-attention mechanism. Comput. Intell. Neurosci., 1–12 (2021)
10. Sachan, R., et al.: Paddy leaf disease detection using thermal images and convolutional neural networks. In: International Conference on Computational Intelligence and Sustainable Engineering Solutions (CISES), pp. 471–476 (2022)
11. Yogesh, et al.: Deep learning based automated fruit nutrients deficiency recognition system. J. Inf. Sci. Eng. **37**(5), 1153–1164 (2021)
12. Nagar, H., et al.: A comprehensive survey on pest detection techniques using image processing. In: 4th International Conference on Intelligent Computing and Control Systems (ICICCS), pp. 43–48 (2020)
13. Wu, X., Zhan, C., Lai, Y.-K., Cheng, M.-M., Yang, J.: IP102: a large-scale benchmark dataset for insect pest recognition. In: 2019 IEEE/CVF Conference on Computer Vision and Pattern Recognition (CVPR) (2019)
14. Domingues, T., Brandão, T., et al.: Machine learning for detection and prediction of crop diseases and pests: a comprehensive survey. Agriculture **12**, 1350 (2022)
15. Li, W., et al.: Recommending advanced deep learning models for efficient insect pest detection. Agriculture **12**, 1065 (2022)
16. Hussain, A., Barua, B., Osman, A., Abozariba, R., Asyhari, A.T.: Low latency and non-intrusive accurate object detection in forests. In: 2021 IEEE Symposium Series on Computational Intelligence (SSCI), pp. 1–6 (2021)
17. Wang, C.-Y., Bochkovskiy, A., Liao, H.-Y.M.: YOLOv7: trainable bag-of-freebies sets new state-of-the-art for real-time object detectors, arXiv preprint arXiv:2207.02696 (2022)
18. Ahmad, I., et al.: Deep learning based detector YOLOv5 for identifying insect pests. Appl. Sci. **12**, 10167 (2022)

Online Grocery Shopping: - Key Factors to Understand Shopping Behavior from Data Analytics Perspective

Pritha Das, Udit Chawla(✉), and Subrata Chattopadhyay

University of Engineering and Management, Kolkata, India
dr.uditchawla@gmail.com

Abstract. Happy customers affect happy retailers and fruitful businesses. In the last few decades' online grocery shopping has relished robust development and after the deadly COVID-19 pandemic, people are forced to stay back at home, which made grocery shopping online. Not only traditional shopping but general online shopping differs from this because of its variability and perishability nature as compared to other products. With the leaping momentum of online grocery shopping, retailers and producers are required to understand the needs and perceptions of their customers towards it to satisfy them to the fullest and improve their business. From this study seven different factors have been found to be affecting the customers' purchasing behavior, 'Ease of Shopping', 'Pandemic Arisen Factors', 'Financial Risk', 'Technology Driven', 'Product Performance and Psycho-Social Risk', 'Location and Quantity Constraint', and 'Entertainment'. Among those, 'Pandemic Arisen Factors' and 'Technology Driven' are significantly impacting consumers' online purchases.

Keywords: Online grocery shopping · product performance · financial risk · purchasing behavior · COVID-19 · e-loyalty

1 Introduction

Consumers' purchasing behavior is revolutionized by the increase in internet usage. Many online shopping platforms were globally introduced through Information and Communication Technology (ICT) and this led to an increase in online grocery shopper's numbers also [52]. Being the world's second-largest (−40%) internet user base, India is still experiencing a low penetration rate of e-commerce. With the increase in smartphone usage, online retail is anticipated at a growth rate of 27% CAGR which is almost more than double from 2019 to 2024 as reported by Goldman Sach. The grocery sector has always been focused on retail as it is an indispensable daily need in all households. Being the backbone (−57%) of the Indian online commercial sector, online grocery is anticipated to grow over 3.5-fold by 2025 [50]. Hence, it is mentioned as the fastest and largest consumer segment in online retail. Indians spend almost more than half of their income on groceries. Its $ 428 billion grocery market makes India one of the world's largest grocery markets. Although less than 1% of it is under the online segment, it is expected 60% CAGR growth rate during 2019–2022.

© The Author(s), under exclusive license to Springer Nature Switzerland AG 2023
M. A. Jabbar et al. (Eds.): AMLDA 2022, CCIS 1818, pp. 166–178, 2023.
https://doi.org/10.1007/978-3-031-34222-6_14

Online grocery shopping was introduced in the last few years of the 1990s in the world, but it was a failure because of additional order preparation and low marginal profit. Being considered an unorganized sector, the grocery sector remains untapped for a long. But today e-commerce is again a combat zone for grocery. This segment is expected to reach $29 billion in size by 2024 in India. Here, the number of internet users is also expected to be 660 million in 2023 [13]. However, online business is restricted mainly to metro cities and selling in non-metro cities is causing huge potential losses [10]. Online grocery shopping stretches many profits to both customers and retailers. Google in the year 2013 has highlighted cash-on-delivery as the most important influencing factor along with other convenience factors like any-time purchases, home delivery, etc., [7, 28]. Compared to next-lane Kirana stores, the product's large variety and assortment with a user-friendly interface are attracting consumers to shop for groceries online more efficiently. In India, 34% of the population are in the '18–35' years age group and are the major online shopping contributors. Hence, it is expected that there will be an increase in per-day online grocery orders to almost 5 million by 2024.

Online grocery shopping can be considered a sporadic innovation [28] and understanding customer behavior for attracting new shoppers is also an uneasy task [53]. For this new process adoption, there are researchers from various viewpoints, such as situational factors [37, 39], consumer behavior and expectations [36, 46] and attitude towards search and information [6]. If a shopper is satisfied with the first order, there is a high opportunity for repeat orders in online grocery. Price discounts as one purchase opportunity will also attract them [9].

Big Basket, Grofers, Flipkart, and Amazon Pantry become the most prominent online grocery retailers in India. When Walmart invested in Flipkart and Alibaba to Big Basket, they became strong competitors and online grocery became the next booming sector. But converting these online grocery shoppers to regular buyers is the next obstacle. Online shoppers are searching and accessing a wide heterogeneity of products available online and comparing the prices of available products over various sites of different vendors online and hence, make their choices based on compared attributes, whether monetary or non-monetary. But shoppers end up searching at a point when the potential benefit is lower than the expected cost and attributes [2]. Although extroverted customers are proactive for any new venture acquaintance and reviews, often termed a "subjective norm", are positively related to customers' purchase desire [43].

Brand loyalty also may affect online purchase decisions. 'Tech-savvy', 'money rich and time poor' people are mainly preferring online grocery purchases. Customers' trust towards retailers is built with time and effort on the part of retailers, which makes customers more loyal. Thus, customer loyalty is an important factor for long-term success in this sector and online grocers should concentrate more on quality than price to draw younger generation people. An increasing online grocery marketplace enables retailers to improve their 'last mile' service in the cities where population is more than 20,000. They are now uncovering product origin specifications to provide enhanced quality information for consumers' food safety. Thus, the availability of food regions motivates consumers to choose online shopping [55] for fresh food purchase. Many researchers found that consumers experience joy during online shopping [21]. [23] emphasized customer experience in the success of a retailer and defined it as a strategic discriminator.

If shoppers enjoy their browsing experience, that enhances online grocery purchase acceptance. The convenience-loving shoppers also like to be on a subscription plan to do more online grocery purchases with more payment for faster home delivery.

Perhaps, the COVID-19 pandemic phenomenon has drastically altered daily food consumption patterns with a massive behavior shifting. Soon after 21-days nationwide lockdown declaration from 24th March, 2020, there were increasing concerns about food availability due to imposed restrictions. Panic customers started stockpiling food, groceries and other essentials. Many customers struggled hard to prolong food dependability since the arrival of this pandemic. Retailers faced unprecedented demand because of supply intrusions due to shortage of freightage and workforce unavailability. But soon online retailers removed this stockpiling risk by providing convenient shopping places along with their risk of getting infected.

After social distancing became the new rule, consumers prefer to have their groceries delivered to their doorstep ignoring the delivery fee attribute. It becomes Indians' long-lasting habit with an increasing consumption demand of nutritional food. Big Basket witnessed 84% customer growth compared to the pre-covid situation. Grofers also observed a 40% increase in basket size during this lockdown. Although, they put restrictions on product quantity to ensure that people did not hoard items. Snack items' demand also increased as the work-from-home pattern has uplifted in-home food consumption with an increase in culinary skill improvement product purchases. Hence, online grocery becomes a new rage and fulfilling customers' expectations is the new success factor.

Thus major objectives and the set of research questions that clearly focus and pinpoints the proposed framework are clearly stated below:

RQ1:- What are the factors influencing consumers' purchasing decisions towards online grocery shopping?

RQ2:- How to develop a conceptual model for the consumers' purchasing decision?

2   Review of Literature

Since the late 2000s, online platforms are the main actors in this era of the digital economy for the sale of a wide product range as well as for the growth of the economy, all over the world. In the future, it is estimated that more than 60% of people in Asia, Africa/Middle East, and Latin America will do online shopping according to the survey by Nielson magazine. Also, this mode of shopping was mentioned as Interactive Home Shopping based on interactions between both buyers and sellers. There, both price and non-price attributes' details were the differentiating factors between electronically connected and disconnected shopping [2].

An online Grocery store is a virtual store over the internet to order food and groceries and get them delivered at a later selected time slot. Therefore, the platform i.e., website design and its characteristics play an important role to attract consumers towards the new purchasing behavior. Already a study on behavioral intentions of website usage supported a positive relationship between perceived efficacy and willingness to use. Information about the website design with easy navigation and non-price attributes of products are described as search convenience to Online shoppers. As shoppers cannot verify the products by touch and feel experience online, they have to trust the secondary non-price attribute information before making a purchase decision [18].

There is always a need for a seamless and superior customer shopping experience in all representatives [19] which were described as "customer corridors". Customer experience in online shopping and its importance was first conceptualized by [23, 45] In the second study, [45] developed an empirical model of Online Customer Experience on its components and outcomes. While shopping online, customers' attitudes and behavior are largely affected by their experience. The Online Customer Experience importance was described as customer satisfaction [40], website improvement [47], and shoppers' purchasing target [17, 35]. Shoppers do not hesitate to break loyalty with online retailers if any discrepancy is experienced with the provided service quality [3]. Hence, customer experience is the main success factor in retail for market success where customers experience consistent, frictionless, and pleasurable shopping. This experience only drives customers' contentment and willingness to stay with the retailer [32, 34, 54]. Online grocery shopping has originated as an alternative to traditional shopping from the demand for time-saving product shopping and such related services. Grocery shopping over the internet is fundamentally different from other online shopping due to food decaying lifespan and frequency of shopping. Here, we discuss grocery shopping not only because of prior findings that suggested this as the most stressful chore [4, 20] but also, because food retailing accounts for more than half of Indian retail market. Due to its rapidly changing nature, online grocery has attracted academic research worldwide, but there are few studies focusing on the Indian online grocery market. Although it is at its nascent stage, it is experiencing rapid growth for the last decade.

Many researchers have already mentioned shopping over the internet as an attractive retail channel in Australia, Europe and the United States. Studies on Online Grocery Shopping were already initiated in the late 90's. Previous research [42] has regulated focus group interviews for United states consumers with at least little online shopping experience. They prefer home shopping either for time convenience or for novelty and delivery fee was also justified with numerous convenience attributes. Here "Hi-Tech Baby Boomers", "Older" and "Physically Challenged" people preferred this shipping method to streamline their life by reducing time pressure and physical difficulty. Thus, Shopping convenience can be mentioned as a time-reduction activity with 5 dimensions decision, access, transaction, benefit, and post-benefit conveniences.

Perceived convenience will familiarize and attract consumers to adopt and use this online grocery shopping [26]. Savings in search cost and labor cost makes consumers shift from offline to online grocery shopping, based on the studies of online consumers' special behavior [8, 22, 25]. Because of time poverty, some consumers consider time as more valuable or equally valuable other than money [19]. Previous research [5] has explained this convenience in terms of access convenience, search convenience, and transaction convenience. Thus, consumers can order groceries without browsing hassle and frequent brand-switching and with personalized lists of products [11]. But for grocery shopping switching from offline to online, consumers need added convenience which should be considered an important success factor in online grocery retailing [43].

Discounting can be termed as a value-added service with a temporary monetary incentive to consumers within a particular time period. Providing discounts on products' prices is a customer delighting tool to adopt particular purchasing behavior [1]. It will be effective if customers are satisfied with current discounts compared with prior ones. Through this approach, there will be an upsurge in discounted product purchases along with basket size [33]. In India, Big Basket offered large discounts on groceries using simple end-to-end discounts. With increased internet penetration, they will make a prominent mark in the Indian grocery market [44]. Undoubtedly retailers will continue to provide more discount options to establish e-loyalty. Consumers always prefer user-friendly websites [31] with large product assortment. Homepage design seems to be a critical one to building a website image in consumers' minds [41]. Not only this, but entertainment value during shopping is also drawing attention which is considered an ancillary benefit [2]. This benefit gives pleasure to consumers during the shopping process. Hedonic shoppers find this entertaining and reflect their emotions in shopping. Thus, cross-cultural e-loyalty is established with a website revisit intention in the future [18].

Cash on delivery and fast delivery are crucial motivators for choosing online grocery shopping. As technology is progressing, same-day delivery and rural delivery are other adoption reasons which are related to personal values and traits. Although shoppers have a low inclination towards paying for home delivery [51], it removes the burden of carrying heavy shopping bags. It is predicted that free home delivery for large orders will grab more online shoppers in the future. Shoppers are willing to buy groceries online only if the products are valued for money [44]. If the product quality is not as per expectation, shoppers will go in return and then get the money refunded. These money-back guarantee tactics are found to be profitable. Not only the discounts available on websites, but their link with financial partners for offering more monetary benefits is increasing online grocery purchase intention [12].

Recently, the coronavirus outbreak in 2020 has brought several things to a halt like never before. The growing panic resulted in major changes in consumers' behavior [16]. This results in an increasing tendency of stockpiling groceries in households [14] which ensures longer stay at home and no eating outside along with less chance of spreading the virus. In a study in India, it is found that this stockpiling behavior will continue post-lockdown [30], but there was a sharp fall in grocery purchases because of sufficient inventory management by retailers. Panic buying is also expected to fade [27]in the coming future. Moreover, nutritional and immunity-boosting food demand is increased due to food and health safety demand. Growing awareness is now inducing consumers to do online grocery shopping to avail of no-touch door-step delivery. The stay-at-home order by the Government allowed consumers to grow culinary skill improvement which resulted in increasing adoption of online grocery shopping. Thus, this new behavior stickiness will be continuing with the prior satisfactory purchase experience.

This pandemic has revolutionized traditional retailing and consumption patterns in this turbulent environment. Consumers' health and hygiene consciousness made them follow the social distancing rule which impacts their online grocery shopping behavior and its contingent future intentions on their age, specifically for older consumers [29]. Recent researches are also there examining various drivers and outcomes of the online grocery shopping experience on the query of whether consumers will stay in online grocery shopping or switch. Consumers' psychological states and their utilitarian and hedonic were also analyzed here [49]. Thus, online grocery shopping has a significant and positive influence on consumer satisfaction so that consumers become trustworthy and loyal in the future [38].

3 Research Methodology

In the present study, there were four metro cities selected on the basis of popularity in India – Kolkata, Delhi, Chennai, and Mumbai. While using Factor and regression, sample size determination is a dicey matter. A wide range of recommendations is available regarding the minimum number of sample sizes for conducting good factor analysis. A number of authors provided various responses required as per the need of factors. These responses are either represented as the sample size (N) or the ratio of this N to the number of variables. Previous research [48] considered a sample size of 50–70 to be sufficient for a model of functional brain connectivity consisting of 4 latent variables. Usually, a sample size of 100–150 is considered the minimum sample size for Factor and Regression Analysis. While few researchers gave the minimum requirement to be 200–250. As per the studies and research, it has been explained the suitable requirement of minimum sample size is – 100 (poor), 200 (fair), 300 (good), 500 (very good), 1000 or more (excellent), for conducting a factor analysis and regression.

In this study, 570 samples were collected from metro cities with the help of a structured questionnaire. Data collection was executed at 5 different housing complexes of each metro city and informal discussions were held with the local residents. The variables of sample characteristics or the demographic factors taken in the study are gender, age, monthly income, occupation, and marital status. From the study, it has emerged that Gender wise, 35.1% Females, 64.9% Males; Age Wise, (18–25) - 25.4%, (26–30) - 34.2%, (31–40) - 21.4%, (>40) - 18.9%; Income wise, (<10k) - 11.4%, (10k to 20k) -19.1%, (20k–30k) - 18.6%, (30k–40k) - 18.4%, (>40k) - 32.5%; Occupation wise, (Business) - 26.7%, (Service) - 56%, (Others) - 17.4%; Marital Status, (Married) - 47.4%, (Unmarried) - 52.6%.

Primarily, 45 quality parameters were identified for analyzing the factors in online grocery shopping. A small pilot test was performed with 50 participants and finally, 40 items were chosen. The variables included in the study have been adapted from existing literature. Previous studies were referred to for scale development and adapted for the research context. Five-point Likert scale ranging from 1-strongly disagree to 5-strongly agree, was introduced for the measurement of each parameter. Data after proper cleaning and validation were used for a number of multivariate analyses to accomplish the objectives of the study. Analysis was done with the help of SPSS 26 software.

4 Analysis and Findings

From the Analysis, the approximate Chi-square statistic is 30593.398 with 78 degrees of freedom, which is significant at 0.05 level (as the p-value is 0.000). The value of the Kaiser Meyer Olkin statistic is good above 0.5 and is excellent up to 1, in our study KMO value is 0.857 which is large and greater than 0.5. From the Total Variance Explained, Factors with eigenvalue 1 or above are considered good and are selected for the study, thus, in our study first seven factors (with eigenvalue 1 or above) are selected to proceed with the factor analysis. Factor 1 accounts for a variance value of 18.603, which is 46.51% of the total variance, likewise, Factor 2 accounts for a variance value of 2.951, which is 7.38% of the total variance, Factor 3 accounts for a variance value of 2.452, which is 6.13% of the total variance, Factor 4 constitutes 1.802 as a value of variance, which is 4.50% of the total variance, Factor 5 constitutes for 1.712 as a value of variance, which is 4.28% of the total variance, while Factor 6 accounts for 1.196 for the variance value, which is 2.99% of total variance and factor 7 constitutes for 1.024 for the value of variance, which is 2.56% of the total variance and thus, the first seven factors combined value accounts for 74.348%.

Table 1. Rotated Component Matrix

	Component						
	1	2	3	4	5	6	7
Online grocery shopping saves time by showing personalized list of food products	.809	–	–	–	–	–	–
Online grocery shopping makes life easier for disabled persons and single parents	.801	–	–	–	–	–	–
Websites with easy navigation and professional design attract customers to do online grocery shopping	.777	–	–	–	–	–	–
No crowd or no queue motivates consumers to shop groceries online	.721	–	–	–	–	–	–
While shopping online, consumers love to browse things on discount to be self–satisfied	.712	–	–	–	–	–	–
Premium subscription (like Amazon Prime) attracts convenience–loving consumers	.693	–	–	–	–	–	–
Consumers prefer more to 'see and touch' groceries which is not available online	.673	–	–	–	–	–	–
Customers always want speedy and timely delivery (specially time-stored families/families with children)	.635	–	–	–	–	–	–
Free shipment is a customer satisfaction factor for increasing online grocery shoppers	.624	–	–	–	–	–	–
Increasing purchase rate of healthier and Nutritional diet/food observed on/after Covid-19 pandemic due to food safety concerns	.604	–	–	–	–	–	–
A large range of product assortment attract online grocery shoppers	.470	–	–	–	–	–	–
Pandemic situation is increasing count of online grocery shoppers due to growing awareness of safety health	–	.791	–	–	–	–	–

(continued)

Table 1. (*continued*)

	Component						
	1	2	3	4	5	6	7
A local store deliver order to the address at the time mentioned by the online store with payment of cash only on delivery	–	.788	–	–	–	–	–
As social distancing becoming the new norm, consumers prefer to get food products through online grocery shopping	–	.754	–	–	–	–	–
Some "Resisting and Responsible" consumers support their local retailers only	–	.754	–	–	–	–	–
Convenient online grocery shopping removes panic food hoarding (stockpiling) risk	–	.732	–	–	–	–	–
Product origin seems to be an influencing factor in online grocery shopping	–	.731	–	–	–	–	–
Consumers seem to be distrustful of online grocery stores because of poor quality control	–	.644	–	–	–	–	–
Contactless delivery attracts safety concerned customers because it is eliminating consumers' risk of getting infected in store crowd	–	.638	–	–	–	–	–
There is time risk if we waste time in searching, but it became a bad purchasing decision	–	–	.763	–	–	–	–
Refunds for returns provide insurance against dissatisfaction	–	–	.749	–	–	–	–
Online customers may need to meet a minimum order requirement to make transactions	–	–	.708	–	–	–	–
Shoppers consider if the goods are value for money	–	–	.703	–	–	–	–
Difficulty in returning spoiled perishable food items stops consumers to do online grocery shopping	–	–	.685	–	–	–	–
If a customer is absent or there is no adult one, then the delivery would be not done	–	–	.672	–	–	–	–
Drivers can refuse to carry goods in to an unsafe property	–	–	.599	–	–	–	–
Some online shoppers' food buying decisions are impulsive	–	–	.597	–	–	–	–
Due to increasing interest towards culinary (cooking) skills, there is an increase in online grocery shopping	–	–	–	.828	–	–	–
Converting online shoppers to regular buyers is the next challenge	–	–	–	.819	–	–	–

(*continued*)

Table 1. (*continued*)

	Component						
	1	2	3	4	5	6	7
A phisher may monitor wireless internet traffic and conduct a phishing attack after detecting a purchase	–	–	–	.418	–	–	–
Online grocery purchase is sticky like if a consumer's last purchase is satisfactory, he/she will go to purchase that food over online only	–	–	–	–	.772	–	–
Poor packaging stops consumers to do online grocery shopping	–	–	–	–	.739	–	–
There is social risk resulting from friends or family thinking that a consumer has made a poor choice	–	–	–	–	.701	–	–
A product might be alright from buyer's prospect but not in the judgment of others	–	–	–	–	.660	–	–
App offers plus bank offers during online payment helps in increasing count of online grocery shoppers	–	–	–	–	.652	–	–
Trust factor is sometimes more than anything while doing online grocery purchase	–	–	–	–	.409	–	–
As social distancing becoming the new norm, consumers prefer to get food products through online grocery shopping	–	–	–	–	–	.914	–
Consumers calculate how much money is wasted if the product does not perform well	–	–	–	–	–	.901	–
One of the advantages of buying over internet is the ease of comparing prices against other product/service offerings	–	–	–	–	–	–	.688
Entertainment while shopping is considered to be an important driver of consumer satisfaction (like some lucky draw/coupon/gifts)	–	–	–	–	–	–	.675

The Rotated Component Matrix table (Table 1) highlights the value of factor loading and the association between the variables and the factors derived from the study. Each variable carries a value that is being used to derive various factors or components, which can be seen from the above table. Factor 1 may be labelled as 'Ease of Shopping', Factor 2 maybe labelled as 'Pandemic Arisen Factors', Factor 3 may be labelled as 'Financial Risk', Factor 4 maybe labelled as 'Technology Driven',, Factor 5 maybe labelled as 'Product Performance and Psychosocial Risk', Factor 6 may be labelled as 'Location and Quantity Constraint', Factor 7 may be labelled as 'Entertainment',

The R-square value is 0.711 which indicates 71.1% of the total variation in the dependent variable, customer purchasing behavior can be explained by the independent variables, 'Entertainment', 'Location and Quantity Constraint', 'Product Performance and

Psychosocial Risk', 'Technology Driven', 'Financial Risk', 'Pandemic Arisen Factors' and 'Ease of Shopping'.

From the ANOVA (Analysis of Variance), it has emerged that the regression model estimates the dependent variable significantly well and it is statistically significant as p-value is less than 0.05 (i.e., 0.000).

From coefficients, it shows the impact factor of the components that we got in our study. From the Analysis, it has emerged that all the factors or the components are statistically significant (except the factor, Product Performance and Psychosocial Risk) to form a regression equation. The regression equation being formed is given below:

Customer Purchasing Behavior = 3.236 + 0.269 * Ease of Shopping + 0.754 * Pandemic Arisen Factors + 0.197 * Financial Risk + 0.363 * Technology Driven + 0.130 * Location and Quantity Constraint + 0.107 * Entertainment

5 Conclusion

A noticeable upsurge has been seen in the usage of online platforms to shop for groceries at the convenience of shopping from home. The COVID-19 pandemic resulted in a skyrocketing rise in its usage due to the restrictions being imposed on people's migration from one place to another which made people order one of their basic needs via online grocery stores. Whether people are working from home, housewives, elders' youngsters, etc. Everyone makes use of online stores to purchase groceries or related items. While shopping for groceries online, customers look after lots of factors (monetary or non-monetary) before making their purchase and they make their purchase only if they feel satisfied with overall expectations they possess from that particular product, hence these factors in turn determine the road of success for the retailers and traders. Retailers make all possible efforts to make their customers satisfied and turn them into their constant and loyal customers. Factors like easy accessibility, convenience in shopping, quick delivery, low delivery charges, attractive discounts, quality products etc., influences the buying behavior of the customers which in turn can be used by the retailers to pave their way towards success.

In this study we tried to understand the various factors responsible for the purchasing behaviors and satisfaction level of the customers while shopping for groceries online, from the study it has been found that impact factor is highest towards the factors during pandemic, this includes lack of movement from one place to another, quick delivery, quality and price effective products which are healthy as well, thus, pandemic made people use online stores for purchasing the groceries more. Other important factor includes ease of shopping, reasonable costs, and discounts, location and quality constraints, etc., all these factors influence the purchasing behavior as well as the satisfaction level of the customer making online purchases of groceries. In addition, to provide superior customer satisfaction by implementing the influencing factors identified here, online grocery retailers can use the study findings as a strategic convoy towards building an easy-flowing and delightful shopping experience. Moreover, it is important to understand consumers' motives for online grocery shopping and the information they count on for making purchase decisions. We hope that our research findings open the way for more wise and promising future research on online grocery shopping.

6 Managerial Implications

On the basis of the findings of this study, 'Product Performance and Psychosocial Risk' does not seem to have much impact on the adoption of online grocery shopping after the entry of the pandemic. Online grocers should not put substantial effort into this factor as customer satisfaction is shifted towards the fulfillment of other attributes' expectations. Another important takeaway from this study is pandemic has made people to be more health and hygiene conscious which is playing the most important role in shoppers choosing online grocery shopping over conventional shopping methods.

7 Limitations and Future Research

Considering major contributions, some limitations need to be communicated. This research result cannot be mapped to other online industries because of its perishability. Secondly, this research is focused on customer satisfaction on basis of several influencing factors. Future research can get a complete picture of customer satisfaction by extending this model. Third, the data was gathered through a questionnaire from the metro cities in India. Culture always has an important role in customer satisfaction. Hence, results may find to be different in other cultures.

References

1. Ailawadi, K.L., Neslin, S.A., Gedenk, K.: Pursuing the value-conscious consumer: store brands versus national brand promotions. J. Mark. **65**(1), 71–89 (2001)
2. Alba, J., et al.: Interactive home shopping: consumer, retailer, and manufacturer incentives to participate in electronic marketplaces. J. Mark. **61**(3), 38–53 (1997)
3. Anton, S.R., Sodano, H.A.: A review of power harvesting using piezoelectric materials (2003–2006). Smart Mater. Struct. **16**(3), R1 (2007)
4. Aylott, R., Mitchell, V.-W.: An exploratory study of grocery shopping stressors. Int. J. Retail Distrib. Manag. **26**(9), 362–373 (1998)
5. Beauchamp, M.B., Ponder, N.: Perceptions of retail convenience for in-store and online shoppers. Mark. Manag. J. **20**(1), 49–65 (2010)
6. Benn, Y., Webb, T.L., Chang, B.P.I., Reidy, J.: What information do consumers consider, and how do they look for it, when shopping for groceries online? Appetite **89**, 265–273 (2015)
7. Chu, J., Arce-Urriza, M., Cebollada-Calvo, J.J., Chintagunta, P.K.: An empirical analysis of shopping behavior across online and offline channels for grocery products: the moderating effects of household and product characteristics. J. Interact. Mark. **24**(4), 251–268 (2010)
8. Clemes, M.D., Gan, C., Zhang, J.: An empirical analysis of online shopping adoption in Beijing. J. Retail. Consum. Serv. **21**(3), 364–375 (2014)
9. Sheehan, D., Hardesty, D.M., Ziegler, A.H., Chen, H.A.: Consumer reactions to price discounts across online shopping experiences. J. Retail. Consum. Serv. **51**, 129–138 (2019)
10. Dattagupta, I.: Walmart's Flipkart buy is a winning deal for consumers (2018)
11. Degeratu, A.M., Rangaswamy, A., Wu, J.: Consumer choice behavior in online and traditional supermarkets: the effects of brand name, price and other search attributes. Int. J. Res. Mark. **17**, 55–78 (2000)
12. Deshmukh, G.K., Joseph, S.: Online shopping in India: an enquiry of consumer's world. J. Bus. Manag. **18**(1), 28–33 (2016)

13. Diwanji, S.: Number of internet users in India from 2015 to 2018 with a forecast until 2023 (2020)
14. Dou, Z., et al.: The COVID-19 pandemic impacting household food dynamics: a cross-national comparison of China and the U.S (2020)
15. Driediger, F., Bhatiasevi, V.: Online grocery shopping in Thailand: consumer acceptance and usage behavior. J. Retail. Consum. Serv. **48**, 224–237 (2019)
16. Duțu, A.: Understanding individuals' behavior under uncertainty: strategy key driver in economic crisis, pp. 57–85 (2020)
17. Fiore, A.M., Kim, J., Lee, H.H.: Effect of image interactivity technology on consumer responses toward the online retailer. J. Interact. Mark. **19**(3), 38–53 (2005)
18. Flavian, C., Guinaliu, M., Gurrea, R.: The role played by perceived usability, satisfaction and consumer trust on website loyalty. Inf. Manag. **43**(1), 1–14 (2006)
19. Foote, N.N.: The image of the consumer in the year 2000, pp. 13–18 (1963)
20. Geuens, M., Brengman, M., S'Jegers, R.: Food retailing: now and in the future: a consumer perspective. J. Retail. Consum. Serv. **10**(4), 241–251 (2003)
21. Giao, H., Vuong, B., Quan, T.: The influence of website quality on consumer's e-loyalty through the mediating role of e-trust and e-satisfaction: an evidence from online shopping in Vietnam. Uncertain Supply Chain Manag. **8**(2), 351–370 (2020)
22. Gong, W., Stump, R.L., Maddox, L.M.: Factors influencing consumers' online shopping in China. J. Asia Bus. Stud. **7**(3), 214–230 (2013)
23. Grewal, D., Levy, M., Kumar, V.: Customer experience management in retailing: an organizing framework. J. Retail. **85**(1), 1–14 (2009)
24. Hansen, T.: Consumer adoption of online grocery buying: a discriminant analysis. Int. J. Retail Distrib. Manag. **33**(2), 101–121 (2005)
25. Heng, Y., Gao, Z., Jiang, Y., Chen, X.: Exploring hidden factors behind online food shopping from amazon reviews: a topic mining approach. J. Retail. Consum. Serv. **42**, 161–168 (2018)
26. Hiser, J., Nayga, R.M., Capps, O.: An exploratory analysis of familiarity and willingness to use online food shopping services in a local area of Texas. J. Food Distrib. Res. **30**, 78–90 (1999)
27. Hobbs, J.E.: Food supply chains during the COVID-19 pandemic. Can. J. Agric. Econ. **68**(2), 171–176 (2020)
28. Huang, Y., Oppewal, H.: Why consumers hesitate to shop online: an experimental choice analysis of grocery shopping and the role of delivery fees. Int. J. Retail Distrib. Manag. **34**(4/5), 334–353 (2006)
29. Itani, O.S., Hollebeek, L.D.: Light at the end of the tunnel: visitors' virtual reality (versus in-person) attraction site tour-related behavioral intentions during and post-COVID-19. Tourism Manag. **84**, 104290 (2021)
30. Jain, S.A.: A study of changes in individual income, spending & saving pattern as a result of COVID-19 situation in India. **19**(13), 339–368 (2020)
31. Kim, H., Niehm, L.S.: The impact of website quality on information quality, value, and loyalty intentions in apparel retailing. J. Interact. Mark. **23**(3), 221–233 (2009)
32. Klaus, P., Maklan, S.: Towards a better measure of customer experience. Int. J. Mark. Res. **55**(2), 227–246 (2013)
33. Leeflang, P.S., Parreño-Selva, J.: Cross-category demand effects of price promotions. J. Acad. Mark. Sci. **40**(4), 572–586 (2012)
34. Lemon, K.N., Verhoef, P.C.: Understanding customer experience throughout the customer journey. J. Mark. **80**(6), 69–96 (2016)
35. Mathwick, C., Malhotra, N., Rigdon, E.: Experiential value: conceptualization, measurement and application in the catalog and Internet shopping environment. J. Retail. **77**(1), 39–56 (2001)

36. Morganosky, M.A., Cude, B.J.: Consumer response to online grocery shopping. Int. J. Retail Distrib. Manag. **28**(1), 17–26 (2000)
37. Muhammad, N.S., Sujak, H., Abd Rahman, S.A.: Buying groceries online: the influences of electronic service quality (eServQual) and situational factors. Procedia Econ. Finan. **37**, 379–385 (2016)
38. Muljono, W., Pertiwi, S.P., Kusuma, D.P.S.: Online shopping: factors affecting consumer's continuance intention to purchase, St. Petersburg State Polytechnical University Journal. НАУЧНО-ТЕХНИЧЕСКИЕ **14**(1), 7–20 (2021)
39. Nilsson, E., Gärling, T., Marell, A., Nordvall, A.C.: Who shops groceries where and how? – the relationship between choice of store format and type of grocery shopping. Int. Rev. Retail Distrib. Consum. Res. **25**(1), 1–19 (2015)
40. Overby, J.W., Lee, E.J.: The effects of utilitarian and hedonic online shopping value on consumer preference and intentions. J. Bus. Res. **59**(10/11), 1160–1166 (2006)
41. Pandir, M., Knight, J.: Homepage aesthetics: the search for preference factors and the challenges of subjectivity. Interact. Comput. **18**(6), 1351–1370 (2006)
42. Park, K., Perosio, D., German, G.A., McLaughlin, E.W.: What's in store for home shopping?(1996)
43. Piroth, P., Ritter, M.S., Rueger-Muck, E.: Online grocery shopping adoption: do personality traits matter? Br. Food J. **122**(3), 957–975 (2020)
44. Sharma, P., Nair, V., Jyotishi, A.: Patterns of online grocery shopping in India: an empirical study, vol. 29, pp. 1–5 (2014)
45. Rose, S., Clark, M., Samouel, P., Hair, N.: Online customer experience in E-retailing: an empirical model of antecedents and outcomes. J. Retail. **88**(2), 308–322 (2012)
46. Seitz, C., Pokrivcak, J., Toth, M., Plevny, M.: Online grocery retailing in Germany: an explorative analysis. J. Bus. Econ. Manag. **18**(6), 1243–1263 (2017)
47. Shobeiri, S., Laroche, M., Mazaheri, E.: Shaping e-retailer's website personality: the importance of experiential marketing. J. Retail. Consum. Serv. **20**(1), 102–110 (2013)
48. Sideridis, G., Simos, P., Papanicolaou, A., Fletcher, J.: Using structural equation modeling to assess functional connectivity in the brain power and sample size considerations. Educ. Psychol. Meas. **74**(5), 733–758 (2014)
49. Singh, R.: Why do online grocery shoppers switch or stay? an exploratory analysis of consumers' response to online grocery shopping experience. Int. J. Retail Distrib. Manag. **47**, 1300–1317 (2019)
50. Sinha, S., Ali, M.H.: Consumer behaviour for e-grocery shopping in India: an overview. **2**(6) (2019)
51. Teller, C., Kotzab, H., Grant, D.: The consumer direct services revolution in grocery retailing: an exploratory investigation. Manag. Serv. Qual. Int. J. **16**(1), 78–96 (2006)
52. Van Droogenbroeck, E., Van Hove, L.: Adoption of online grocery shopping: personal or household characteristics? J. Internet Commer. **16**(3), 255–286 (2017)
53. Van Droogenbroeck, E., Van Hove, L.: Triggered or evaluated? a qualitative inquiry into the decision to start using e-grocery services. Int. Rev. Retail, Distrib. Consum. Res. **30**(2) 103–122 (2020)
54. Verhoef, P.C., Lemon, K.N., Parasuraman, A., Roggeveen, A., Tsiros, M., Schlesinger, L.A.: Customer experience creation: determinants, dynamics and management strategies. J. Retail. **85**(1), 31–41 (2009)
55. Zheng, Q., Wang, H.H., Lu, Y.: Consumer purchase intentions for sustainable wild salmon in the Chinese market and implications for agribusiness decisions. Sustainability **10**(5), 1377–1392 (2018)

A Novel Approach: Semantic Web Enabled Subject Searching for Union Catalogue

Dharmeshkumar Shah[1,4]($\boxtimes$) (iD), Harshal Arolkar[2](iD), and Ronak Panchal[3](iD)

[1] Scientist-B (CS), Information and Library Network (INFLIBNET) Centre, Gandhinagar, Gujarat 382007, India
dashah@inflibnet.ac.in

[2] PG Programme, FCT & FCAIT, GLS University, Ahmedabad, Gujarat 380006, India
harshal.arolkar@glsuniversity.ac.in

[3] R.N.G. Patel Institute of Technology, Bardoli 394620, India
ronakvtcbb@gmail.com

[4] GLS University, Ahmedabad, Gujarat, India

Abstract. Most students and academicians use anonymous item search strategies to fetch books or other library materials, including subject keywords. Also, most of the search follows keyword-based search which returns irrelevant information as a result, and in the end, result success rates will be low. To overcome such problems, especially in the library catalogue, this paper presents an ontological approach to convert syntactic search strategy to semantic search and identify major subjects using Dewey Decimal Classification (DDC), available in the Union Catalogue of Gujarat Colleges (GujCat). The semantic web is creative and relevant and provides information in a way the computer can understand. Currently, GujCat follows keyword-based searching techniques, giving only exact text-matching results. This paper has suggested a structure that implements semantic concepts with the DDC scheme that can improve the subject-wise search and the overall search result quality of GujCat. Semantic-based search requires a Resource Description Framework (RDF) or Ontology concepts. The Simple Protocol and RDF Query Language (SPARQL) is a query language recommended by World Wide Web Consortium (W3C) to access and explore the ontology and data. The DDC classification scheme refers to a hierarchy of classes to enhance and improve subject-wise search for all the subjects available in the books.

Keywords: Ontology · DDC · MARC · Semantic Web · RDF · SPARQL · Protege

1 Introduction

Information and Library Network (INFLIBNET) Centre has developed an online interface, Online Union Catalogue for Indian Universities (IndCat). "IndCat is

India's most comprehensive free online union catalogue of books, theses, and serials from major university/institute libraries. IndCat is primarily used for collection development, copy cataloguing, inter-library loans (ILL), and retro-conversion of metadata. Similarly, the Online Union Catalogue of Gujarat Colleges (GujCat) is a subset of INFLIBNET's IndCat. It is a unified online library catalogue of books available in significant college libraries in Gujarat state. Guj-Cat comprises metadata information like title, author, place, publisher, ISBN, edition, publication year, etc. Currently, it is a dedicated web-based interface developed to access the integrated catalogues of libraries in Gujarat" [1]. Guj-Cat has around 5 lakh plus unique metadata and 7 lakh plus records withholding details of 39 colleges of Gujarat state. The GujCat is a vital information retrieval tool in libraries. According to previous studies, subject searching is the most challenging aspect of any online catalogue search therefore it is necessary to enhance the Graphical User Interface (GUI) of the GujCat website by assisting the searcher in selecting the appropriate keywords for fruitful results. The "**free search**" or "**exact search**" method, also referred to as a keyword search, can look for can look for words or phrases that might appear in one or more fields of the record (e.g., title, author, place, publisher, subject headings). Moreover, keyword searches with more than one word are processed as Boolean operator 'AND', 'OR', and 'NOT' queries and access metadata containing the specified word anywhere in the record, as shown in Fig. 1.

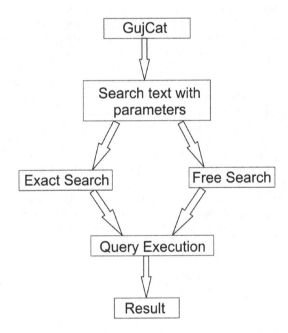

Fig. 1. Existing search flow of GujCat website

"The current GujCat website uses a keyword-based information retrieval system that generates results based on exact matches", which has a low precision rate. Using ontology-based semantic search for keyword-based search can improve the limitation of search technique. It will also aid in bridging the gap between the terminology typically used to describe the index information assets within GujCat metadata and the information the users need. The meaning of the user's search and the connections between the ideas in the text can be interpreted using an ontology-based search. In the preceding context, this study proposes an ontology-based subject-searching structure. The suggested structure aims to develop an approachable system with high retrieval performance with the ability to understand query intent. In addition, the developed ontology will assist in query expansion and search results. This structure would function because it makes advantage of DDC's semantically enhanced design to comprehend the query's intent.

2   Literature Review

Subject searching is one of the library system's most crucial search options because it uses controlled vocabulary, which can provide a meaningful descriptor for subject access [2]. Many other reasons affect the result of search tasks, like spelling and typographical mistakes with the search text [6]. Users feel dissatisfied with the results when they use keyword-based searches. "Few of the users are not even aware about the existence of subject terms" [7]. The ontology-based searching structure would replace the current keyword-based GujCat website by building an inverted index based on the semantic entities related to the documents. Instead of disclosing the expressiveness of the Library of Congress Subject Headings (LCSH)-based strings to the end user, the keyword-based retrieval primarily relies on exact matching using a statistical algorithm [2]. "An Integrated ontology using various kinds of ontology built by multiple experienced organisations using metadata of research publication. Mapping of ontology based on DDC, a classification system, to fit other domain ontologies into one based on the metadata. The metadata is essential in making ontology, obtained from research publications, have properties, i.e., Title, Subject, Authors Name, Affiliation, Keywords, etc.". [8]. "Classification-based ontologies could be helpful for practically implementing the semantic web. It was proved by Giunchiglia et al., where the author converted the generic classification schemes to OWL ontology" [12].

3   Problem Statement

Subject searching is done by users in the current MAchine-Readable Cataloging (MARC) based GujCat [1]. It exclusively shows a successful outcome when the terminology of the searcher matches the terminology of the underlying topic headings in the database. Figure 1 allows users to select the areas in which searches are performed. Figure 2 shows the current result from GujCat, In which subject mapping is not implemented with DDC; hence users are getting only what they searched for. This kind of searching reduces the DDC's capacity for semantic expressiveness. Furthermore, DDC must connect better with the Boolean searching provided by present keyword-based systems [2].

"The most challenging aspect of online catalogues is subject searching" [3]. Most users are unfamiliar with DDC's primary subject hierarchy and terminology, so they are facing difficulty in overall subject searching. Sometimes, it may lead to irrelevant output [4,5]. According to Sridhar, M S. (2004), different subject-searching problems [11] as identified from works of literature and presented are:

- Too many irrelevant searches or no records being found
- Failure to use subject vocabulary supported by the system
- Insufficient or missing cross-references
- Very few or numerous metadata records to a subject heading &
- The inability of users to persist.

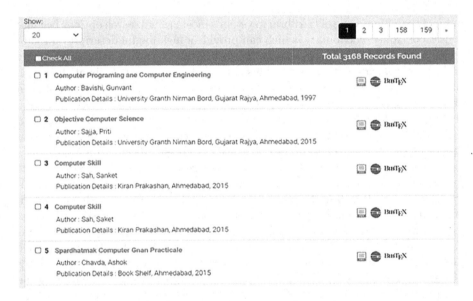

Fig. 2. Current search result from GujCat website Source (https://gujcat.inflibnet. ac.in)

The present MARC-based GujCat ignores the semantic meaning of words and only matches words syntactically. Therefore, as a result, the false detection rate is high, and the precision rate is low. Another area for improvement is that users find searching challenging when unfamiliar with the proper search terms. It is evident from the discussion above that GujCat needs a semantic-enabled subject-searching system. To solve these problems, this study proposes an ontology-based searching strategy for the GujCat website.

4   Objectives

- To analyse the existing search facility available with GujCat.
- Analysis of current metadata based on classification number.
- Propose a method to convert syntactic search strategy to semantic search in GujCat.

5   Analysis of Existing Data

At present, the GujCat website contains book metadata from 39 colleges. Most records include class number values with MARC tag 082 or 084, which follows the DDC classification scheme. OCLC Online Computer Library Center, Inc publishes the DDC scheme. Each DDC class is represented using Arabic numerals with a specific format, i.e. In a class number, a decimal point comes after the third digit. The main class is represented by the first digit of each three-digit class number. The division is indicated by the second digit in each three-digit class number. The section is indicated by the third digit in each three-digit number. This notational hierarchy is demonstrated by the underlined digits in the following example:

```
000   Computer Science, Information and General Works
000    Computer Science, Knowledge and Systems
005      Computer Programming, Programs and Data
005.8          Computer Security
005.82          Cryptography and Steganography
```

In the above example, Cryptography and Steganography are more specific than Computer programming, programs and data. DDC Scheme includes ten significant classes available in GujCat, i.e. Philosophy and Psychology, Religion, Social Science, Language, Pure Science, Technology, Arts and recreation, Literature, History and geography, and Computer Science, Information and General Works. Based on existing data, Fig. 3 shows the analysis of the significant domains of DDC scheme classes available in GujCat.

6   Research Methodology

The proposed methodology for creating an ontology-based searching structure for GujCat is depicted in Fig. 4. In this proposed design, users can search a book using various metadata parameters like title, author name, ISBN, place, publisher etc., on the GujCat user interface. This search text is formalised in SPARQL query language instead of the database-structured query language. It executes on DDC class scheme ontology and returns relevant results to the user interface.

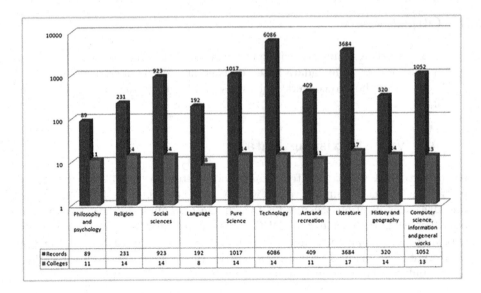

Fig. 3. DDC domain analysis

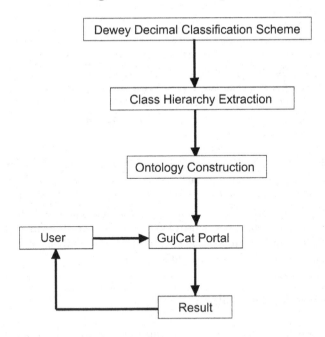

Fig. 4. Proposed Workflow

In the proposed system, the ontology is implemented using the DDC scheme for GujCat book searching.This ontology contains all the important DDC class domains. The proposed Ontology lists all ten main fields as shown in Fig. 3 of this classification scheme. This paper outlines a method for creating ontologies that divides each DDC scheme category into class and subclass relations. These classes are referred to by Ontology as Level-1, Level-2, and Level-3 until a more specific to general class is reached [9].

7 Suggested Structure

In this part, we discuss our suggested structure for increasing the quality of GujCat search results.

7.1 Basics to Construct GujCat Ontology Elements Based on DDC and Book Attributes

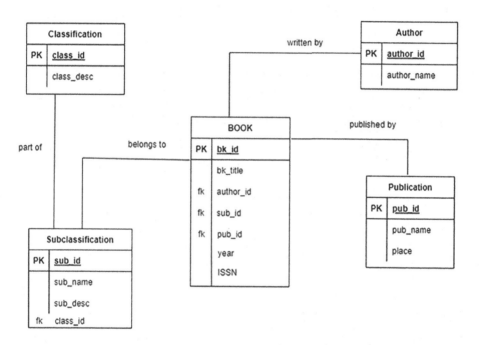

Fig. 5. Relationship between ontology classes with ER Diagram

GujCat ontology consists of different classes, with Book as the main class. There are various subclasses of Book class i.e. Author, Place, Publisher, Language, Subject. The DDC scheme forms a hierarchy of subjects levelwise. Among the subclasses, Subject is directly mapped with DDC scheme hierarchy. Each class has two types of properties, namely object property and data property. Each book has various parameters like author, place, publisher, year, edition, subject with the values. Each Parameter has some value which is known as property.

For example, a book has an author which gives the object property 'has written by' as shown in Fig. 5 [4]. The Book has an edition which provides the object with the property 'has edition'. The Book has ISBN, which gives the data type property 'has ISBN'. All book parameters consist of values. These values are the individuals. Suppose a book has the title 'Introduction to Algorithms.' This is the individual for class 'Book', which has the object property "has a title." Book has the author 'Thomas H. Cormen.'This is another individual object property "has the author." The Book has ISBN 9780262046305'. ISBN is a type of integer. As a result, this is a data type property. Class and subclass connections can be used to structure Web ontology language classes (OWL).

It is simple to integrate the classes in the library ontology in class and subclass relations since the classes in the DDC scheme are organised in a hierarchical way. The proposed system associates individuals and classes with object and data type attributes. OWL can make advantage of a variety of features. Annotations and other information can also be added to properties.

7.2 Construction of Book Ontology

Using DDC scheme mapping as shown in Fig. 6 (Neo4j is used to draw the diagram) of the Book ontology into library ontology concepts is done to construct concepts. This study examined the DDC scheme and extracted the hierarchy of the classes. Install Protégé and begin creating ontologies with the protégé editor.

– Choose the directory that will store the ontology;
– Start ontology construction with the "Thing" main class and list the sub-classes;
– Start including people to each class;
– Add object attributes and data-type characteristics &
– Add properties to annotation.

Ontology construction is carried out using Protégé 5 (Protege) [10], Protégé is an ontology editor tool.

7.3 Basics to Build and Evaluate Outcome from Ontology

The below-proposed steps explain how to apply a semantic approach on GujCat for searching the books using their metadata.

1. Class to Class Relation Using RDF Graph Diagram in Protege Tool. As shown in Fig. 7, the significant classes in ontology are book, author and publisher and classes are related to each other using relationships.

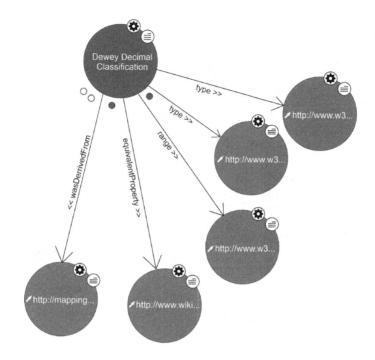

Fig. 6. Dewey Decimal Classification (DDC) Mapping

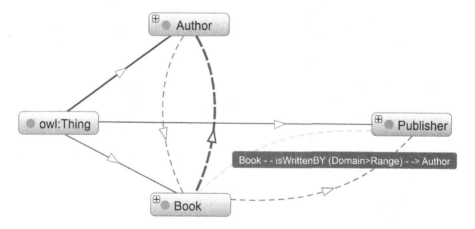

Fig. 7. Book ontology classes

2. Ontology Relation Diagram with Classes, Object Properties and Data Properties: In ontology, the class contains object properties, i.e. written, written by, published by, etc., and data properties, i.e. title, publisher name, ISBN etc., as shown in Fig. 8.

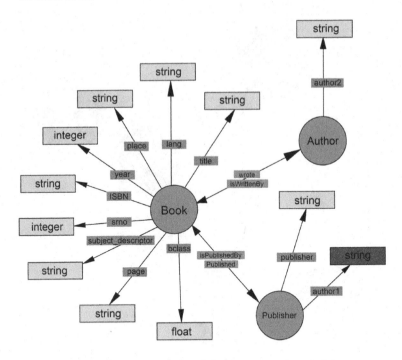

Fig. 8. Object property and data property in ontology

3. SPARQL Query from Ontology with Book Class. The below program is the SPARQL query to retrieve author and publisher wise book details from the union catalogue metadata.

```
PREFIX rdf: <http://www.w3.org/1999/02/22-rdf-syntax-ns#>
PREFIX owl: <http://www.w3.org/2002/07/owl#>
PREFIX rdfs: <http://www.w3.org/2000/01/rdf-schema#>
PREFIX xsd: <http://www.w3.org/2001/XMLSchema#>
PREFIX infl: <http://gujcat.inflibnet.ac.in/ontology#>
SELECT *
WHERE
{
     ?book a infl:Book.
     ?book infl:title ?booktitle.
     ?book infl:isWrittenBy ?author.
     ?author infl:author1 ?firstauthor.
     ?book infl:isPublishedBy ?publisher.
     ?publisher infl:publisher ?pubname.
}
```

Output: To explore the concept of the ontology using the protege tool, sample records are taken from the GujCat database to evaluate the data retrieved from ontology. Figure 9 shows the data obtained from sample ontology using the SPARQL query.

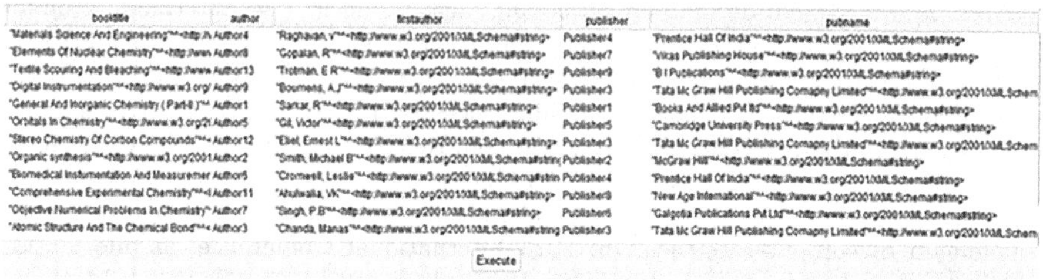

booktitle	author	firstauthor	publisher	pubname
"Materials Science And Engineering"^^<http://t	Author4	"Raghavan, V"^^<http://www.w3.org/2001/XMLSchema#string>	Publisher4	"Prentice Hall Of India"^^<http://www.w3.org/2001/XMLSchema#string>
"Elements Of Nuclear Chemistry"^^<http://www	Author8	"Gopalan, R"^^<http://www.w3.org/2001/XMLSchema#string>	Publisher7	"Vikas Publishing House"^^<http://www.w3.org/2001/XMLSchema#string>
"Textile Scouring And Bleaching"^^<http://www	Author13	"Trotman, E R"^^<http://www.w3.org/2001/XMLSchema#string>	Publisher9	"B I Publications"^^<http://www.w3.org/2001/XMLSchema#string>
"Digital Instrumentation"^^<http://www.w3.org/	Author9	"Boumens, A.J"^^<http://www.w3.org/2001/XMLSchema#string>	Publisher3	"Tata Mc Graw Hill Publishing Comapny Limited"^^<http://www.w3.org/2001/XMLSchem
"General And Inorganic Chemistry (Part-II)"^^	Author1	"Sarkar, R"^^<http://www.w3.org/2001/XMLSchema#string>	Publisher1	"Books And Allied Pvt ltd"^^<http://www.w3.org/2001/XMLSchema#string>
"Orbitals In Chemistry"^^<http://www.w3.org/2(	Author5	"Gil, Victor"^^<http://www.w3.org/2001/XMLSchema#string>	Publisher5	"Cambridge University Press"^^<http://www.w3.org/2001/XMLSchema#string>
"Stereo Chemistry Of Corbon Compounds"^^<	Author12	"Eliel, Ernest L"^^<http://www.w3.org/2001/XMLSchema#string>	Publisher3	"Tata Mc Graw Hill Publishing Comapny Limited"^^<http://www.w3.org/2001/XMLSchem
"Organic synthesis"^^<http://www.w3.org/2001	Author2	"Smith, Michael B"^^<http://www.w3.org/2001/XMLSchema#string	Publisher2	"McGraw Hill"^^<http://www.w3.org/2001/XMLSchema#string>
"Biomedical Instumentation And Measuremer	Author6	"Cromwell, Leslie"^^<http://www.w3.org/2001/XMLSchema#strin	Publisher4	"Prentice Hall Of India"^^<http://www.w3.org/2001/XMLSchema#string>
"Comprehensive Experimental Chemistry"^^<	Author11	"Ahulwalia, VK"^^<http://www.w3.org/2001/XMLSchema#string>	Publisher8	"New Age International"^^<http://www.w3.org/2001/XMLSchema#string>
"Objective Numerical Problems In Chemistry"^	Author7	"Singh, P.B"^^<http://www.w3.org/2001/XMLSchema#string>	Publisher6	"Galgotia Publications Pvt Ltd"^^<http://www.w3.org/2001/XMLSchema#string>
"Atomic Structure And The Chemical Bond"^^<	Author3	"Chanda, Manas"^^<http://www.w3.org/2001/XMLSchema#string	Publisher3	"Tata Mc Graw Hill Publishing Comapny Limited"^^<http://www.w3.org/2001/XMLSchem

Execute

Fig. 9. shows the sample output derived using SPARQL query in protege tool

8 Conclusion and Future Work

The field of information retrieval has seen a lot of development, however, not a single appropriate work has been done so far for efficient subject search for the union catalogue using a semantic approach. Thus, this work proposes that the GujCat's semantic search feature can be implemented using concepts from the semantic web. It is exploratory work; therefore, Initially, the causes of GujCat search issues were investigated, followed by significant experimental work to gain information in this subject. A sample ontology for this domain data has been produced in accordance with the primary recommendation. SPARQL queries of various types have been successfully conducted, demonstrating the inference capacity and ontology capability that can lead to semantic search projects for GujCat. The current GujCat website provides only a traditional keyword search facility. The proposed approach enables semantic-based search using ontology with the help of a DDC scheme which covers the hierarchy of the significant subject most efficiently.

As future work, we will implement the same with the DDC subjects available in GujCat and some necessary improvements in the suggested structure can be implemented to improve the efficiency of the search functionality using some machine learning algorithms.

References

1. GujCat Homepage, https://gujcat.inflibnet.ac.in. Last Accessed 10 Dec 2022
2. Rosalien, R.: Enhancement of subject searching in OPAC using ontology. Revista ESPACIOS **39**(44), (2018)
3. O'Brien, A.: Online catalogs: enhancements and developments. Annual Rev. Inform. Sci. Technol. (ARIST) **2**(5), 219–242 (1994)

4. Drabenstott, K.M., Weller, M.S.: Failure analysis of subject searches in a test of a new design for subject access to online catalogs. J. American Soc Inform. Sci. **47**(7), 519–537 (1996). https://doi.org/10.1002/(SICI)1097-4571(199607)47:7%3C519::AID-ASI5%3E3.0.CO;2-X

5. Aluri, R., Olson, Hope A.: A: Subject analysis in online catalogs, 2nd edn. Libraries Unlimited Inc, (2001)

6. Yee, M.M.: System design and cataloging meet the user: User interfaces to online public access catalogs. J. American Society Inform. Sci. **2**(5), 78–98 (1991). https://doi.org/10.1002/(SICI)1097-4571(199103)42:2⟨78::AID-ASI2⟩3.0.CO;2-2

7. Antell, K., Huang, J.: Subject searching success: transaction logs, patron perception, and implications for library instruction, Reference & User Services Quarterly. American Library Assoc. **48**(1), 68–76 (2008)

8. Ali, S.: An Integrated ontology for classification of research publication in the domain of computer science. In: 2013 International Conference on Information Systems and Computer Networks on Proceedings, pp. 125–128. IEEE, Mathura, India (2013). https://doi.org/10.1109/ICISCON.2013.6524187

9. Dar, A.R., Razza, S.: Building ontology for library management system using dewey decimal classification scheme. J. Comput. Eng. Inform. Technol. **7**(1), 1–8 (2018). https://doi.org/10.4172/2324-9307.1000194

10. Protégé Homepage, http://protege.stanford.edu/. Last Accessed 12 Dec 2022

11. Sridhar, M.S.: Subject searching in the OPAC of a special library: problems and issues. Int. Digital Library Persp. **20**(4), 183–191 (2004). https://doi.org/10.1108/10650750410564691

12. Giunchiglia, F., Zaihrayeu, Ilya., Farazi, F.: Converting Classifications into OWL Ontologies : Retrieved from University of Trento, Department of Information Engineering and Computer Science, Italy (2008)

How People in South America is Facing Monkeypox Outbreak?

Josimar Chire-Saire[1] (ID), Anabel Pineda-Briseño[2]([✉]) (ID),
and Jimy Frank Oblitas[3] (ID)

[1] Institute of Mathematics and Computer Science (ICMC), University of São Paulo
(USP), São Carlos, Brazil
jecs89@usp.br
[2] División de Estudios de Posgrado e Investigación, Tecnológico Nacional de
México/Instituto Tecnológico de Matamoros, H. Matamoros, Tamaulipas, Mexico
anabel.pb@matamoros.tecnm.mx
[3] Facultad de Ingeniería, Universidad Privada del Norte, Trujillo, Peru
jimy.oblitas@upn.edu.pe

Abstract. During the ongoing Covid-19 pandemic, a new outbreak of
Monkeypox was confirmed in the United Kingdom at the beginning of
May of 2022, and from there it has spread throughout the world. Monkeypox is a re-emerging zoonotic disease caused by monkeypox virus.
The first case was detected in monkeys in 1958. Nevertheless, in humans
it was not until 1970 that it had its first manifestation in the Democratic
Republic of the Congo. On the other hand, social media platforms had
proved to be an important source of valuable information. People use this
kind of tools, specifically Twitter, to express their ideas, feelings, opinions, interests, in addition to information related to their both physical
and mental health. Therefore, Twitter is real-time source of public information extremely useful on public health issues. This work presents a
methodology to monitoring epidemiological events. A sentiment analysis
of Twitter users of South America was carry out based in this proposal.
Tweets with Monkeypox-related information for this study were collected
from May 31, 2022 to November 30, 2022. Afterwards, the data was pre-
processed, and from there text mining techniques and machine learning
algorithms were applied to know how people is facing Monkeypox outbreak, a new public health emergency of international concern.

Keywords: Sentiment Analysis · Machine Learning · Text Mining ·
Monkeypox

1 Introduction

Monkeypox (MPOX) is a viral zoonosis, a virus transmitted from animals to
humans [1]. Human monkeypox was first identified in humans in 1970 in the

---

J. Chire-Saire and J. F. Oblitas—These authors contributed equally to this work.

© The Author(s), under exclusive license to Springer Nature Switzerland AG 2023
M. A. Jabbar et al. (Eds.): AMLDA 2022, CCIS 1818, pp. 191–201, 2023.
https://doi.org/10.1007/978-3-031-34222-6_16

Democratic Republic of the Congo, but before in monkeys 1958 [2]. Since early 2022, even during the Covid-19 pandemic, cases of MPOX have been reported from countries where the disease is not endemic, and continue to be reported in several endemic countries [3]. On May 7, 2022 first case of MPOX was confirmed in the United Kingdom [4]. After that, the virus has been spreading rapidly throughout the world. For this reason, on July 23, 2022 the World Health Organization (WHO) declared the highest level of alert [5], so this represents a global health emergency.

On the other hand, social media platforms had proved to be an important source of information on the Internet due the amount of information that is shared by people (citizens and official sources). People use this kind of tools to express their ideas, feelings, opinions, interests, in addition to information related to their both physical and mental health. In this context, social networks represent an attractive source of data that can be exploited to monitor public health [6–8]. Particularly the social network Twitter provides a real-time source of public information that is extremely useful on public health issues, as for example [9–11].

The main contribution of this work is the design of a methodology able to validate the usefulness of monitoring epidemiological events. We performance a sentiment analysis of Twitter users of South America was carry out based in this proposal. With this approach we exploits the potential of Twitter data usefully because we take advantage of the social media users whom share feelings and thoughts every time.

The rest of this paper is structured as follows. Section 2 presents an overview of MPOX global situation overview around the world. In Sect. 3 the methodology employed in this study is described. In Sect. 4 the results of our research are presented. Last, Sect. 5 exposes the conclusions and the future work.

2   Monkeypox Global Situation Overview

Since January 1, 2022, cases of MPOX have been reported to WHO from 110 member countries across 6 regions into which the WHO is divided. The regions are: Region of the Americas, European Region, African Region, Western Pacific Region, Eastern Mediterranean Region, and South-East Asia Region. As of November 30, 2022, a total of 81,608 laboratory confirmed cases worldwide, including 59 deaths, have been reported to WHO. In each country, an outbreak is considered when there is confirmation of a case of MPOX. The MPOX global situation exposed above can be observed in the map shown in the Fig. 1. In early May, 2022 MPOX cases were reported in non-endemic countries such as the UK, Spain, and elsewhere in Europe. The MPOX epidemiological information used in this section was obtained from [12].

Confirmed cases of Monkeypox by country in the World

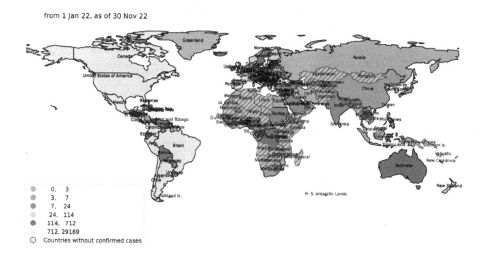

Fig. 1. 2022 Monkeypox Outbreak Global Map.

In the Table 1 you can see the 10 most affected countries globally. Together, these countries account for 85.99% (n = 70,180) of the cases reported globally. It is important to point out that this list is in order to contextualize the general situation of MPOX in the world and does not consider the total population of the countries.

On the other hand, the Fig. 2 shows the number of confirmed cases and deaths monthly from January 1, 2022 to November 30, 2022. It can be seen in the Fig. 2 that the MPOX virus began to increase from May until reaching the peak of infections in July. After that, the cases reported were decreasing month after month. Regarding deaths, the number has gradually increased as the virus spreads, as can be seen in the Fig. 2. It is important to note that due to this behavior, the WHO declared to MPOX an international health emergency on July 23, 2022 [5].

Table 1. The 10 most affected countries globally (MPOX).

#	Flag	Country	Cases - cumulative total (Nov 30)	Deaths - cumulative total (Nov 30)
1		United States of America	29,127	15
2		Brazil	10,007	13
3		Spain	7,408	3
4		France	4,107	0
5		Colombia	3,852	0
6		United Kingdom	3,725	0
7		Germany	3,671	0
8		Peru	3,466	0
9		Mexico	3,361	4
10		Canada	1,456	0

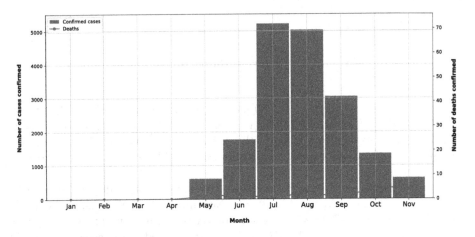

Fig. 2. Map of confirmed cases and deaths of MPXV in the World.

The WHO keeps the level of global risk under constant evaluation. According to reports for November 30, 2022, the WHO maintains the status of the MPOX outbreak as an international public health emergency. This was determined in the third meeting of the International Health Regulations (2005) (IHR) Emergency Committee regarding the multi-country outbreak of MPOX, which was held on Friday, 11 November 2022 [13].

2.1   Monkeypox Spreading in South America

This section introduces the context of MPOX spreading in South America from January 1, 2022 to November 30, 2022. Since the first case of MPOX was diagnosed in Argentina on Jun 03, 2022 [14], around 10,224 cases have been confirmed by Ministers of Health of South America until November 30, 2022. Figure 3 illustrates the distribution of confirmed MPOX cases throughout the South America.

Confirmed cases of Monkeypox by country in South America

from 1 Jan 22, as of 30 Nov 22

Fig. 3. Map of confirmed cases of MPOX in South America.

The Table 2 presents a summary of total confirmed cases and deaths by country in South America. In addition, we have included the total number of inhabitants by country, the date on which the first case was registered and the date on which each country reported the first contagion to the WHO. The datasets used in this section was obtained from [12]. Until November 30, 2022, the total cases confirmed was 10,224, while the total deaths was 5. This represents 12.52% of confirmed cases and 8.47% of deaths globally, respectively.

As can be seen in the Fig. 4 and at the cut-off date, in South America, the country with the highest number of confirmed cases per 100 thousand inhabitants was Peru with 11, the second most affected countries were Chile and Colombia with just 8 cases per every 100,000 people. Countries with 3 or fewer cases per each 100,000 settlers were Bolivia, Argentina, Ecuador, Venezuela, Paraguay and Uruguay.

3   Methodology

This work explores people' opinions on Twitter, regarding the MPOX virus through sentiment analysis using natural language processing (NLP) and machine learning algorithms (ML). Data were processed in and visualized using Python. The methodology is summarized in Fig. 5.

Table 2. Information about Latin American countries, population (thousands).

Flag	Country	Population	Cases (cumulative total)	Deaths (cumulative total)	First Case	First case (reported to WHO)
	Argentina	45,479,000	944	1	May 27 [14]	Jun 03
	Bolivia	11,640,000	257	0	Aug 01 [15]	Aug 03
	Chile	18,187,000	1,311	2	Jun 17 [16]	Jun 18
	Colombia	49,085,000	3,852	0	Jun 23 [17]	Jun 25
	Ecuador	16,905,000	346	2	Jul 06 [18]	Jun 14
	Peru	31,915,000	3,466	0	Jun 26 [19]	Jun 28
	Paraguay	7,192,000	24	0	Aug 25 [20]	Aug 26
	Uruguay	3,388,000	14	0	Jul 29 [21]	Jul 31
	Venezuela	2,020,000	10	0	Jun 12 [22]	Jun 12

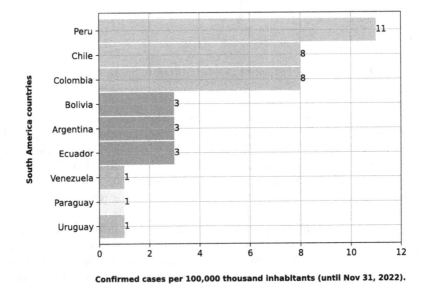

Confirmed cases per 100,000 thousand inhabitants (until Nov 31, 2022).

Fig. 4. 2022 MPOX Confirmed Cases in South America.

3.1 Data Collection

For this work, a total of 33,263 Spanish language tweets were collected between May 31, 2022, and November 30, 2022. The collection was using the Twitter application programming interface (API). The keywords used for collecting the tweets were "viruela" and "viruela del mono". The search was carried out within a radius of 50 km with epicenter the central point of each capital city. The latitudes and longitudes of each central point by country are displayed in the Table 3.

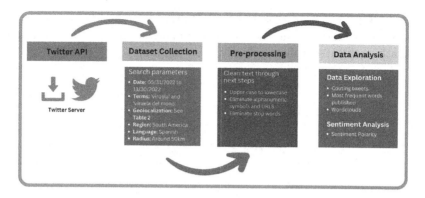

Fig. 5. Methodology proposed for this research.

Table 3. List of search epicenters by country in South America.

	Country Name	Capital Name	Capital Latitude	Capital Longitude
1	Argentina	Buenos Aires	−34.58	−58.67
2	Bolivia	La Paz	−16.50	−68.15
3	Chile	Santiago	−33.45	−70.67
4	Colombia	Bogota	4.60	−74.08
5	Ecuador	Quito	−0.22	−78.50
6	Paraguay	Asuncion	−25.27	−57.67
7	Peru	Lima	−12.05	−77.05
8	Uruguay	Montevideo	−34.85	−56.17
9	Venezuela	Caracas	10.48	−66.87

3.2 Data Pre-processing

This step is important in order to clean or extract from the text, any symbols, which are words that don't add value to the intended analysis from this work. First, the text was converted from uppercase to lowercase letters. Next, punctuation marks such as commas, periods, semicolons, question marks, exclamation marks, among others were eliminated. Also, stop words, retweets, and non-printable characters as emojis were removed. Finally, keywords such as HTTPS, HTTP, URL, to name a few, were eliminated.

3.3 Data Analysis

The processed tweets were counted and analyzed using word frequencies of single terms (unigrams). Then, they were visualized through word clouds to help to measure public opinion. Immediately, a Twitter sentiment analysis based in a Machine Learning approach was realized to determine the polarity of people' opinions. The sentiment analyzer classifies information as either positive or negative. Each tweet is assigned a polarity based on the sentiment level using the criteria in Table 4. The model used is a Multinomial Naive Bayes, which performs really well for text classification [23]. Finally, we present the top 10 terms per month, and the sentiment polarity of each term.

Table 4. Criteria for sentiment level.

Criteria	Sentiment Polarity
Sentiment Level >=0.5	Positive
Sentiment Level <0.5	Negative

4   Results

In this section we are going to present the main findings of this research. In the first part (Sect. 4.1), we will present a data exploration about the publication frequency per month of Twitter users. And in the second part (Sect. 4.2), we are going to show the results of a sentiment analysis polarity about MPOX.

4.1   Data Exploration

In order to trace what was the domain of opinion during the spread of the MPOX virus, the number of tweets and the most frequently appearing terms were obtained. In Fig. 6 the number of Tweets posted per month between May 31, 2022 and November 30, 2022 is shown. As you can see, the number of tweets increased considerably since may until its peak on August. Subsequently, the number of tweets was decreasing the following three months (September, October and November).

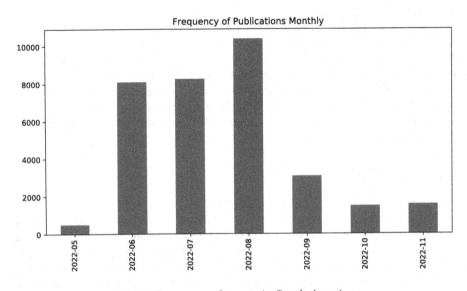

Fig. 6. Frequency of tweets in South America.

To help identify the topics of interest or central topics in the period explored, single word clouds (unigrams) were implemented per month, which are shown in Fig. 7. According to the word clouds, the most popular keywords per month were: "viruelasmallpox", "mono/monkey", "casos/cases", "caso/case", "saludhealth", and "simicaape". As can be seen in Fig. 7, this behavior remains constant during the seven months explored, even when there is variability in the number of tweets published. The main cause of the peak of the number of publications in August was the international health emergency regard MPOX declared by WHO on July 23, 2022 [5].

Fig. 7. The word clouds of the most popular keywords per month in South America.

4.2   Sentiment Analysis Polarity

After a first exploratory data analysis, a sentiment analysis was carried out which aimed to classify the tweets as positive or negative. From the data collected, the 8.27% were positive and 91.73% negative. This performance was consistent throughout the seven months of the disease progresses according to Fig. 8.

5   Conclusions and Future Work

This paper presented a methodology used to validate the usefulness of monitoring epidemiological events through sentiment analysis. With this proposal we were able to identify the peoples' opinions of Twitter users from South America during the first seven months of the propagation of the MPOX virus. The Tweets collected correspond to May 31, 2022 to November 30, 22 period. In a first data exploration, the results reported the disease peak on August, and the most post terms were: "viruela/smallpox", "mono/monkey", "casos/cases",

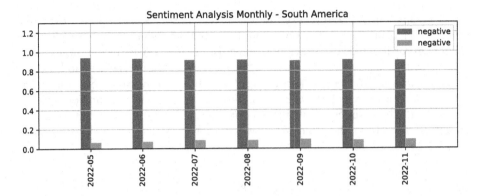

Fig. 8. Sentiment analysis of tweets about MPOX in South America.

"caso/case", "salud/health", and "simica/ape". Additionally, a sentiment analysis was carried out to classify the tweets into positive or negative. The machine learning algorithms classified the tweets as 8.27% positive and 91.73% negative. Along with the previous classification, we employ NLP techniques to determine the top 10 keywords per month and their sentiment polarity. The term "viruela/smallpox", was the most widely used and it was classified as "positive" by machine learning algorithms after the sentiment analysis, and more than 60% of the keywords were classified as negative.

As future work derived from this research, it is intended to expand the field of study to other areas such as education, economy, and mental health. Additionally, a work dedicated exclusively to monitoring the development of MPOX on the US-Mexico border.

Acknowledgments. The authors thank to Research4tech, an Artificial Intelligence (AI) community of Latin American Researcher with the aim of promoting AI, build science communities to catapult and enforce development of Latin American countries supported on science and technology, integrating academic community, technology groups/communities, government and society. This work was sponsored in part by the Tecnologico Nacional de Mexico/Instituto Tecnologico de Matamoros and by the Consejo Nacional de Ciencia y Tecnologia de Mexico (CONACyT).

References

1. WHO: Monkeypox (2022). https://www.who.int/healthtopics/monkeypox#tab=tab_1. Accessed 01 Nov 2022
2. Magnus, P.V., Andersen, E.K., Petersen, K.B., Birch-Andersen, A.: A pox-like disease in cynomolgus monkeys. Acta Pathologica Microbiologica Scandinavica **46**(2), 156–176 (1959)
3. Bunge, E.M., et al.: The changing epidemiology of human monkeypox–a potential threat? a systematic review. PLoS Neglected Trop. Dis. **16**(2), 0010141 (2022)
4. Saxena, S.K., et al.: Re-emerging human monkeypox: a major public-health debacle. J. Med. Virol. **95**, e27902 (2023)

5. WHO: WHO Director-General's Statement at the Press Conference Following IHR Emergency Committee Regarding the Multi-Country Outbreak of Monkeypox–23 July 2022 (2022). https://www.who.int/directorgeneral/speeches/detail/who-director-general-s-statement-on-the-pressconference-following-IHR-emergency-committee-regarding-the-multi-country-outbreak-of-monkeypox-23-july-2022. Accessed 20 Aug 2022

6. Christaki, E.: New technologies in predicting, preventing and controlling emerging infectious diseases. Virulence 6(6), 558–565 (2015)

7. Paul, M.J., et al.: Social media mining for public health monitoring and surveillance. In: Biocomputing 2016: Proceedings of the Pacific Symposium, pp. 468–479. World Scientific (2016)

8. Bodnar, T., Salathé, M.: Validating models for disease detection using twitter. In: Proceedings of the 22nd International Conference on World Wide Web, pp. 699–702 (2013)

9. Ahmed, W., Bath, P.A., Sbaffi, L., Demartini, G.: Moral panic through the lens of twitter: an analysis of infectious disease outbreaks. In: Proceedings of the 9th International Conference on Social Media and Society, pp. 217–221 (2018)

10. Jordan, S.E., Hovet, S.E., Fung, I.C.-H., Liang, H., Fu, K.-W., Tse, Z.T.H.: Using twitter for public health surveillance from monitoring and prediction to public response. Data 4(1), 6 (2019)

11. Sivasankari, S., Kavitha, M., Saranya, G.: Medical analysis and visualisation of diseases using tweet data. Res. J. Pharm. Technol. 10(12), 4306–4312 (2017)

12. Organization., W.H.: Monkeypox Outbreak: Global Trends (2022). https://worldhealthorg.shinyapps.io/mpxglobal. Accessed 30 Sept 2022

13. WHO: Multi-country outbreak of monkeypox, External situation report #9 - 2 November 2022 (2022). https://www.who.int/publications/m/item/multi-country-outbreak-ofmpox-external-situation-report-11-1-december-2022. Accessed 03 Nov 2022

14. CNN: Argentina confirma su primer caso de la viruela del mono (2022). https://cnnespanol.cnn.com/. Accessed 08 Oct 2022

15. PL: Bolivia alerta por primer caso de viruela símica (2022). https://www.prensa-latina.cu. Accessed 08 Oct 2022

16. MINSAL: MINSAL confirma el primer caso de Viruela del Mono en Chile (2022). https://www.minsal.cl/. Accessed 08 Oct 2022

17. MINSALUD: Minsalud e INS confirman tres casos de viruela símica en Colombia (2022). https://www.minsalud.gov.co/. Accessed 08 Oct 2022

18. INFOBAE: Ecuador detecta primer caso de viruela del mono (2022). https://www.infobae.com/. Accessed 08 Oct 2022

19. MINSA: Minsa confirma primer caso de la viruela del mono en el Perú (2022). https://www.gob.pe/. Accessed 08 Oct 2022

20. LaNación: Salud Pública confirma primer caso de viruela símica en Paraguay (2022). https://www.gub.uy/. Accessed 08 Oct 2022

21. MSP: Primer caso importado de viruela símica en Uruguay (2022). https://www.lanacion.com.py/. Accessed 08 Oct 2022

22. BBC: Viruela del mono: detectan el primer caso en Venezuela (2022). https://www.bbc.com/. Accessed 08 Oct 2022

23. Hofman, E.: Senti-py. https://github.com/aylliote/senti-py. Accessed 17 Dec 2022

Multilevel Classification of Satellite Images Using Pretrained AlexNet Architecture

A. Josephine Atchaya, J. Anitha, Asha Gnana Priya, J. Jacinth Poornima, and Jude Hemanth[✉]

Department of ECE, Karunya Institute of Technology and Sciences, Coimbatore, India
judehemanth@karunya.edu

Abstract. Remote Sensing has been a hot topic in recent years. As satellite imagery has improved spatially and spectrally in recent years, its quality has improved as well. Remote Sensing (RS) has been able to provide a lot of information that is easily interpreted. High-tech remote sensing imagery still faces the problem of selecting and combining appropriate features according to their spectral and spatial properties. In this study, the pretrained AlexNet technique is proposed to classify the satellite images. The pretrained deep learning network Alexnet is implemented for enhanced image and the raw data. For the enhancement technique, an Adaptive Median Filter has been used. A deep learning technique based on Adaptive Median Filter can be used to classify satellite images accurately based on the results obtained. AlexNet gives 87.5% accuracy for 8 class classification for enhanced image and AUC value of the enhanced image is 0.8915.

Keywords: Remote Sensing · Deep Learning · Adaptive Median Filter · AlexNet

1 Introduction

The features of larger image patches or sub-images should be analyzed in order to better interpret high-resolution satellite images [1]. Context data should also be taken into account in order to increase their interpretation accuracy [2]. The detail information increases intra class variation within the spectral domain but decreases interclass variation within it, making it more difficult to classify [3]. In light of these two perspectives, more effective spatial spectral features are recommended. Researchers in RS are able to expand their horizons by tackling a number of issues with deep learning [4]. However, operational challenges still remain.

Through the development of valuable and advanced algorithms such as DL, AI played a key role in the fight against COVID-19 [5]. With regards to drug development and diseases associated with drugs, AI is demonstrating a significant improvement [6]. A significant amount of high-quality data is required for Machine Learning algorithms to learn and predict highly accurate results[7]. Hence, it is essential to ensure that the images are well-processed, annotated, and generic when it comes to RS image processing [8]. A deep learning algorithm allows computer systems to learn from data by themselves, also known as deep artificial neural networks [9]. The goal of deep learning (DL) is to directly

© The Author(s), under exclusive license to Springer Nature Switzerland AG 2023
M. A. Jabbar et al. (Eds.): AMLDA 2022, CCIS 1818, pp. 202–209, 2023.
https://doi.org/10.1007/978-3-031-34222-6_17

learn useful representations of features from data using neural networks [10]. The neural network requires some enhancing technique to process the feature extraction [11]. But DL enables machines to identify and extract features from images without the need for features as input and enhancing techniques [12]. Data that has been categorized or labeled previously can also be analyzed with DL to evaluate patterns [12]. Deep learning (DL) techniques offer a solution to this problem and are becoming increasingly important in image processing applications [14]. The learning ability of deep neural networks can be enhanced by unstructured data [15]. The cost of convolutional neural networks (CNNs) is higher than transfer learning because more data is required [16]. The suggested approach uses a deep learning network that has been pretrained in AlexNet [17]. Prior to training on the Remote sensing dataset, all pre-trained models were initialized with the ImageNet database [18]. There are several layers in the architecture, including a convolutional layer, a normalization layer, a ReLU layer, a pooling layer, a fully connected layer, and a SoftMax layer.

In this work the performance has been done by two cases. In first case the classification can be done after enhancing the data [19]. In second case the raw data directly given to classifier and then the performances are calculated. Based on our requirements, the pre-trained architecture can be modified to increase performance. The performances matrices are evaluated by using the UC Merced dataset of size 256×256. The data set has 21 classes, each class having 100 images.

2 Proposed Method

An objective of Remote Sensing (RS) is to obtain information about a place or phenomenon by analyzing the data collected by a remote sensor. Agricultural crops can also be predicted, urbanization increased, weather monitored, floods prevented, and fires controlled using satellite imagery in addition to tracking earth resources and mapping geography. But the quality of the satellite images is affected by some disturbances. Inaccurate picture capture leads to noisy images because pixel values don't accurately represent actual image intensity. There are several types of noise affects the satellite images. So some sort of preprocessing is needed. By applying some enhancement technique it maintains the image quality. Image quality has been enhanced using different filtering techniques. This issue can be solved via spatial filtering. One such type is Adaptive Median Filter (AMF). It gives the better outperformance than other filters. Figure 1 shows the block diagram of proposed method. There are two Performance done in this work. In first case the enhanced image sends to classifier and then the performance analysis can be done. In second case the raw image directly process to the classifier and the performance analysis can be done. Based on this the accuracy can be calculated.

2.1 Filtering

Digital images suffer from degradation due to unwanted entities such as noise, which corrupts valuable information. Images are contaminated by noise caused by in devices, errors in data acquisition, natural phenomena, compression, denoising, and transmission. Images are de-noised to remove noise effects. Images produced by scanners and digital

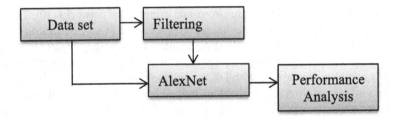

Fig. 1. Block diagram of proposed method

cameras often have image noise, a variation in brightness or color. It is possible that the original image cannot be processed and analyzed in this scenario. The first and most important step in handling an image is to enhance it before processing or analyzing it. When it comes to removing noise from an image, researchers still face challenges due to the fact that the process causes artifacts and blur. In addition to detecting noise, median filters and Gaussian filters cannot distinguish between noise and fine details simultaneously. So we have processed an Adaptive Median Filter (AMF) as an improvement over the standard median filter. This filter is used to identify which pixels have been affected by impulse noise in an image. Spatial processing is performed by the Adaptive Median Filter. We tested the performance with Remote Sensing images (RS). Figure 2 and Fig. 3 shows the output of AMF. The images are corrupted when Salt & Pepper Noise.

(a)   (b)   (c)

Fig. 2. Output of Salt &Pepper noise: (a) Original image: (b) Noisy image: (c) Image after filtering

2.2 AlexNet

A convolutional neural network called AlexNet is credited with being one of the most significant contributions to deep learning, particularly in terms of machine vision. A great deal of power and accuracy can be achieved with AlexNet even on very challenging datasets. AlexNet's performance will be significantly reduced if any of the convolutional layers are removed. Computer vision and artificial intelligence problems can benefit from

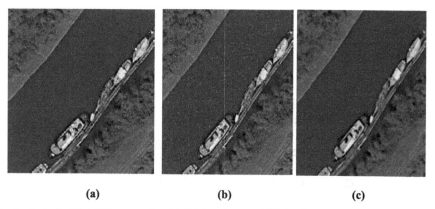

| (a) | (b) | (c) |

Fig. 3. Output of Salt&Pepper noise: (a)Original image: (b)Noisy image: (c)Image after filtering

the use of AlexNet, a leading architecture for object-detection tasks. As image tasks become more complex, AlexNet may replace CNNs more frequently. Natural language processing and medical image analysis have also benefited from AlexNet's deep learning. This is a milestone in making deep learning more widely applicable. Figure 4 illustrates the proposed pretrained ALEXNET architecture.

Steps for AlexNet's implementation.

1. The pre-trained AlexNet architecture has 25 layers. The network's input layer is 227 * 227 * 3 with zero centre normalisation.
2. This architecture consists of two 11 * 11 convolutional layers with stride 2 and zero padding, followed by cross channel normalisation with 5 channels per element and four 3 * 3 grouped convolutions with stride 1 and padding 1.
3. The network's pooling layer is a Maxpooling layer of 3 * 3 kernels with 2 stride and zero padding.
4. Finally, there are three fully connected layers, each with two 4096 channel and one 1000 channel that can be changed depending on the classification layers (8) as required.

2.3 Performance Analysis

Each technique's performance is measured using metrics including classification accuracy (AC), sensitivity (SE), specificity (SP), positive predictive value (PPV), and negative predictive value (NPV). Classification The ratio of correctly categorised photos to all images is how accuracy is measured. The network's capacity for positive result identification is referred to as sensitivity, and its capacity for negative result identification is referred to as specificity. The following are the mathematical formulas for the performance measures.

$$AC = \frac{TP + TN}{TP + TN + FP + FN} \qquad (1)$$

$$SE = \frac{TP}{TP + FN} \qquad (2)$$

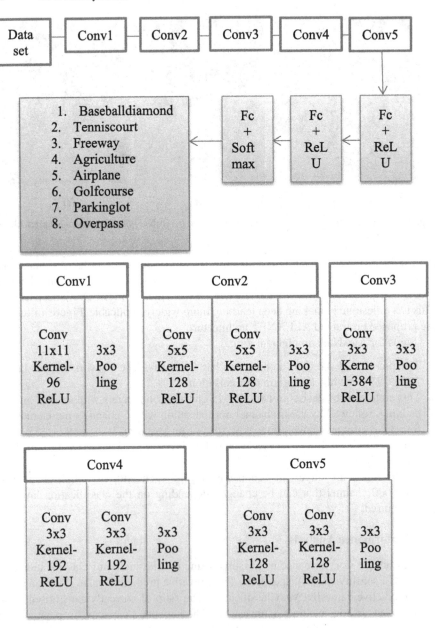

Fig. 4. AlexNet Architecture

$$SP = \frac{TN}{TN + FP} \qquad (3)$$

$$PPV = \frac{TP}{TP + FP} \qquad (4)$$

$$NPV = \frac{TN}{TN + FN} \qquad (5)$$

Performance metrics are calculated utilizing True Positives (TP), True Negatives (TN), False Positives (FP), and False Negatives (FN) values from the aforementioned equations. The amount of photos in each class that were properly and wrongly identified is represented by the TP, TN, FP, and FN numbers. When classifying data at eight levels, these factors are employed. Table 1 lists the deep learning performance metrics.

Table 1. Performance analysis of AlexNet.

Image	AC	SE	SP	PPV	NPV
Normal Image	85.7	84.3	97.9	94.2	92.7
Enhanced Image	87.5	85.6	98.2	96.1	95.2

There is a relationship between the detection rate and the false positive rate on the ROC curve. The accuracy is higher if the values are above the saturation point. Thus, the performance and classification of the model is consider as the best classification model. The ROC curve for the classification of satellite images are given in Fig. 5. The AUC value for the normal image is 0.9184 and for the enhanced image is 0.8915.

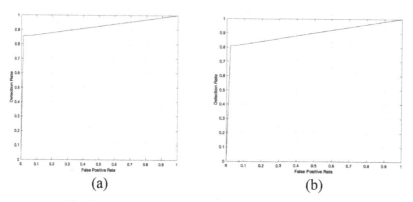

(a)   (b)

Fig. 5. ROC curves: (a)Normal image (b)Enhanced image.

3 Conculsion

Deep learning technique (AlexNet) for remote sensing images are thoroughly explained in this work. The dataset used for this work is UCmerced dataset. The classification has been done in two different ways. After enhancing the image, classification was performed in the first case. A second case involves directly presenting the raw data to the classification process. As part of the enhancement process, an adaptive median filter was utilized. AlexNet's performance is measured in terms of classification accuracy (AC), sensitivity (SE), specificity (SP), and positive predictive value (PPV). Compared with raw data, the enhanced classification method provides better outperformance. In order to reliably categorize satellite images, a deep learning approach based on an adaptive median filter can be used.

Despite this, there are still ways to improve the deep learning technique for satellite images. For example, identifying which preprocessing technique is suitable for high resolution satellite images is not yet provided. It is also a key problem in detecting satellite images. Therefore, suitable enhancement and classification processes for remote-sensing images will be discussed in our future work.

References

1. Cresson, R.: A framework for remote sensing images processing using deep learning techniques. IEEE Geosci. Remote Sens. Lett. **16**, 1–5 (2018). https://doi.org/10.1109/LGRS.2018. 2867949
2. Li, Y., Zhang, H., Xue, X., Jiang, Y., Shen, Q.: Deep learning for remote sensing image classification: a survey. Wiley Interdisc. Rev. Data Mining Knowl. Disc. **8**(6), e1264 (2018). https://doi.org/10.1002/widm.1264
3. Hong, D., et al.: More diverse means better: multimodal deep learning meets remote-sensing imagery classification. IEEE Trans. Geosci. Remote Sens. **59**(5), 4340–4354 (2020)
4. Han, W., Feng, R., Wang, L., Cheng, Y.: A semi-supervised generative framework with deep learning features for high-resolution remote sensing image scene classification. ISPRS J. Photogramm. Remote Sens. **145**, 23–43 (2018). https://doi.org/10.1016/j.isprsjprs.2017. 11.004
5. Tiwari, S., Dogan, O., Jabbar, M.A., Kumar, S.: Applications of machine learning approaches to combat COVID-19 : a survey. Elsevier Inc. (2022)
6. Tiwari, S.M., Akhil, J.: Review of machine learning approach for drug development process (2021). https://doi.org/10.1201/9781003161233-3
7. Al-amri, S.S., Kalyankar, N.V., Khamitkar, S.D.: A comparative study of removal noise from remote sensing image. Int. J. Comput. Sci. **7**(1), 32–36 (2010)
8. Xu, X., Chen, Y., Zhang, J., Chen, Y., Anandhan, P.: A novel approach for scene classification from remote sensing images using deep learning methods. Eur. J. Remote Sens. **54**(sup2), 1–13 (2020). https://doi.org/10.1080/22797254.2020.1790995
9. Hamida, A.B., Benoit, A., Lambert, P., Amar, C.B.: 3-D deep learning approach for remote sensing image classification. IEEE Trans. Geosci. Remote Sens. **56**(8), 4420–4434 (2018). https://doi.org/10.1109/TGRS.2018.2818945
10. Li, F., Feng, R., Han, W., Wang, L.: High-resolution remote sensing image scene classification via key filter bank based on convolutional neural network. IEEE Trans. Geosci. Remote Sens. **58**(11), 8077–8092 (2020). https://doi.org/10.1109/TGRS.2020.2987060
11. Li, J., et al.: Deep discriminative representation learning with attention map for scene classification. Remote Sens. **12**(9), 1366 (2020)
12. Chen, Y., Zhu, L., Ghamisi, P., Jia, X., Li, G., Tang, L.: Hyperspectral images classification with gabor filtering and convolutional neural network. IEEE Geosci. Remote Sens. Lett. **14**(12), 2355–2359 (2017)
13. Wang, X., Shen, S., Ning, C., Huang, F., Gao, H.: Multi-class remote sensing object recognition based on discriminative sparse representation. Appl. Opt. **55**(6), 1381–1394 (2016)

14. Zhao, W., Guo, Z., Yue, J., Zhang, X., Luo, L.: On combining multiscale deep learning features for the classification of hyperspectral remote sensing imagery. Int. J. Remote Sens. **36**(13), 3368–3379 (2015). https://doi.org/10.1080/2150704X.2015.1062157

15. Mohanty, S.P., et al.: Deep learning for understanding satellite imagery: an experimental survey. Front. Artif. Intell. **3**, 1–21 (2020). https://doi.org/10.3389/frai.2020.534696

16. Chaudhuri, B., Demir, B., Chaudhuri, S., Bruzzone, L.: Multilabel remote sensing image retrieval using a semisupervised graph-theoretic method. IEEE Trans. Geosci. Remote Sens. **56**(2), 1144–1158 (2017)

17. Shi, Q., Tang, X., Yang, T., Liu, R., Zhang, L.: Hyperspectral image denoising using a 3-D attention denoising network. IEEE Trans. Geosci. Remote Sens. **59**(12), 10348–10363 (2021). https://doi.org/10.1109/TGRS.2020.3045273

18. Zhong, Y., Han, X., Zhang, L.: Multi-class geospatial object detection based on a position-sensitive balancing framework for high spatial resolution remote sensing imagery. ISPRS J. Photogramm. Remote Sens. **138**, 281–294 (2018). https://doi.org/10.1016/j.isprsjprs.2018.02.014

19. Cao, Y., et al.: Feature extraction of remote sensing images based on bat algorithm and normalized chromatic aberration. IFAC-PapersOnLine **52**(24), 318–323 (2019). https://doi.org/10.1016/j.ifacol.2019.12.429

Handwriting Recognition for Predicting Gender and Handedness Using Deep Learning

Mala Saraswat[1]([✉]) [iD] and Ayushi Agarwal[2]

[1] School of Computer Science Engineering and Technology, Bennett University, Greater Noida, UP, India
malasaraswat@gmail.com
[2] ABES Engineering College, Ghaziabad, UP, India

Abstract. This research focuses on predicting the gender and handedness and also combined prediction through Handwriting Recognition. In this paper we have analyzed various Deep learning approaches using different CNN models. Our proposed approach uses two data sets IAM English dataset and Real-Time dataset that was collected by us for recognizing the handwriting pattern to perform the defined task. Using different Deep learning approaches, experiments were conducted to analyze the performance on the given two datasets for predicting. Gender and handedness. Experiments showed Google Net using CNN is the most efficient for the prediction and recognition with the handwriting samples. For combined prediction the accuracy rate is around 94% with Real-Time dataset and 95% with the IAM dataset.

Keywords: Deep Learning · CNN model · Handwriting Recognition · gender · handedness

1 Introduction

Handwriting recognition in the current scenario is the increasing research field and being explored more now for different experimentation. Research says that the handwriting recognition technique can be used or utilized for predicting and recognizing many different traits and features [1]. In many criminal investigation it is used for maintaining the data for each suspect they have. Their handwriting recognition is performed manually for having the right suspect who has to be punished. But this manually recognition is time consuming and the availability for their experts is also less. So to make the process fast the departments can maintain their own handwriting recognition system as per their requirement so as to have accurate outcomes.

The main focus of this research is predicting the gender, handedness and combination of both the features by using handwriting recognition. For the implementation of the task different types of deep learning models have been used. The models used in this work are CNN, Alex Net, Res Net, Google Net and VGG. The implementation task is performed by utilizing the default models present in the source. Discussing about these networks Alex Net, Res Net, VGG and Google Net are all different types of CNN models [2].

© The Author(s), under exclusive license to Springer Nature Switzerland AG 2023
M. A. Jabbar et al. (Eds.): AMLDA 2022, CCIS 1818, pp. 210–221, 2023.
https://doi.org/10.1007/978-3-031-34222-6_18

Basically all are the upgraded versions of CNN. Each model is better than the other in terms of final result output because of the difference in the number of intermediate layers. Like in case of Alex Net, it is similar to the Le Net. But the difference comes with respect to the filters. The Alex Net has many defined filters in comparison to the Le Net. The Alex Net can categorize a lot more objects precisely and efficiently. Fig. 1 depicts basic layout of Alex Net. Furthermore, it also deals with the over fitting problem by using the dropout option rather than the regularization.

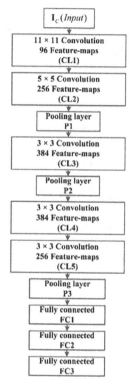

Fig. 1. Basic Layout of Alex Net Architecture.

The Res Net, is inspired by VGG-19 and consists of 34 layers. Thus the deeper concept behind this network is that the deeper layers should not have any kind of training mistake and also enhance the final resultant. But now a days in the implementation with the deep learning concepts the Google Net is most prominently utilized for the work and also being utilized for many computer vision applications which includes the face detection, identification and adversarial training and many more. The Google Net network model is made up of 22 Layers and 27 are for pooling layers which make it very much efficient model among the deep learning models. Figure 2 depicts the intercept module for Google Net Network Model.

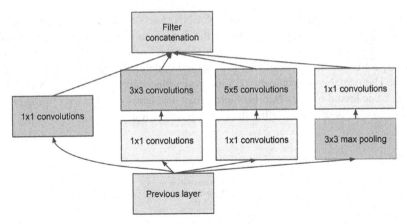

Fig. 2. The Intercept Module for the Google Net Network Model.

While implementing the task with different models along with the machine learning algorithms as well, it was seen that there is huge hike in the percentage of the accuracy rate. Where the maximum efficiency with the machine leaning models is around 75–80% the same prediction rate got increased up to 95% with deep learning models. Thus this has helped in making the dataset good for working on the prediction and recognition task and feature efficient content.

Another among the deep learning models is the VGG network, created with 19 layers deep to replicate and establish the relationship between depth and network representational capability. The small size images readability can be dome efficiently with the help of CNN model. But the stack of 3 x 3 filters, made the readability more efficient and prominent. Thus, makes the algorithm more stable for recognition. Since, the feature extraction is the most important phase in the recognition phase. If the clarity for the feature extraction is good and prominent the result for the final prediction is more promising. The VGG network is promoted in phases with much experimentation. Currently VGG-19 is the best among other VGG nets.

2   Related Work

Much research is performed for the prediction of different handwriting traits. But all have their own challenges, pros and cons and difficulty level. Agarwal et. al, in their they have showcased the difference in the accuracy rate with machine learning and deep learning for the prediction problems through recognition of content form handwriting samples [3, 4].

In the proposed work by Singh et al. [5] there has been an attempt in designing a self-controlled RDP, which is the Ramer-Douglas-Peucker algorithm approach for feature extraction in online handwriting recognition using deep learning. When comes about the related works regarding for the defined task of predicting the gender and handedness by handwriting recognition. It has been observed that there are differences in handwriting of each individual and specific difference among male and female as well as to handedness of either group of people. With respect to the characteristic differences among the handwriting of each gender group each can be predicted.

Deep learning has also been used for Fake news classification. Sharma et. al performed fake news classification by employing user characteristics as well as tweet text to news. It uses XGBoost algorithm and BERT transformer to classify the tweets [6].

Saraswat et. al proposes a convolutional neural network (CNN)-based engineering architecture for age, gender and emotion classification. The model is trained to categorize input images into eight groups of age, two groups of gender and six groups for the emotion [7]. Saraswat et. al employed Deep learning using RNN for genre classification for recommending book [8]. In the previous works, firstly by Bi et al. [9], with the implementation based upon Kernel Mutual Information (KMI) and SVM for predicting gender got 72% successful by using ICDAR English and RDF Chinese datasets, in each dataset. In another work by Ahmed, et al. [10], by using ICDAR and QUWI datasets implementing with ANN, SVM and KNN discriminated gender got successful with 69% with KNN and 70% successful with SVM. Gattal et al. in their work used oriented basic image features (oBIFs) histograms and SVM and 72% successfully predicted gender. Thus in the works of other writers as well where they had used the ML techniques and algorithms got maximum success up to 72% for predicting gender and approximately 89% for handedness. This much of high percent success also depend upon the large set of data as more the data for training and testing more is the accuracy rate [11]. While coming to the works for the defined tasks by Deep learning algorithms and models [12] the accuracy rate got increased up to around 80% for gender prediction and 90% in handedness prediction and combined accuracy was about 83% with IAM English dataset which consists of 115, 320 isolated words from the handwriting samples collected from 657 writers. In the other works with different approaches in research papers by Liwicki et al. [13–15] had reached up to 80.72% maximum accuracy in case of gender prediction and 100% prediction accuracy for handedness by using IAM dataset [16]. In other work Kumar et al. utilize CNN for signature verification [17].

3 Proposed Approach

The methodology followed for the implementation with the deep model is followed. As initially the handwritten data is collected and image is processed for the feature extraction. The feature extraction is important process for the recognition and prediction. Correct image feature extraction is very necessary for the training if the error persists than the content has to be trained again. Then the data is converted into the digital form by managing the data images in 64 X 64 sizes. Although the deep models are not sensitive to the size of the data still maintaining the similar size makes the working to the point and then leading to the prediction of the trait. This can be understood with the help of the flow diagram shown (Fig. 3).

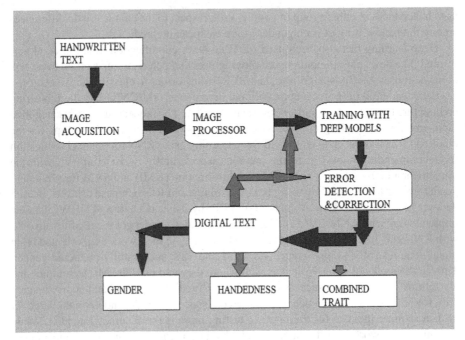

Fig. 3. Process followed for the Deep models implementation.

4   Experiments and Results

This phase of the work comprises of the information regarding the datasets. Since there were two datasets used independently so there content details have been discussed in the further section. Along with this it also cover the method followed for the computation for the prediction. Then in the last phase of this section it covers the results discussion for the accuracy rates calculated from the computation of the content for the prediction of gender, handedness and combined through handwriting recognition

4.1   Datasets

For implementing the proposed approach in this work two datasets viz. IAM- English Dataset and Real-Time Dataset that we collected form college students. For IAM dataset, according to the official information available for this dataset it comprises of around 655 people's handwriting samples which were further partitioned as sentences collection and words collection along with their traits details so as to rectify our implemented prediction results. Here, we could not extract whole dataset due to the limitation of our system but we have successfully achieved around 4899 data samples out which 1000 were female data sample and 3899 male. Out of which only 552 people were left handed in the ratio of 220 female and 332 male left handed people and rest all were right handed data. We have performed training with 3233 data samples and testing with around 900-1000 data in each phase.

In case of Real-Time dataset, we collected the writing samples of 2900 students from ABES Engineering College, Ghaziabad. For collecting and managing the data according to the need it took around 60 days for completing it. Among them 1900 were male gender pupil and 1000 female gender, 2600 right handed and 300 left handed. For male gender prediction training is done with 2900 data and 2000 data for testing. For female gender 2700 data is used for training and 2300 is used for testing. For right handedness 2800 data is used for training and 2420 data is used for testing. For left handedness 980 data is used for training and 300 data is used for testing. For the combined prediction for right-handed male 2690 data is used for training and 1473 data is used for testing. For left handed male 529 data is used for training and 180 used for testing. For right-handed female 2430 data is sued for training and 1155 data is used for training and lastly for left handed female 740 data is sued for training and 280 data is used for testing.

This collection and its peer processes were performed and the samples are managed in image format of 64X64 pixels size. This similarity in the image size is made to make the precision about the input of the data to the model. Following the image processing steps and managing the data took around 45 days so that we can work on our implementation. Simultaneously the IAM data set is implemented to understand and create a comparison among both the datasets from accuracy point of view. And to symbolize that new researches can be performed with the real-time datasets rather than just depending upon the existing data samples. The handwriting samples are scanned using scanner and converted to the image format. Noise is removed for the content having any kind of discrepancy, then the features are extracted for the study. The model is thus trained and tested with 34–66% data. And the validation is been performed with 90% of the whole data. The Jupiter open platform is used for implementing the code with CNN models. In the previous published work of ours we have already worked with the Machine Learning algorithm and basic Deep Learning model that is CNN model. Now since there are many other CNN models are available so there rise a perspective that states there can be changes in the accuracy with other CNN models.

Previous work researchers utilized different datasets such as IAM, KHATT, QUWI, MNIST. In this work we have collected and utilized real time dataset. Few researchers even have used datasets in different languages as well to understand and evaluate the difference in the prediction rate for the traits with different languages. In many cases there were differences in the accuracy rate for prediction of the same trait with same group of people in different language. So we are focusing on research where irrespective of the handwriting language the algorithms should remain good.

4.2 Results

As discussed in previous section, we have used two datasets. This section discusses the result by predicting Gender: Male and Female, Handedness: Right handed and Left Handed and Combined: Right Handed Male (RM), Right handed Female (RF), Left Handed Male (LM), Left handed Female (LF).

4.2.1 IAM Dataset

Table 1 shows the accuracy for Gender Prediction using IAM dataset.

Table 1. Accuracy for **GENDER** Prediction using **IAM DATASET**

LEARNING MODEL USED	ACCURACY FOR GENDER	
	MALE	FEMALE
Machine Learning Algorithms	79%	79%
CNN	82%	86%
Alex Net	89%	92%
Res Net	90%	90%
VGG	94%	93%
Google Net	97%	94%

Here, one can very well understand the difference that the machine learning algorithms have least accuracy and among the deep learning models VGG and Google Net is nearly equally accurate in doing the prediction accurately. With the Google Net the maximum accuracy came out to be the 97%. This is the highest among all the other networks. Table 2 shows the accuracy for Handedness Prediction with IAM dataset.

Table 2. Accuracy for Handedness prediction with IAM DATASET

LEARNING MODEL USED	ACCURACY FOR HANDEDNESS	
	RIGHT HANDED	LEFT HANDED
Machine Learning Algorithms	79%	74%
CNN	83%	80%
Alex Net	92%	89%
Res Net	93%	93%
VGG	94%	93.45%
Google Net	95%	94.72%

Similarly, here for the handedness prediction the accuracy rate is high in comparison to the gender prediction. But here in this case the same variation could be seen that the machine learning has least rate of accuracy. Whereas when comes to the CNN model, it is moderate in both the cases with gender as well as with the handedness. Here, Google net again gained the maximum accuracy rate. The difference in the filters, networks middle layers and the pooling layers, it has made this network the most efficient of all.

4.2.2 Real Time Dataset

Table 3 depicts the performance for Gender Prediction with Real-time dataset.

Table 3. Accuracy Table for Gender Prediction using **REAL-TIME DATASET**

LEARNING MODEL USED	ACCURACY FOR GENDER	
	MALE	FEMALE
Machine Learning Algorithms	75%	79%
CNN	87%	85%
Alex Net	90%	90%
Res Net	95%	95%
VGG	96%	95.67%
Google Net	95.64%	95.32%

The results from the previous section are form the IAM dataset where the maximum accuracy for the gender prediction came out to be 97% for the gender and for handedness the maximum is 95% approximately. Here with the real time database an effort has been made to match with this much of accuracy rate for the predefined dataset. So here with the gender it was around 95% accurate. Table 4 shows the accuracy Handedness Prediction with IAM dataset.

Table 4. Performance for Handedness Prediction using Real Time Dataset

LEARNING MODEL USED	ACCURACY FOR HANDEDNESS	
	RIGHT HANDED	LEFT HANDED
Machine Learning Algorithms	72%	75%
CNN	79%	76%
Alex Net	85%	89%
Res Net	89%	89%
VGG	90%	90%
Google Net	92%	90%

When the rate of accuracy comes to the handedness was around 92%. This can be seen that the accuracy rate is quite close with the IAM dataset. Thus this also shows that not only the predefined and official datasets can be used for performing the prediction through recognition but a real time collected data can also perform well. This type of technique of working also gives good exposure to the image processing and handwriting recognition phases.

4.2.3 Combined Prediction

In this phase of work, it is summarized data of the observation with combined prediction for both the datasets. Here, both gender and handedness are predicted in combination.

For this the attributes are segregated as four characters namely, RM that is right handed male. For doing the training of this particular category the data was available with us in good quantity, next comes the LM that is left handed male, RF that is right handed female and LF that is left handed female. While working for creating the real-time dataset it was observed that the right handed data is easily available, while struggle comes when comes to the left handed data collection. Still we managed and collected good amount of left handed handwriting sample for training and testing.

For the IAM dataset the data is already available to us in different folders according to their prediction of trait. So, we do not have to struggle for segregating the data according to the feature for which we were doing implementation. Although according to the official information for the IAM dataset, it is available in different languages but here in this work we have focused precisely on English dataset. Table 5 shows the Combined Prediction by IAM dataset and Fig. 5 depicts the accuracy graphically for IAM dataset using machine learning and different CNN models

Table 5. Combined Prediction using **IAM DATASET.**

MODEL USED	COMBINED PREDICTION			
	RM	RF	LM	LF
Machine Learning Algorithms	72%	69%	72%	67%
CNN	80%	84%	81.23%	80%
Alex Net	85%	84.56%	85%	84.34%
Res Net	90%	89.51%	90.32%	90%
VGG	94%	93.56%	94%	93.23%
Google Net	95%	94.68%	95.34%	95%

Here, the average accuracy for the combined prediction with the IAM dataset is around 95%. Here, for the combined prediction as described above the features are segregated as four feature traits. The left handed people are less in comparison with the right handed people so to work with left handed data is little tricky. Thus for making the left handed content equally efficient with the right handed the complete data is introduced with the online data augmentation. The data augmentation is a technique of replicating the same content with different combinations of the data. With this technique involvement the accuracy rates were computed accordingly. Here the VGG net and the Google Net were equally efficient. Table 6 shows the Combined Prediction by Real Time dataset and Fig 6 depicts accuracy graphically (Fig. 4).

It can be observed from the results that the accuracy rate with the Google Net is the maximum in each case. And VGG network is also nearly equally efficient. Thus, for prediction and recognition task with the deep learning models the VGG network and the Google Net is most efficient. And among both the Google Net is the most efficient. For combined prediction the accuracy rate is around 94% with Real-Time dataset and 95% with the IAM dataset.

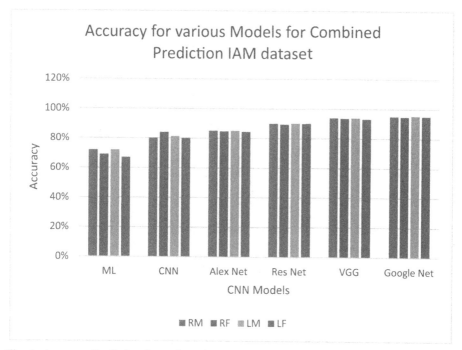

Fig. 4. Accuracy Prediction for various CNN models for Combined Gender and Handedness Prediction using IAM dataset

Table 6. Combined Prediction using Real Time Dataset.

MODEL USED	COMBINED PREDICTION			
	RM	RF	LM	LF
Machine Learning Algorithms	69%	65%	70%	67%
CNN	80%	82.96%	80%	80%
Alex Net	82.56%	83.16%	83%	84%
Res Net	90%	88.50%	90%	88%
VGG	93.46%	93%	92%	92%
Google Net	93.89%	93.68%	92.34%	90%

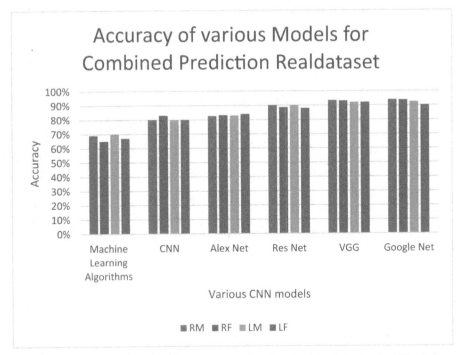

Fig. 5. Accuracy Prediction for various CNN models for Combined Gender and Handedness Prediction using Real Time dataset.

5   Conclusion

From the experiments, we conclude that the Google Net is most efficient for the prediction and recognition with the handwriting samples. But in comparison to the machine learning models for algorithms like the SVM, KNN, Random Forest, Naïve Bayes and many other supervised learning algorithms the CNN models are more efficient. Even the basic CNN model gives around 10% more efficient results. The real-time dataset came out to be nearly efficient for these algorithms.

Future work can be done for the predicting the same trait such as gender or handedness for same group of people but with their different handwriting sample that means same person with two or more handwriting pattern in different languages. This would make the algorithms more efficient.

The application of our research is that it can help in understanding the basic mood and traits for the different gender people. There is other future work possible where we can work for finding the gender and handedness and combined trait, with comparing the different language handwriting patterns for the same group of people, so as to imbibe an embedded algorithm model that would be suitable for any language type of handwriting pattern and predict the correct desired trait. There is also other gender in our society. Their handwriting patterns can also be collected to understand their handwriting pattern so that all the gender category that is present in the present scenario will be considered for the research perspective and not only two basic genders.

References

1. Wang, Y., Xiao, W., Li, S.: Offline handwritten text recognition using deep learning: a review. J. Phys. Conf. Ser. **1848**(1), 012015 (2021). IOP Publishing
2. Sankara Babu, B., Nalajala, S., Sarada, K., Muniraju Naidu, V., Yamsani, N., Saikumar, K.: Machine learning based online handwritten telugu letters recognition for different domains. In: Kumar, P., Obaid, A.J., Cengiz, K., Khanna, A., Balas, V.E. (eds.) A Fusion of Artificial Intelligence and Internet of Things for Emerging Cyber Systems. ISRL, vol. 210, pp. 227–241. Springer, Cham (2022). https://doi.org/10.1007/978-3-030-76653-5_12
3. Agarwal, A., Saraswat, M., Arora, A.: Leveraging handwriting for gender and handedness prediction using various machine learning approaches. NeuroQuantology **20**(7), 461–469 (2022). https://doi.org/10.14704/nq.2022.20.7.NQ33060
4. Agarwal, A., Saraswat, M.: Analyzing Handwriting for Gender, Handedness and Combined Prediction using Machine Learning Algorithms. In: 13th International Conference on Advances in Computing, Control, and Telecommunication Technologies, ACT 2022. vol. 8, pp. 966–972 (2022)
5. Singh, S., Chauhan, V.K., Smith, E.H.B.: A self controlled RDP approach for feature extraction in online handwriting recognition using deep learning. Appl. Intell. **50**(7), 2093–2104 (2020). https://doi.org/10.1007/s10489-020-01632-4
6. Sharma, S., Saraswat, M., Dubey, A.K.: Fake news detection using deep learning. In: Villazón-Terrazas, B., Ortiz-Rodríguez, F., Tiwari, S., Goyal, A., Jabbar, M.A. (eds.) KGSWC 2021. CCIS, vol. 1459, pp. 249–259. Springer, Cham (2021). https://doi.org/10.1007/978-3-030-91305-2_19
7. Saraswat, M., Gupta, P., Yadav, R.P., Yadav, R., Sonkar, S.: Age, Gender and emotion estimation using deep learning. In: Saraswat, M., Harish Sharma, K., Balachandran, J.H., Kim, J.C., Bansal, (eds.) Congress on Intelligent Systems: Proceedings of CIS 2021, Volume 2, pp. 59–70. Springer Nature Singapore, Singapore (2022). https://doi.org/10.1007/978-981-16-9113-3_6
8. Saraswat, M.: Leveraging genre classification with RNN for Book recommendation. Int. J. Inf. Technol. 1–6 (2022)
9. Bi, N., Suen, C.Y., Nobile, N., Tan, J.: A multi-feature selection approach for gender identification of handwriting based on kernel mutual information. Pattern Recogn. Lett. **121**, 123–132 (2019)
10. Ahmed, M., Rasool, A.G., Afzal, H., Siddiqi, I.: Improving handwriting based gender classification using ensemble classifiers. Expert Syst. Appl. **85**, 158–168 (2017)
11. Gattal, A., Djeddi, C., Siddiqi, I., Chibani, Y.: Gender classification from offline multi-script handwriting images using oriented basic image features (oBIFs). Expert Syst. Appl. **99**, 155–167 (2018)
12. Siddiqi, I., Djeddi, C., Raza, A., Souici-meslati, L.: Automatic analysis of handwriting for gender classification. Pattern Anal. Appl. **18**(4), 887–899 (2014). https://doi.org/10.1007/s10044-014-0371-0
13. Liwicki, M., Schlapbach, A., Loretan, P., Bunke, H.: Automatic detection of gender and handedness from on- line handwriting. J. Soc. Psychol. 179–18 (2007)
14. Liwicki, M., Schlapbach, A., Bunke, H.: Automatic gender detection using on-line and off-line information. PAA. Pattern Anal. Appl. **14**(1), 87–92 (2011)
15. Liwicki, M., Schlapbach, A., Loretan, P., Bunke, H.: Automatic detection of gender and handedness from online Handwriting. In: Proceedings of the 13th Conference of the International Graphonomics Society (2007)
16. IAM Homepage. http://www.fki.inf.unibe.ch/databases/iamon-line-handwriting-database
17. Kumar, R., et al.: Deformation adjustment with single real signature image for biometric verification using CNN. Comput. Intell. Neurosci. **2022**, 4406101 (2022)

Retrieval of Weighted Lexicons Based on Supervised Learning Method

Asdrúbal López-Chau[1]([✉]) [iD], Rafael Rojas-Hernández[1] [iD], David Valle-Cruz[2] [iD], and Valentin Trujillo-Mora[1] [iD]

[1] Laboratorio de Investigación en Ingeniería y Ciencias Aplicadas, CU UAEM Zumpango, Universidad Autónoma del Estado de México, 55600, Zumpango Estado de México, México
alchau@uaemex.mx
[2] Unidad Académica Profesional Tianguistenco, Universidad Autónoma del Estado de México, 52640 Santiago Tianguistenco, Mexico

Abstract. Lexicons are a lexical resource that has been used successfully in sentiment analysis and other areas of natural language processing. Although there are several unweighted lexicons and weighted lexicons, they all achieve poor performance in many applications. This is because they are created in general contexts, and adding more terms to an existing lexicon is complicated. Furthermore, current methods for generating weighted lexicons are complex and not very intuitive. In this article, we show the results of a method to generate weighted lexicons from a tagged corpus. The terms that make up the lexicon, as well as the corresponding weights, are obtained by means of a distance measure that is closely related to the probability that a document belongs to its label. The preliminary results obtained with a corpus of 405 documents show that the method reaches an accuracy of 92.3%.

Keywords: Lexicon · Weighted lexicon · NLP

1 Introduction

Lexicons are one of the simplest resources to use for sentiment analysis and have been widely used to understand different types of phenomena. Some examples are the analysis of voter sentiment in political campaigns, the understanding of customer preferences and tastes, the segmentation of profiles in marketing and the understanding of financial sentiment in the stock [2,9,10].

In addition to the lexicon-based approach, the polarity of a text can be identified with machine learning or deep learning methods. This polarity can represent two completely different values, such as positive or negative, big or small, acceptance or rejection. It is necessary to have labeled data, vectorize documents, and adjust models, among other intermediate steps; in contrast, basic sentiment analysis with lexicons just requires identifying the polarities of the words in the text by matching the list of words in the lexicon. The main

M. A. Jabbar et al. (Eds.): AMLDA 2022, CCIS 1818, pp. 222–230, 2023.
https://doi.org/10.1007/978-3-031-34222-6_19

advantage of a lexicon based approach for sentiment analysis is that neither labeled data nor the fitting of predictive models are required.

Some lexicons are just lists of words (NWL, Non Weighted Lexicons) grouped into categories, like positive or negative; while other lexicons are weighted (WL, Weighted Lexicons), i.e., each word has also a number associated, which indicates the intensity of sentiment or polarity. Some examples of the former type of lexicons are Bin Liu [4] and Sentiment140 [3]; whereas examples of WLs are SentiWordNet [1], WordNet [7], AFINN [8] and VADER [5].

Although there are WLs whose weights were assigned manually, this way of building lexicons is a slow process and not very scalable. On the other hand, creating WLs automatically has a broader field of application, and the process can be easily scaled.

There are currently several approaches to create WL. One of these approaches is to map each word of a corpus onto a vector space. This is usually done with a method that produces non-sparse representations, such as word2vect. Next, a group of seed words (whose polarities/weights are known) are mapped onto that space, afterwards, clusters of words are identified. Then, using the known weights of elements in the word set, the weights of words in clusters are assigned. Other approach to create WL is to train a committee of predictive models (classifiers) with data labeled or partially labeled. Finally, the scores are assigned considering a voting scheme.

As can be seen, the construction of WLs based on classifier training has the potential to adapt to the detection of polarities in different types of text, but it can be challenging in terms of precision and performance. For this reason, this paper presents the results of a method to create WL using a supervised learning method. Our method is based on the following observations:

- Words that are used frequently in similar contexts tend to have a similar meaning. This abstract idea comes from the semantic theory of language usage.
- In many disciplines, simple models are preferable than complex ones. It is well know in machine learning that the complexity of a model is related with the form of the decision boundary in the input space, simplest decision boundaries are linear. We choose the Logistic regression classifier as prediction model with linear decision boundary. Other choice, very used in sentiments analysis, can be Linear Support Vector Machine.

The document is divided into 6 sections, including the introduction. The Sect. 2 presents the related work on lexicon design. The Sect. 3 presents the preliminary terminology to understand the construction of the automatic lexicon. The Sect. 4 presents the methods. The fifth section shows the experiments and results. The Sect. 5 is the conclusions of the study.

2   Preliminaries

2.1   POS Tagging

In many languages, three of the most important parts in a sentence are nouns, verbs and adjectives. Therefore, our method takes into account this to create the weighted lexicon.

In natural language processing, Part-Of-Speech tagging is the process of identifying and labeling each word in a text as noun, pronoun, verb, adjective, etc. In this paper, we use the library Spacy, that performs POS Tagging on a given text. Spacy refers these parts of the speech as NOUN, VERB and ADJ, respectively.

2.2   Logistic Regression

Suppose we have a training set X_{tr} that is a subset of X, whose structure is show in Eq. (1):

$$X = \left\{ (x_i, y_i) : x_i \in \mathbf{R}^d, y_i \in \{0, 1\}, i = 1, ..., N \right\} \tag{1}$$

where the tuple (x_i, y_i) is the i-th instance and its corresponding label, d is the number of dimensions or attributes, and N is the cardinality of X.

Logistic regression is a linear classification method that models the probability that the class y_i of an instance x_i belongs to certain category. Logistic function, shown in Eq. (2), models this probability.

$$p(x_i) = \frac{e^{\beta_0 + \beta^T x_i}}{1 + e^{\beta_0 + \beta^T x_i}} \tag{2}$$

with $\beta_0 \in \mathbf{R}$ and $\beta \in \mathbf{R}^p$ are the coefficients or parameters of the model. Parameter β_0 is called the intercept.

Maximum likelihood method is used to fit coefficients of logistic function for a given X_{tr}. This can be achieved by minimizing the following cost function:

$$\mathcal{L}(\beta) = \sum_{i=1}^{N} y_i ln(p(x_i)) + (1 - y_i) ln(1 - p(x_i)) + \frac{\lambda}{2} \beta^T \beta$$

This optimization problem is usually solved with Newton conjugate gradient or quasi-Newton methods. Modern libraries use methods as Broyden-Fletcher-Goldfarb-Shanno (BFGS), gradient methods (SAGA) or Liblinear packages.

2.3   Distance from a Point to a Linear Decision Boundary

Let be $\beta_0 + \beta^T x$ the equation of a hyperplane in a d-dimensional space, where $\beta_0 \in \mathbb{R}$, $\beta \in \mathbb{R}^d$ are the coefficients; and $x \in \mathbb{R}^d$. The shortest *distance* from a point v to the hyperplane can be computed as shown below, in Eq. 3:

$$distance = \frac{\beta^T v + \beta_0}{\beta^T \beta} \tag{3}$$

If a hyperplane corresponds to the decision boundary of a prediction model, then the distance between a correctly classified object and the hyperplane can be interpreted as a relationship with the probability (or degree of membership) that such an object belongs to the predicted class. The greater the distance, the greater the probability that the object belongs to the class. Figure 1) shows this graphically. The object_1 has greater probability of belonging to Class_1 than object_2, because distance_1 ¿ distance_2.

We will explain the method to create a weighted lexicon below.

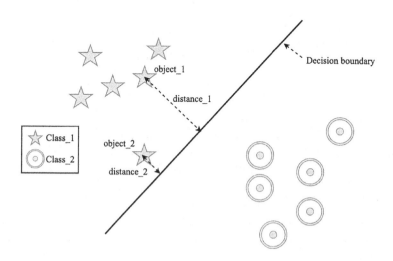

Fig. 1. Distance from point to decision boundary

3 Method

Let $C = \{(d_i, y_i), i = 1, ..., N\}$ bet a corpus with N documents. Each document d_i has been tagged with a label y_i. Also, let $h(d_i)$ be a prediction model (classifier) that has an acceptable performance; $h(d_i)$ correctly predicts $M \leq N$ documents in C. Furthermore, suppose the M documents obey the distributional hypothesis, then these words appear frequently and have similar meanings [ref].

The reasoning of the proposed method is that if the above assumptions hold, and taking into account that the absolute distances from each document to the linear decision boundary are associated with the probability that the class of document is the predicted class, then the words in a document also follow a similar relationship with the class.

In our approach, we use the class of document as the sentiment (for example, positive or negative) and the distances are used as an indicator of the polarity, i.e., to compute the weight of words.

The details of the method are described below:

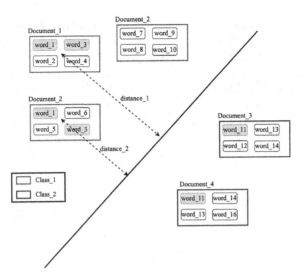

Fig. 2. Linear decision boundary classifies five documents: Document_1, Document_2 and Document_3 are all of the same category (class_1); whereas Document_3 and Document_4 belong to the opposite category (class_2). The words word_1 and word_3 are used in Document_1 and Document_2. The word word_11 is used in Document_3 and Document_4.

1. **Data preprocessing.** In this stage, characters other than letters and spaces are eliminated, accented vowels are exchanged for the corresponding unaccented vowels, all letters are converted to lowercase. Stop words are also removed.
2. **Vectorization of documents.** A process to represent documents as vectors is applied to TF-IDF is used to vectorize the documents. Each document is represented by a high dimensional sparse vector.
3. **Model generation.** A linear decision boundary classification method is used to classify the vectorized documents. The classifier parameters are adjusted to obtain the best performance using cross validation.
4. **Identify correctly classified documents.** Retain those documents correctly classified, and get rid of those that are not.
5. **Identify the words** that are only used in documents belonging to certain class but that are not used in the documents of the other classes. Repeat this for each one of the classes.
6. **Apply POS-tagging** to identify words that are NOUN, VERB or ADJECTIVE.
7. **Compute the distance** of each correctly classified document to the linear decision boundary.
8. For each word identified as NOUN, VERB or ADJECTIVE, **calculate the average of the distances** of the documents that contain that word.
9. Consider **words that are frequently used in documents.**

To exemplify the method, Fig. 2, shows five documents that are correctly classified by a linear classifier.

4   Experimentation and Results

We tested the method explained in the previous section using the data set "Paper Reviews" [6]. This contains 405 scientific paper reviews, that correspond to submissions to an international conference on computing and informatics. Each review has a preliminary decision, i.e., the preliminary decision of acceptance or rejection of a paper taken by the conference committee. There are 257 accepted papers, and 122 rejected papers.

The vectorization of documents thought IF-DTF produces a sparse matrix, with 6183 columns. This number represents the total of different words used in the corpus. That matrix is used to fit a Logistic Regression classifier.

Table 1 shows the performance achieve by the Logistic Regression classifier on the whole data set.

Table 1. Performance of classifier

Class	Precision	Recall	f1-score
accept	0.92	0.95	0.94
reject	0.89	0.83	0.86

Due to accuracy of the classifier is not perfect (i.e., it is lower than 1.0), only the documents correctly classified are retrieved: 242 accepted and 91 papers rejected.

The number of words exclusively used in the accepted papers is 2998. The number of words exclusively used in the rejected papers is 1136. The type of these words is verb, noun, adjective, or other. We focus only on adjectives, nouns and verbs, a summary is shown in Table 2.

Table 2. Type and number of words per class

Class	Adjetive	Noun	Verb
accept	712	880	789
reject	310	307	349

Some of the terms shown in Table 2 are used only in one document, i.e., these words are not considered frequent. We chose the words that are used at least in three documents. Figures 3 and 4 show a graphical representation of the lexicon found. The size of the word corresponds with its weight. Table 3 shows the number of words of each type in the lexicon.

Table 4 shows an example of the obtained results, it shows a subset of the weighted words that are adjectives.

Fig. 3. Wordcloud of Lexicon for class reject: Adjectives, Nouns and Verbs.

Fig. 4. Wordcloud of Lexicon for class accept: Adjectives, Nouns and Verbs.

Table 3. Size of weighted lexicon

Class	Adjetive	Noun	Verb
accept	121	185	153
reject	27	44	37

4.1   Evaluating the Weighted Lexicon

Currently, there are few studies on metrics to evaluate the quality of a weighted lexicon. The classification accuracy is the most commonly metric used as the performance evaluation. This is computed by performing the classification task with a lexicon on a labeled data set.

For our case, the classes are "accepted" and "rejected". To determine the class of a document, it is necessary to assign to each word w_i in the document D_j, its corresponding weight, according to the lexicon and class. Therefore, a document has associated two scores, one for the class "accept" and other for the class "reject". Equations (4) and (5) show how to compute these scores.

$$rejected\_w\_j = \sum_{w_i \in D_j} weight\_term(w_i) \qquad (4)$$

$$accepted\_w\_j = \sum_{w_i \in D_j} weight\_term(w_i) \qquad (5)$$

The prediction is computed considering the greatest score, this is shown in equation (6).

$$prediction = \begin{cases} accept & \text{if } accepted\_w\_j > rejected\_w\_j \\ reject, & \text{otherwise} \end{cases} \qquad (6)$$

The classification accuracy achieved with this lexicon for the data set is 92.34%.

Reviewing the terms that make up the lexicon found, it is observed that some of these terms correspond to the same word in plural, singular, masculine, feminine, and that some verbs are repeated, but in different tenses (future, past or present). Therefore, it is necessary to perform a deeper processing of the data. Although it might seem that this can be solved using a stemming algorithm, a large number of the corpus documents are written in Spanish. When carrying out preliminary tests, it was found that applying the Snow Ball algorithm for stemming, the accuracy is significantly degraded.

Table 4. Fragment of the lexicon generated for the class accept

Type	term	weight	Frequency
ADJ	st	2.41192564	215
ADJ	puesta	0.583409861	63
ADJ	not	0.476257609	25
ADJ	ast	0.388487729	27
ADJ	fico	0.356428181	45
ADJ	table	0.306731739	27
ADJ	adecua	0.226343251	24
ADJ	grafico	0.206070716	24
ADJ	relevant	0.202129201	23
ADJ	comput	0.195437364	19
ADJ	grafica	0.191855849	23
ADJ	low	0.190412804	8
ADJ	mental	0.172052728	12
ADJ	more	0.168628721	7
ADJ	segund	0.149278718	17
ADJ	estable	0.127274299	17
ADJ	rico	0.114880231	16
ADJ	research	0.112514203	5
ADJ	roto	0.112210131	12

5   Conclusions

This research presents results of experiments with an automatic lexicon to determine if an article can be accepted or rejected, based on the type, number, and size of adjectives, pronouns, and verbs it contains. Although it is not intended to replace experts when ruling or reviewing this type of document, the three elements mentioned (adjectives, pronouns and verbs) can be useful to approximate the prediction of the scientific review results. The findings obtained are promising and motivate us to continue carrying out experiments with other machine learning techniques applied to different areas of knowledge.

As future works, it is required to use lexical resources to identify misspelled words; verb conjugations that correspond to the same verb; plural, singular forms of Spanish words; and gender variants of the terms (masculine and feminine). Work is currently underway to expand the corpus in order to generate a lexicon that can be used in a general way, and not only in a specific context such as the one shown in this paper.

References

1. Baccianella, S., Esuli, A., Sebastiani, F.: SentiWordNet 3.0: an enhanced lexical resource for sentiment analysis and opinion mining. In: Proceedings of the Seventh International Conference on Language Resources and Evaluation (LREC 2010). European Language Resources Association (ELRA), Valletta, Malta (2010). http://www.lrec-conf.org/proceedings/lrec2010/pdf/769_Paper.pdf

2. Cambria, E., Li, Y., Xing, F.Z., Poria, S., Kwok, K.: Senticnet 6: ensemble application of symbolic and subsymbolic AI for sentiment analysis. In: Proceedings of the 29th ACM International Conference on Information & Knowledge Management, pp. 105–114 (2020)

3. Go, A., Bhayani, R., Huang, L.: Twitter sentiment classification using distant supervision. Processing **150** (2009)

4. Hu, M., Liu, B.: Mining and summarizing customer reviews. In: Proceedings of KDD 2004, the ACM SIGKDD International Conference on Knowledge Discovery and Data Mining, pp. 168–177. ACM Press (2004). https://www.microsoft.com/en-us/research/publication/mining-and-summarizing-customer-reviews/

5. Hutto, C., Gilbert, E.: Vader: a parsimonious rule-based model for sentiment analysis of social media text (2015)

6. Keith, B., Fuentes, E., Meneses, C.: A hybrid approach for sentiment analysis applied to paper reviews (2017). https://archive.ics.uci.edu/ml/datasets/Paper+Reviews

7. Miller, G.A.: Wordnet: a lexical database for English. Commun. ACM **38**(11), 39–41 (1995). https://doi.org/10.1145/219717.219748

8. Äruprup Nielsen, F.: A new anew: evaluation of a word list for sentiment analysis in microblogs. CoRR abs/1103.2903 (2011). http://arxiv.org/abs/1103.2903

9. Valle-Cruz, D., Fernandez-Cortez, V., López-Chau, A., Sandoval-Almazán, R.: Does twitter affect stock market decisions? financial sentiment analysis during pandemics: a comparative study of the h1n1 and the covid-19 periods. Cogn. Comput. **14**(1), 372–387 (2022)

10. Valle-Cruz, D., Lopez-Chau, A., Sandoval-Almazan, R.: How much do twitter posts affect voters? analysis of the multi-emotional charge with affective computing in political campaigns. In: DG. O2021: The 22nd Annual International Conference on Digital Government Research, pp. 1–14 (2021)

Performance Evaluation of Smart Flower Optimization Algorithm Over Industrial Non-convex Constrained Optimization Problems

Akhilesh Kumar Singh and Shikha Mehta[(✉)]

Computer Science Engineering and Information Technology, Jaypee Institute of Information Technology, Noida, India
shikhamehta301277@gmail.com

Abstract. The large number of dimensions, complexity and constraints of real world problems is the deriving force to assess the algorithms in diverse applications scenarios. Over a past decade, nature inspired algorithm are seen as potential solutions to solve continuous optimization problems. These are non-deterministic algorithms with proven abilities to find near optimal solutions. However, according to not a single free lunch theorem, nor an any algorithm is suitable for solving all kinds of problems. This work present performance evaluation of recent metaheuristic algorithm that is Sun Flower Optimization Algorithm (SFOA) over Non-Convex Constrained Optimization problems industrial problems from domains like mechanical engineering, chemical processes and Process synthesis and design problems. SFOA is compared with IUDE, MAgES, iLSHADE 424 for 15 problems with varied number of equality and inequality constraints. Results reveal that SFOA performs better for two out of four industrial chemical problems and five out of six process design and synthesis problems. Problems by mechanical engineering, IUDE, MAgES, iLSHADE 424 outperform SFOA for 4 out of five problems.

Keywords: Smart Flower Optimization Algorithm · industrial optimization problems · mechanical engineering problems · process synthesis and design problems · chemical engineering problems · metaheuristic algorithm

1 Introduction

Over the period of past few decades, technological revolutions have lead to the emergence of new problems with huge number dimensions, inherent complexity with equality and inequality constraints in engineering and allied domains. These problems are modeled mathematical optimization problems that are used or access to find out the decision variables to minimize or maximize the objective function significance even though sustaining the constraints of valuable decision space. From the above concept, mobile robot's navigation, satellite observation planning, communication applications, image processing applications, data mining problem, IIR filter design, big data, transformer fault diagnosis, power system economics and security, path planning, renewable energy, cyber

M. A. Jabbar et al. (Eds.): AMLDA 2022, CCIS 1818, pp. 231–239, 2023.
https://doi.org/10.1007/978-3-031-34222-6_20

physical systems, knapsack problem, gesture segmentation and many other optimization problems has been successfully employed through various important current fields. Majority of the optimization problems exist in engineering domains are NPhard, that is, it is almost impossible to find solutions to these problems in polynomial interval in time. Besides, these optimization problems are too complex for developing the model mathematically. Heuristic and metaheuristic algorithms that are seen as potential solutions to handle the complex nature of the problems. These are non-deterministic population based algorithms which search for the solutions from multiple points in parallel thereby accumulative the possibility of attaining global optima. Large number of meta-heuristic algorithms have been developing to solve the complex problems in diverse domains. These types of algorithms are categorized as evolutionary algorithms that based on nature inspired and swarm based algorithms. These algorithms have common advantages like they do not require any domain knowledge to find the solutions, they are gradient free algorithms so inherently simple and that are use arbitrary variables, which moderate the likelihood of life trapped in local optimum point. Numerous meta-heuristic algorithms are developed over the years like Genetic algorithms, particle swarm optimization algorithms shuffled frog leaping algorithms, artificial bee colony etc. According to no free lunch theorem, no algorithm is suitable for solving all kinds of problems. Therefore, the behavior of these algorithms must be analyzed for all kinds of problems to establish the claims. Every year Congress on Evolutionary computation (CEC) organizes competitions and provides benchmark suites of constrained and unconstrained problems. For unconstrained algorithms, a miscellaneous collection of experiment problems with various points of problems are proposed or exist in [5–8]. Likewise, numerous collections of experiment problems that are recommended for forced algorithms in [9–11]. For unconstrained algorithm, a collection of real-world entities problems that are studied, examined and Processed in [12].

This paper presents performance evaluation of recently developed Smart Flower Optimization algorithm (SFOA) over non-convex industrial optimization problem from 3 categories-industrial chemical processes, design and process synthesis problems and mechanical engineering problems. The SFOA is inspired by the development method of the immature sunflower which depict heliotropic movement during the sunny days. Rest of the paper is planned as follows: Section 2 presents related work followed by details of SFOA in following section. Experiments and results are shown in Sect. 4 and conclusion is given in Sect. 5.

2 Related Work

The most common group of real-world optimization problems are constrained type where presence of constraints and low feasible region might vitiate the effectiveness and strength of at all optimization algorithm. Additionally, majority of the nature inspired algorithms are usually designed for unconstrained optimization problems.

Consequently, an additional strategy named Constraint Handling Technique (CHT), mandatory for handling the constraints of the practical challenges and problems. Numerous CHTs are recommended in the literature. In the past, the basic approach to handle the restrictions was to penalize the fitness value of non-feasible solutions. Due to restrictions of the penalty factor, lots of CHTs have been suggested or offered in the last two decades. Few known or current CHTs are supremacy of feasible [13], self-adaptive penalty function [14], epsilon constraint handling [15], a meta-heuristic nature inspired density-based subspace clustering algorithm for high-dimensional information or data [16] and Firefly Algorithm for Optimization of Association Rules [17]. In addition, the role of search methods in constrained algorithms needs to be analyzed on constrained optimization problems. In recent years, this research topic has become popular among researchers. Newly developed algorithms have been bench-marked on numerous engineering optimization problems [18–20]. Mathematically, the real-world constrained optimization problems are represented as follows.

$$Minimize\ f(\bar{x}),\ \bar{x} = (x1, x2, ...xn) \tag{1}$$

$$Subject\ to:\ g_p(\bar{x}) \le 0, p = 1, \ldots n$$

$$h_q(\bar{x}) = 0,\ q = n + 1, \ldots m$$

3   Smart Flower Optimization Algorithm (SFOA)

In third section presents SFOA [22] algorithm in detail. The Sun Flower Optimization Algorithm is motivated by the growing mechanism of the undeveloped sunflower. Immature or undeveloped sunflower generates heliotropic movement during the sunny day. There are two factors by which growing mechanisms are controlled in the heliotropic movement: Auxin (also called growth hormone) and biological clock. Smart flower optimization algorithm(SFOA) can work in two different way sunny mode and cloudy mode or rainy mode. In sunny mode, the movement of sunflower in normal condition. On the other way, the second mode i.e. cloudy or rainy, the effect of development hormone decreases or may non-existent. From the above condition abnormal growth is caused. Pseudocode of the SFOA is as follows:

$$|hq(x)|0, q = n + 1, m \ldots \ldots \tag{2}$$

$$d = damping_{max} - Itr * \frac{(damping_{max} - damping_{min})}{Itr_{max}} \ldots \ldots \tag{3}$$

$$L_{Itr+1}^{newSF} = \begin{cases} L_{Itr}^{oldSF} + d * \sin(\omega) * \left[Aux * L_{Itr}^{bestSF} - L_{Itr}^{oldSF}\right], Hoursday \le 24 \\ L_{Itr}^{oldSF} + d * \sin(\omega)\left[L_{Itr}^{bestSF} - L_{Itr}^{oldSF}\right], otherwise \ldots \ldots \end{cases} \tag{4}$$

$$L_{(new,SF)}^{(Itr+1)} = L_{(old,SF)}^{Itr} + d * \sin(\omega) * \left[L_{(best,SF)}^{Itr} - L_{(old,SF)}^{Itr}\right] \tag{5}$$

In the above algorithm, the default parameter values maximum damping is 1.5, minimum damping is 0, Aux is [0, 1], is [0, 1600], Hours day is [0, 100], and Sun parameter are set as 1 (Fig. 1).

Input: population size (M), Maximum number of iteration(ItrMAX) number of decision variable (Dim), Sun parameter (Sun)

Output: Lbest, fbest

Algorithm

1. Initialization a population and set as the current population.
2. Find the best solution/ best length (L_{best}) in the initial population.
3. For Itr= 1 to Itr$_{MAX}$
4. Generate the dumping parameter (d) using equation (1).
5. For i=1 to M
6.   Generate the parameter ω is the angle of sine function ε [0,160].
7.   For j=1 to Dim
8.   If Sun =1   % means sunny day
9.   Generate the parameters: growth hormone (Aux) , Biological clock (Hours' day)
10.   Update the jth element of the ith population (L_i) using equation (2).
11.   else   % means (Sun =0) cloudy or rainy day.
12.   Generate the Hours 'day parameter only.
13.   Update the jth element of the ith population (L_i) using equation (3).
        end if Sun
14.   Update the angle parameter by adding phase shift value φε [0,0,1]
15.   ω^{j+1}= ω^j + φ
16.   end for j
17. end for i
18. Calculate objective function values of the newly generated population and find the best one ($L_{best, new}$)
19. Replace L_{best} by $L_{best, new}$ if f($L_{best, new}$) < f (L_{best})
20. end for Itr.

Fig. 1. Pseudocode of the SFOA

4 Experiment Analysis

Numerous experiments were performed to assess the efficiency of Smart Flower optimization algorithm with respect to well-known algorithms IUDE [25], sMAgES [26] and iLSHADE [27] All these above algorithms are implemented in Python 3.0 and executed in Google Collaborator environment. For evaluating the algorithm on CEC benchmark 2020 has been run 30 times per function and average values of fitness functions are presented. The stopping criteria is used to stop the optimization process in each algorithm. It is based on the various number of decision variables in each problem as discussed in [21]. The maximum fitness or optimized function evaluations are fixed for the considered industrial optimization problems during the optimization process as follows (Fig. 2, Tables 1, 2 and 3):

$$MaxFES = 1*10^5, if D \leq 10, 2*10^5, if 10 \leq D \leq 30, 4*10^5,$$
$$if 30 \leq D \leq 50, 8*10^5, if 50 \leq D \leq 150, 10^6, if 150 \leq D \tag{6}$$

Analysis for Industrial Chemical Process Problems. Table 1 depicts the performance of SFOA [22] in positions of worst, average and best and standard deviation values of SFOA for optimization. That problems are related to industrial chemical processes. These problems are highly complex with numerous inequality and in-equality

Sr. No.	Industrial Problem Category	Number of Input/number of dimension	Number of InEquality Constraints	Number of Equality Constraints
	Industrial Chemical Process			
1	Heat Exchanger Network Design	9	0	8
2	Heat Exchanger Network Design (Case 2)	11	0	9
3	Reactor Network Design	6	1	4
4	Haverly's Pooling Problem	9	2	4
	Process Synthesis and Design Problem			
5	Process Synthesis Problem	2	2	0
6	Process Synthesis and Design Problem	3	1	1
7	Process Flow Sheeting Problem	3	3	0
8	Two-reactor Problem	7	4	4
9	Process Synthesis Problem	7	9	0
10	Process design Problem	5	3	0
	Mechanical Engineering Problem			
11	Weight Minimization of a Speed Reducer	7	11	0
12	Optimal Design of Industrial refrigeration System	14	15	0
13	Tension/compression spring design (case 1	3	3	0
14	Welded beam design	4	5	0
15	Three-bar truss design problem	2	3	0

Fig. 2. Industrial Non-Convex Constrained Optimization Problems

Table 1. Industrial Chemical Process Problems

Function	Value	SFOA	IUDE[25]	sMAgES[26]	iLSHADE[27]
F1	Best	3.42E+02	1.91E+02	1.89E+02	**1.89E+02**
	Worst	2.11E+01	0.00E+00	1.92E+02	2.03E+02
	Average	1.67E+02	2.85E+02	1.90E+02	1.97E+02
	Std	7.35E+01	1.99E+02	7.96E-01	6.58E+00
F2	Best	1.19E+05	7.05E+03	7.05E+03	**7.05E+03**
	Worst	8.33E+03	5.94E+03	2.66E+04	7.05E+03
	Average	4.29E+04	6.93E+03	1.05E+04	7.05E+03
	Std	2.84E+04	3.70E+02	6.54E+03	5.57E-13
F3	Best	**-9.24E-01**	-3.87E-01	-3.88E-01	-3.75E-01
	Worst	-1.00E+00	-5.52E-01	-3.86E-01	-3.75E-01
	Average	-9.64E-01	-5.05E-01	-3.88E-01	-3.75E-01
	Std	2.44E-02	7.80E-02	7.55E-04	1.21E-06
F4	Best	**-8.92E+02**	-4.00E+02	-4.00E+02	-4.00E+02
	Worst	-2.99E+03	-8.30E-03	-1.47E+02	-6.30E-03
	Average	-1.93E+03	-3.56E+02	-2.44E+02	-1.01E+02
	Std	5.03E+02	1.33E+02	9.30E+01	1.57E+02

constraints. In such problems non-linearities are introduced in design relations of process equipment, equations of mass and heat balance etc. In this category, F1 and F2 functions are without any inequality constraints. For these two functions, best values of sMAgES and iLSHADEs are better as compared to IUDE and SFOA. For F3 and F4 problems which are Reactor network design and Haverly's pooling problem with both

Table 2. Process Design and Synthesis Problems

Function	Value	SFOA	IUDE[25]	sMAgES[26]	iLSHADE[27]
F5	Best	**6.84E-01**	2.00E+00	2.00E+00	2.00E+00
	Worst	-5.16E-01	2.00E+00	2.00E+00	2.00E+00
	Average	1.42E-01	2.00E+00	2.00E+00	2.00E+00
	Std	2.27E-01	1.92E-16	5.83E-05	2.36E-16
F6	Best	**1.17E+00**	2.56E+00	2.56E+00	2.56E+00
	Worst	5.36E-01	2.93E+00	2.56E+00	2.69E+00
	Average	8.46E-01	2.60E+00	2.56E+00	2.66E+00
	StD	2.04E-01	1.23E-01	0.00E+00	2.74E-01
F7	Best	**1.23E-01**	1.08E+00	1.08E+00	1.08E+00
	Worst	1.00E-01	1.25E+00	1.08E+00	1.25E+00
	Average	1.03E-01	1.10E+00	1.08E+00	1.21E+00
	Std	5.58E-03	5.78E-02	2.36E-16	7.65E-02
F8	Best	**9.57E+01**	9.92E+01	9.92E+01	9.92E+01
	Worst	2.69E+01	1.07E+02	6.88E+00	1.10E+02
	Average	5.92E+01	1.02E+02	1.05E+02	1.03E+02
	Std	1.70E+01	4.07E+00	1.13E+02	4.60E+00
F9	Best	2.44E+04	**2.92E+00**	**2.92E+00**	**2.92E+00**
	Worst	2.29E+04	4.21E+00	4.63E+00	2.92E+00
	Average	2.37E+04	3.08E+00	3.64E+00	2.92E+00
	Std	4.08E+02	4.21E-01	6.72E-01	3.85E-08
F10	Best	**2.51E+04**	2.69E+04	2.69E+04	2.69E+04
	Worst	2.29E+04	2.69E+04	2.69E+04	2.69E+04
	Average	2.36E+04	2.69E+04	2.69E+04	2.69E+04
	Std	5.10E+02	3.86E-12	3.86E-12	3.86E-12

equality and inequality constraints, SFOA overtakes all the algorithms IUDE, sMAgES and iLSHADEs.

Analysis for Process Synthesis and Design Problems. Table 2 shows the results of all algorithms obtained for process design and synthesis problems. These problems fall under the category of mixed-integer nonlinear constrained optimization problems. Out of 6 problems, SFOA performs better over 5 problems that is F5, F6, F7, F8 and F10. For F9 problem, IUDE, sMAgES and iLSHADEs attain same values and perform better than SFOA. This problem has few constraints but large number of constants due to which SFOA is not able to get optimal result.

Analysis of Mechanical Engineering Problems. Table 3 presents the performance of SFOA for mechanical engineering problems. Out of five problems, SFOA performs better only for one problem and for all other problems, existing IUDE, sMAgES and iLSHADEs algorithms perform better. On the whole, SFOA is a good choice for problems related to design and processes synthesis problem and industrial chemical processes problems. IUDE, sMAgES and iLSHADEs are more suitable for mechanical engineering problems.

Table 3. Mechanical Engineering Problems

Function	Value	SFOA	IUDE[25]	sMAgES[26]	iLSHADE[27]
F11	Best	3.29E+03	**2.99E+03**	**2.99E+03**	**2.99E+03**
	Worst	2.71E+03	2.99E+03	2.99E+03	2.99E+03
	Average	2.99E+03	2.99E+03	2.99E+03	2.99E+03
	Std	1.50E+02	0.00E+00	0.00E+00	0.00E+00
F12	Best	2.30E+06	**3.22E-02**	**3.22E-02**	**3.22E-02**
	Worst	3.40E+04	3.22E-02	4.45E-02	3.25E-02
	Average	8.56E+05	3.22E-02	3.40E-02	3.23E-02
	Std	5.93E+05	4.91E-18	4.09E-03	1.11E-04
F13	Best	5.88E-01	**1.27E-02**	**1.27E-02**	**1.27E-02**
	Worst	1.29E-02	1.27E-02	1.27E-02	1.27E-02
	Average	1.06E-01	1.27E-02	1.27E-02	1.27E-02
	Std	1.41E-01	1.27E-02	1.27E-02	1.27E-02
F14	Best	2.78E+00	**1.67E+00**	**1.67E+00**	**1.67E+00**
	Worst	3.37E-01	1.67E+00	1.67E+00	1.67E+00
	Average	1.16E+00	1.67E+00	1.67E+00	1.67E+00
	Std	6.72E-01	2.08E-16	2.08E-16	1.07E-11
F15	Best	**8.41E+01**	2.64E+02	2.64E+02	2.64E+02
	Worst	9.00E+00	2.64E+02	2.64E+02	2.65E+02
	Average	3.82E+01	2.64E+02	2.64E+02	2.64E+02
	Std	1.87E+01	0.00E+00	0.00E+00	4.47E-01

5 Conclusion

In this work performance evaluation of Smart Flower Optimization Algorithm is done over Non-Convex Constrained Optimization problems. Smart Flower Algorithm Optimization is motivated from the immature sunflower growth mechanisms. The SFOA is evaluated with respect to well-known existing algorithm such as IUDE, sMAgES and iLSHADEs for industrial optimization problems with equality and inequality constraints. SFOA performs better for industrial chemical processes and process synthesis and design problems. IUDE, sMAgES and iLSHADEs are more suitable for mechanical engineering problems. The comparative analysis of this algorithm reports that the problems are tough to solve for newly developed constrained optimization algorithms.

References

1. Lourenço, H.R., Martin, O.C., Stützle, T.: Iterated local search. In: Handbook of metaheuristics, pp. 320–353. Springer, Berlin (2003)
2. Doğan, B., Ölmez, T.: A new metaheuristic for numerical function optimization: vortex search algorithm. Inf Sci **293**, 125–145 (2015)
3. Mladenović, N., Hansen, P.: Variable neighborhood search. Comput Oper Res **24**(11), 1097–1110 (1997)
4. Kirkpatrick, S., Gelatt, C.D., Vecchi, M.P.: Optimization by simulated annealing. Science **220**(4598), 671 (1983). https://doi.org/10.1126/science.220.4598.671
5. Suganthan, P.N., et al.: Problem definitions and evaluation criteria for the CEC 2005 493 special session on real-parameter optimization, KanGAL report (2005)

6. Liang, J., Qu, B., Suganthan, P., Hernandez-Díaz, A.G.: Problem definitions and evaluation criteria for the CEC 2013 special session on real-parameter optimization, Computational Intelligence Laboratory, Zhengzhou University, Zhengzhou, China and Nanyang Technological 496 University, Singapore, Technical Report 201212, pp. 281–295, 497 (2013)

7. Liang, J., Qu, B., Suganthan, P.: Problem definitions and evaluation criteria for the CEC 2014 special session and competition on single objective real-parameter numerical optimization. Computational Intelligence Laboratory, Zhengzhou University, Zhengzhou China and Technical Report, Nanyang Technological University, Singapore 635 (2013)

8. Awad, N., Ali, M., Liang, J., Qu, B., Suganthan, P.: Problem definitions and evaluation criteria for the CEC 2017 special session and competition on single objective bound constrained real-parameter numerical optimization, Technical report (2016)

9. Liang, J., et al.: Problem definitions and evaluation criteria for the CEC 2006 special session on constrained real-parameter optimization. J. Appl. Mech. **41**, 8–31 (2006)

10. Mallipeddi, R., Suganthan, P.N.: Problem definitions and evaluation criteria for the CEC 2010 competition on constrained real-parameter optimization, Nanyang Technological University, Singapore 24 (2010)

11. Wu, G., Mallipeddi, R., Suganthan, P.: Problem definitions and evaluation criteria for the CEC 2017 competition on constrained real-parameter optimization, National University of Defense Technology, Changsha, Hunan, PR China and Kyungpook National University, Daegu, South Korea and Nanyang Technological University, Singapore, Technical Report (2017)

12. Das, S., Suganthan, P.N.: Problem definitions and evaluation criteria for CEC 2011 competition on testing evolutionary algorithms on real world optimization problems, pp. 341–359. Jadavpur University, Nanyang Technological University, Kolkata (2010)

13. Deb, K.: An efficient constraint handling method for genetic algorithms. Comput. Methods Appl. Mech. Eng. **186**, 311–338 (2000)

14. Tasgetiren, M.F., Suganthan, P.N.: A multi-populated differential evolution algorithm for solving constrained optimization problem. In: 2006 IEEE International Conference on Evolutionary Computation, pp. 33–40. IEEE (2006)

15. Takahama, T., Sakai, S., Iwane, N.: Constrained optimization by the constrained hybrid algorithm of particle swarm optimization and genetic algorithm. In: Australasian Joint Conference on Artificial Intelligence, pp. 389–400. Springer (2005)

16. Agarwal, P., Mehta, S., Abraham, A.: A meta-heuristic density-based subspace clustering algorithm for high-dimensional data. Soft. Comput. **25**(15), 10237–10256 (2021). https://doi.org/10.1007/s00500-021-05973-1

17. Mehta, S., Singh, M., Kaur, N.: Firefly algorithm for optimization of association rules. In: 2020 6th International Conference on Signal Processing and Communication (ICSC), pp. 143–148 (2020). https://doi.org/10.1109/ICSC48311.2020.9182770

18. Dhiman, G., Kumar, V.: Spotted hyena optimizer: a novel bio-inspired based meta-heuristic technique for engineering applications. Adv. Eng. Softw., 48–70 (2017)

19. Dhiman, G., Kumar, V.: Seagull optimization algorithm: theory and its applications for large-scale industrial engineering problems. Knowl.-Based Syst. **165**, 169–196 (2019)

20. Zhang, J., Xiao, M., Gao, L., Pan, Q.: Queuing search algorithm: a novel metaheuristic algorithm for solving engineering optimization problems. Appl. Math. Model. **63**, 464–490 (2018)

21. Kumar, A., Wu, G., Ali, M.Z., Mallipeddi, R., Suganthan, P.N., Das, S.: A test-suite of non convex constrained optimization problems from the real-world and some baseline results. Swarm Evol. Comput. **56**, 100693 (2020). https://doi.org/10.1016/j.swevo.2020.100693

22. Sattar, D., Salim, R.: A smart metaheuristic algorithm for solving engineering problems. Eng. Comput. **37**(3), 2389–2417 (2020). https://doi.org/10.1007/s00366-020-00951-x

23. Kumar, A., Wu, G., Ali, M.Z., Mallipeddi, R., Suganthan, P.N., Das, S.: A test-suite of non-convex constrained optimization problems from the real-world and some baseline results. Swarm Evol. Comput. **56**, 100693 (2020). ISSN 2210-6502. https://doi.org/10.1016/j.swevo.2020.100693
24. Agarwal, P., Mehta, S.: Nature-inspired algorithms: state-of-art, problems and prospects. Int. J. Comput. Appl. **100**(14), 14–21 (2014)
25. Trivedi, A., Srinivasan, D.: An improved unified differential evolution algorithm for constrained optimization problems. In: 2018 528 IEEE Congress on Evolutionary Computation (CEC), pp. 1–10 (2018)
26. Hellwig, M., Beyer, H.-G.: A matrix adaptation evolution strategy for constrained real-parameter optimization. In: 2018 IEEE Congress on Evolutionary Computation (CEC), pp. 1–8, July 2018. https://doi.org/10.1109/CEC.2018.8477950
27. Fan, Z., Fang, Y., Li, W., Yuan, Y., Wang, Z., Bian, X.: LSHADE44 with an improved constraint-handling method for solving constrained single-objective optimization problems. In: 2018 IEEE Congress on Evolutionary Computation (CEC), pp. 1–8, July 2018. https://doi.org/10.1109/CEC.2018.8477943

Author Index

M. A. Jabbar et al. (Eds.): AMLDA 2022, CCIS 1818, pp. 241–242, 2023.
https://doi.org/10.1007/978-3-031-34222-6

Printed in the United States
by Baker & Taylor Publisher Services